The Structure of Communication in Early Language Development

THE CHILD PSYCHOLOGY SERIES
EXPERIMENTAL AND THEORETICAL ANALYSES OF CHILD BEHAVIOR

EDITOR
DAVID S. PALERMO
DEPARTMENT OF PSYCHOLOGY
THE PENNSYLVANIA STATE UNIVERSITY
UNIVERSITY PARK, PENNSYLVANIA

The Perception of Stimulus Relations: Discrimination Learning and Transposition, HAYNE W. REESE, 1968

Cognitive Development: The Child's Acquisition of Diagonality, DAVID R. OLSON, 1970

The Ontogenesis of Grammar: A Theoretical Symposium, DAN I. SLOBIN, 1971

An Ethological Study of Children's Behavior, W. C. McGREW, 1972

The Child's World of Make-Believe: Experimental Studies of Imaginative Play, JEROME L. SINGER, 1973

The Study of Behavioral Development, JOACHIM F. WOHLWILL, 1973

Studies in the Cognitive Basis of Language Development, HARRY BEILIN, 1975

Infant Perception: From Sensation to Cognition, Volume I, Basic Visual Processes; Volume II, Perception of Space, Speech, and Sound, (Eds.), LESLIE B. COHEN AND PHILIP SALAPATEK, 1975

The Structure of Communication in Early Language Development, PATRICIA MARKS GREENFIELD AND JOSHUA H. SMITH, 1976

The Structure of Communication in Early Language Development

Patricia Marks Greenfield
University of California
Los Angeles, California

Joshua H. Smith
Stanford University
Stanford, California

ACADEMIC PRESS New York San Francisco London 1976

A Subsidiary of Harcourt Brace Jovanovich, Publishers

ACADEMIC PRESS, INC.
111 Fifth Avenue, New York, New York 10003

United Kingdom Edition published by
ACADEMIC PRESS, INC. (LONDON) LTD.
24/28 Oval Road, London NW1

Library of Congress Cataloging in Publication Data

Greenfield, Patricia Marks.
   The structure of communication in early language
development.

      (Child psychology series)
      Bibliography: p.
      1.   Children–Language.   I.   Smith, Joshua H., joint
author.   II.   Title.   [DNLM: 1.   Language development–
In infancy and childhood.   2.   Verbal behavior–In
infancy and childhood.   LB1139.L3 G812u]
LB1139.L3G69   372.6   75-32027
ISBN 0–12–300250–8

To Dot with thanks

Contents

Preface

As we come to know more about language in general and language development in particular, it becomes ever clearer that communication and knowledge of the world are intrinsic to the organization of human language. Our
study traces the child's emerging grammar from these two points of origin: the
child's world of action and perception and the communicative processes in
adult interpretation and adult–child dialogue.

In 1967 and 1968, I was struck by the communicative power of my daughter
Lauren's single-word utterances. I also noticed developmental change in the
range of messages she was able to convey by a single word. Upon closer observation, I concluded that she was achieving this communication by systematically
combining her word with nonverbal elements in the situation—action, object,
gesture, intonation, and so forth. I also noted that these same messages were
later actualized in dialogue, as Lauren used her single words to respond to my
comments and questions. I thought, moreover, that other people would
recognize the same basic messages, given the same contextual cues. This book
is an attempt to convince others of these facts, through systematic investigation
of the phenomena that originally caught my attention.

The two children studied were Matthew Greenfield, my second child, and
Nicholas Thompson, the first child of Dorothy and Robert Thompson, whose
lives were interwined with ours in various ways. When we started, it was very
suspect to study anything one knew about from personal experience—one
might not be "objective." In the years since, it has been liberating to watch
this attitude of distrust and suspicion lift—as students of child language have
come to realize that abstracting language from its lived context destroys just
what one wished to study in the first place. In part, this book is an attempt to
show that scientific method does *not* depend upon studying something one
knows and cares nothing about.

Both children were born in 1968. Discussion of my earlier observations of

Lauren with David McNeill, just before Matthew's birth, were influential in my decision to carry out the study. I am very grateful to him, both for his encouragement and for introducing me to Joshua Smith, the co-author of this book. Despite McNeill's important role, our theoretical interpretation of single-word utterances is, nevertheless, quite different from the one he proposed for my original observations of Lauren (McNeill, 1970a, 1971).

Our data were collected in 1969 and 1970. Joshua Smith analyzed a portion of the data for an undergraduate honors thesis in linguistics at Harvard in 1970. This was the first step in the fruitful collaboration that culminated in this book. A first draft of our book manuscript, called *Communication and the Beginnings of Language* by P. M. Greenfield, J. H. Smith, and B. Laufer, was complete in early 1972. It is to this draft that many citations in the literature refer. At that point, a delay occurred, caused by the necessity of retranscribing our tapes. One advantage of the delay has been to allow us some perspective on what amounted to an explosion of interest in this early period of langauge development. Hence, we have been able to discuss a number of studies carried out simultaneously with ours.

A book can hardly capture the rich and subtle means by which word and event interact in early language. When Matthew was 22 months old, the end of the period under study, I had the opportunity to make a sound film with Allegra May, a talented and sensitive film maker. Through the medium of film, it was possible to present Matthew's early messages to eye and ear, as they were intended. This project was an exciting and rewarding collaboration on many levels. After the film was edited, Jerome Bruner joined us to help develop and to present the narration. Partly because it was designed for a nontechnical audience, partly because it represents a compromise between our differing points of view on the material, and partly because it was formulated several years ago, the narration deviates in places from the analytic concepts presented in this book. Nonetheless, *Early Words* (1972), the film that resulted from our collaborative effort, shows how Matthew lived the phenomena that are at the heart of this research.

The plan of our book is basically chronological. Chapter 1 is an historical and theoretical account of the relevant body of knowledge that existed before our study. It is an attempt to show that a semantically based account of grammar provides a point of contact between the early diary studies, which have been ignored for so long, and modern studies of grammatical development. Chapter 2 describes our empirical framework, with its methodological and theoretical rationale, as well as its limitations. Chapter 3 presents the basic data of semantic development in the period under study. (Although the researcher should find the detail of Sections 3.3 through 3.16 useful, other readers may prefer to read only the summaries in Sections 3.3 through 3.16 or even just the overall summary Section 3.17.) Chapter 4 has three major parts: The first relates semantic development to cognitive development; the second concentrates on analyzing the role of adult-initiated dialogue in the child's transition to syntax; and the third shows how the principle of informativeness (in the information theory sense) can be used to predict *what* the child says *when*. In this chapter, the ratio of ideas to data is higher than in Chapter 3 and will, we hope, stimulate other researchers to further empirical investigation. Chapter 5, the final chapter, relates our study to work that has been reported since our data were collected. (Because of this chronological organization, Bloom's (1973) book on one-word speech is discussed in Chapter 5, whereas her earlier book is discussed in Chapter 1.) This chapter also discusses linguistic models, and draws some general conclusions.

Because both our subjects happened to be male, we refer to the language learner as "he" throughout this work. For analagous reasons, the adult interacting with the child is always referred to as "she." This, unfortunately, compounds the much more general problem of sexist bias in language. We hope, nevertheless, the reader will keep in mind that children of both sexes learn to speak and that adults of both sexes are capable of teaching them.

We would like to express our thanks to many people who helped at various points along the way: Bernice Laufer, who served as the observer for the formal observations; Alexis Koen, Linda Schantz, Christine Hodson, and Wanda Wong, all of whom played important roles in the data analysis; Edy Veneziano for a number of insightful ideas; Alvin Hall, who gave me careful and detailed comments on our first draft; Susan Braunwald, Patricia Zukow, Elinor Keenan, and Bambi Schieffelin, who read and discussed the manuscript with me; Martha Platt, who carefully prepared the index.

Much of the work was done while I was a Research Fellow at the Center for Cognitive Studies, Harvard University. I profited greatly from discussing the first draft with a group there that included Jerome Bruner, Paul Harris, Susan Carey Block, and Jeremy Anglin. I also received support from the Milton Fund, Harvard University and from a University Research Grant, University of California, Santa Cruz.

Most of all I would like to express my appreciation to Dorothy Thompson, who paid the same careful attention to Nicky's language as I did to Matthew's.

P. M. G.

chapter 1

Single Words and Grammatical Development: An Historical and Theoretical Perspective

W hen toward the end of the first year of life, children begin to speak their mother tongue, each utterance consists of but a single word. About 6 months after this modest beginning, they start to produce two-word utterances as well. By the age of 3 or 4 years, children are well on their way to linguistic mastery. A number of studies carried out in the 1960s (Braine, 1963; Brown and Fraser, 1964; Miller and Ervin, 1964; Blount, 1969; Kernan, 1969; Bloom, 1970; Bowerman, 1973) investigated the nature of child language at various ages after the appearance of two-word utterances. In contrast, child language before the appearance of two-word combinations was virtually ignored during this period.

There is ample reason why more effort was not expended on one-word utterances. Later speech is easier to understand because the child's repertoire of sounds, or phonological system, is more adult; it is considerably more accessible, since there is more of it; and fewer assumptions need be made to study it. When a child begins speaking in single words, an investigator will be lucky to obtain more than a handful of examples during several hours of observation. For these single words to yield data of interest, moreover, it is necessary to relate them to the circumstances in which they were uttered. Even though parents have been doing this for years, modern investigators of child language have just begun to do so (Bloom, 1970). A further complication to the study of this early period in the development of language is the fact that little is known about how adults

1

use contextual information in real life to understand emerging speech. In other words, what are the cues that enable adults to interpret and expand many of the earliest one-word utterances?

Our study was an attempt to rethink and reformulate these "complications," taking them as intrinsic, rather than extrinsic, to linguistic communication, especially language acquisition. We followed two children during this early period of one-word speech and attempted to connect single-word utterances with later grammatical development.

When our project began in 1969, there existed two main lines of relevant research. The more recent line might be called "grammatical studies." These studies applied various tools that had been developed in American structural and transformational linguistics to the analysis of child language in the two-word stage and later. The second, older line of research consists of studies that have touched on one-word speech, often termed "holophrastic speech." These studies show less unity of approach, but they have developed some analytic concepts and a rich body of data that complement the linguistic methods of the grammatical studies.

1.1 Grammatical Studies

PIVOT GRAMMAR

Three independent studies begun in the early 1960s (Braine, 1963; Brown and Fraser, 1964; Miller and Ervin, 1964) form the beginning of the modern grammatical approach to child language. In this approach, children's speech is taken as a language to be discovered, not merely an imperfect replica of adult speech. These studies found child language to have relatively similar properties. Their findings have been unified (McNeill, 1966) and criticized (Bloom, 1970; Bowerman, 1973; Brown 1973)[1] in subsequent reviews of the literature. Here, we will briefly present the unified version of their results and some criticisms of those results, and will proceed to discuss the theoretical bases of their methods.

Pivot and Open Classes

These early studies found that young children's two-word sentences were made up of two types of words, which later came to be called the "pivot" and

---

[1] These three references report earlier work that was available to us in unpublished form at an early point in our study: Bloom's book is based on a 1968 thesis, Bowerman's on a 1970 thesis. Brown's book is the final comprehensive account of a study begun in 1962; we read a preprint of his chapter on two-word speech in 1970.

"open" classes. A key characteristic of the pivot class is that each member occurs only in a fixed sentence poisition (either initial or final) (Bowerman, 1973, p. 29). In the sentences *allgone shoe, allgone train,* and *allgone record, allgone* functions as an initial pivot. There are also final pivots in some children's speech. In *shoe on, record on,* and *hat on, on* is a final position pivot. Some other characteristics are often ascribed to pivots: There are relatively few pivot words, but they are used frequently; new words are rarely added to the pivot class (McNeill, 1966, p. 20); pivot words occur neither alone nor in combination with other pivot words; pivot words are usually function words, which build on the reference of another word but do not have reference of their own (p. 20). However, the pivot class need not be uniform (Brown, 1973). *Hi, allgone, on, mommy, that,* and *no* are common examples of pivot words (McNeill, 1966, p. 22). The open class is essentially the complement of the pivot class (Bowerman, 1973, p. 34). A specific open-class word can occur both initially and finally; open-class words may occur alone or together with other open-class words, as well as with pivots; new words are easily added to the open class and need not be used frequently. Most of the words in a child's vocabulary belong to this class. These words are content words, like nouns and verbs in adult language.

A child's grammar, at this point, may be described by the rules (McNeill, 1966, pp. 21, 23)

$$(1) \qquad\qquad S \rightarrow \begin{Bmatrix} P \\ O \end{Bmatrix} \qquad O$$

(S = sentence; P = pivot; O = open; → = "consists of"; the brackets { } enclose alternatives.) An extra transformation is needed to move some pivots to final position.

Bowerman (1973, p. 68) has shown that the characteristics just given do not actually define a single class of pivot words in child speech; that is, all pivot words do not really have the same privileges of occurrence. In the data of the original studies, she found words of high frequency and function-word meaning which variously occurred alone (*more*), occurred with other pivots (*do,* in *want do*), and occurred in both initial and final position with open-class words (*that*). She also found words with characteristics of both classes. For example, *truck* had the high frequency and constant position characteristic of the pivot class, but the concrete reference characteristic of the open class. Although one can reassign words to different classes and include some words in both classes to maintain the original form of a pivot grammar, most of the generalizations that it was intended to capture would be lost. With this in mind, let us turn to the original studies and consider what methods led these investigators to those characteristics of child language that were formalized as pivot grammar and caused them to dismiss apparent "exceptions" to the rules of this grammar.

Assumptions Underlying Pivot Grammar

The investigators who first applied grammatical techniques to the study of child language shared a number of assumptions. The most basic among these was the assumption that child language was sufficiently similar to adult language that it could be studied by the same techniques. This assumption led to other assumptions implicit in the techniques of grammatical analysis which these investigators borrowed from American structural linguistics. These techniques, treated in detail by Bloomfield (1933) and Harris (1951), are summarized and discussed by Gleason (1961) and Lyons (1970). It is primarily this second set of assumptions with which we shall be concerned.

Structural linguistics was concerned primarily with methods for the statement of regularities in a particular corpus of material (body of actual speech data) in a language (Harris, 1951, pp. 1–5, 12–13). Harris (1951) and other workers formulated a number of procedures for discovering those regularities without recourse to information about the meaning of the corpus. These methods for discovering grammatical regularities in a sample of an unknown language are often called "discovery procedures." Both these aspects of linguistic methodology were well suited to the study of child language.

First, the notion of grammar as a description of a corpus fitted the position of the investigator who collected samples of child speech and then proceeded to analyze them (cf. Miller and Ervin, 1964). Although children talk all the time, it is difficult to guide their production. To investigate a particular aspect of their language, one must await the right data in the corpus. Collecting a sufficiently large corpus is a substitute for being able to elicit information about specific aspects of a language.

Second, the separation of grammatical description from meaning solved a difficult problem for these investigators. It is often felt that the assignment of meanings to child language causes much to be read in which is not there (Bloom, 1970). Investigators would prefer to exclude the incorrect meanings. It is difficult, however, to specify an objective basis for differentiating valid and invalid semantic interpretations. One way to avoid using invalid interpretations is to disregard meanings altogether. In doing, so, one can claim not to be making any prior assumptions about the nature of child language. This solution to the problem of meaning in child language found theoretical justification in linguistics. Since meanings were peripheral to the study of language (Chomsky, 1957, Ch. 9), it was not apparent that they should be included in studies of child language. The discovery procedures that had been developed in linguistics gave a principled method for analyzing child language while excluding considerations of meaning.

An approach to language based on discovery procedures entailed a number of more specific assumptions. Discovery procedures must be of a relatively restricted nature. Since nothing is known beforehand about words, one must justify grouping any of them together. The basic datum about any word is its distribution, the set of linguistic contexts in which it occurs (Harris, 1951, p. 5). Words are put in the same class on the basis of similarities of distribution. This procedure is easily applied to child language. Braine's (1963) initial pivot class is a good example of a class of words which were grouped by this procedure. Both *bye bye* and *see* occurred only in two-word sentences in initial position. Both occurred with a number of other words in second positions; and, in addition, both occurred before some of the same words. Thus, not only were their distributions similar, they also overlapped. On these grounds, Braine put them in the same class. Other words were added to the class on similar grounds. Grammars that are based on discovery procedures like these take the form of statements about the distribution of classes of words. The statements concern the order of classes and co-occurrence restrictions among them. Although other discovery procedures can reveal constituent structure,[2] these depend on the possibility of substituting single words for strings of words in fixed contexts. Such substitution is meaningless in a corpus whose greatest sentence length is two words (Bloom, 1970).

To investigators using these methods, relative frequency and position were the most obvious characteristics of words in the search for grammatical regularities. The pivot class appeared to combine both fixed positions and high frequency of use, whereas little could be said about the residual open class. Thus, pivot grammar was the inevitable outcome of an analysis based exclusively on distributional facts, that is, on privileges of occurrence. The fact that the contrast between pivot and open words appeared to parallel the contrast between function and content words in adult speech was taken as confirmation of the analysis (McNeill, 1966, pp. 20–21). However, Bowerman's demonstration that pivot grammars do not capture all the facts about the distribution of words in two-word speech suggests that this method of analysis may not be appropriate to the data.

Although constructions involving pivot and open-class words were emphasized in the early grammatical investigations (Bowerman, 1973), a grammar for this stage also had to include sentences that consisted entirely of open-class words. It is interesting to see how the early studies interpreted these open–open sentences, for such constructions were later to dramatize most effectively the futility of basing early child grammars on distributional facts alone.

Braine (1963) did his best to ignore the open–open type of sentence. He

[2]Constituent structure is the hierarchical pattern of units and subunits composing the internal structure of a particular sentence. A constituent is any morpheme, word, or construction which enters into some larger construction. When a single word can be substituted for a group of words, this group is taken to constitute a simple constituent.

considered that the child's syntax consisted of ordering and that the child knew the ordering properties only of pivot words; he therefore concluded that sequences of open-class words "have no discernable structure" (p. 12).

Of the early investigators, Miller and Ervin (1964) take the most tentative view of their results. This is probably because their procedure went beyond that described above, and because the children that they studied were slightly older than the children in the other studies (Bowerman, 1973). After they had isolated a few pivot-like words in their corpus on the basis of distributional criteria, they observed that much of the corpus remained undescribed. They then assigned words to classes on the basis of their class membership in adult speech. A few pairs of the child's classes that did not differ significantly from each other in distribution were lumped together, but such pairs were rare. The result was a large number of classes, each with a unique distribution and some correspondence to adult language. A simple set of distributional rules could not describe the corpus; they wrote as follows:

> The regularity displayed in the table shows that this method [of grouping words by adult class membership] yields information about structure, [footnote:] A grammar cannot be derived from the tables. The table only shows that elements are ... systematized. The best explanation for the systematization is that the child has word classes, classes that have at least some properties of word classes in adult speech [Miller and Ervin, 1964, p. 23].

That is, they found that adult word classes had correlates in child language, but they had no way to describe the relationship of one of a child's classes to another when the two occurred together in a sentence. Their paper serves to demonstrate that the notion of word class alone is inadequate to describe child language in any significant way.

GRAMMATICAL RELATIONS: McNEILL

The solution to the description of sentences that consist of two open-class words came from new developments in transformational linguistics. These developments allowed a limited and definable use of meaning to describe the relationship of words that stand in sequential order.

Chomsky (1965) observed that the concept of deep structure allowed one to state a simple set of grammatical relations which held between the elements of a sentence across a wide range of superficial forms. He defined these relations between parts of a sentence and their subparts. That is, a grammatical relation holds between two nodes of a hierarchy that are in a hierarchical (dominance) relation to one another. For example, the relation *subject of* is defined between a sentence (S) and a noun phrase (NP) by the rule:

(2) $$S \rightarrow NP \quad VP$$

The sentence *John hit someone* consists of the noun phrase *John* and the verb phrase *hit someone*. The noun phrase *John* is the *subject of* the sentence. *John* is also *subject of* the sentence *Someone was hit by John,* despite its different surface form, because that relation is present at the level of deep structure.

NcNeill (1966) realized that these relations could be used to describe the structure of children's two- and three-word sentences and gave an argument that they were, indeed, present. He observed that, if sentences that consisted of two open-class words were actually without structure, then all possible word orders should occur. However, some orders do not occur. McNeill claimed that a description using grammatical relations could explain why they do not.

For one of Brown's subjects (Adam), he wrote such a description. The words were divided into nouns (N), verbs (V), and pivots (P). Because a pivot class does not appear in adult grammar, a list of examples may be helpful: *my, that, a,* and *dirty.* The grammatical relations were defined by a set of three rules, originally proposed in 1966, then revised in 1970 (a,b). In the latest version, the rules are presented as follows:

(3)   S → (NP⁀VP)

(The linked parentheses mean that both elements are optional, but at least one must be present.)

(4) $NP \rightarrow \begin{Bmatrix} (P) & N \\ N & N \end{Bmatrix}$

(Brackets again enclose alternatives; a single pair of parentheses denotes an optional element.)

(5)   VP → (V) NP

(McNeill, 1970a, p. 28).

McNeill proposes that the grammatical relations implied by these rules are part of a child's innate knowledge about language, although the order of constituents, of course, is not. These rules generate four possible combinations of two classes (P N, N N, V N, N V). If all three classes (P, N, V) could appear in random order, there would be nine possible two-word combinations. In fact, only those combinations of classes occur that are produced by the rules given above. The same is true for three-word sentences; only 8 of 27 possible combinations occur. McNeill concludes that this limitation of actually occuring sequences implies that child speech is not random, but has structure. The success of grammatical relations in accounting for the limitation suggests that they are present in child speech. More generally, the fact that child speech is not random but highly limited in form allows us to attribute structure to it even when we cannot be certain that our interpretations are correct.

We note in passing that some combinations (e.g., N V) are unambiguous (a subject and a verb), but others are not. According to McNeill's rules, N N could be either a subject and an object or a modified object. McNeill did not recognize the potential for ambiguity in 1966 (or 1970b) and did not say whether both these possibilities occurred, or how he would determine which one was present in a given sentence. This is not crucial to his argument, but is quite important for the application of his analysis to real speech.[3]

A completely formal argument for grammatical relations could not be entirely successful. The grammar's greatest problem is that it is very powerful: It can produce much longer sentences than children can. If all options were chosen, a sentence five words long would be generated. From McNeill's description, it seems doubtful that this ever happened. In fact, the child rarely produced sentences that even had subjects. From McNeill's discussion of the child's production, it appears that each individual possibility in the rules was used at some point. What is missing is a general account of why some sentence types are more frequent and develop before others.

GRAMMATICAL RELATIONS AND SITUATIONAL INFORMATION

Bloom's thesis, published in 1970, was the first grammatical study to make explicit use of nonlinguistic information in the investigation of child language.[4] That is, she used the context in which a sentence was uttered to interpret that sentence. However, to avoid overinterpreting children's sentences, she restricted her interpretations to specifying the relationship between overt elements. Bloom's treatment actualizes claims about child language that were implicit or explicit in McNeill (1966, 1970b) and gives a much clearer picture of the way in which a child uses his language in specific situations.

A careful record of the contexts in which sentences were used revealed that a given combination of words could be used in very different situations, with correspondingly different relations between the constituent words. The clearest examples of this occurred with a sentence of two nouns: The two nouns in *mommy sock* would stand in the relationship of subject—object if said when her mother was putting on the child's sock, or possessor—possessed if said when the child picked up her mother's sock. Noun—noun strings, treated as a single construction in earlier investigations, could also express three other relations,

---

[3]His views were altered in 1970 (a) after the appearance of Bloom's (1968) thesis, which will be discussed next, but his original formulation about grammatical relations is most important to a history of the transformational approach to child language.

[4]Because Bloom's (1973) analysis of earlier stages in language development was carried out simultaneously with our data collection, it did not serve as background to this study; it is therefore discussed in Chapter 5.

depending on the situation: locative[5] (e.g., *sweater chair*, said when pointing to a sweater on a chair), attributive (e.g., *baby book* used to describe a book about a baby), and conjunction (e.g., *umbrella boot*, said when her mother was bringing her umbrella and boots). Data from the Berkeley cross-cultural studies (Ervin–Tripp, 1971) suggested the universality of these and other semantic relations described by Bloom.

Bloom (1970) argued that the fact that a single sequence could be used in several very different situations did not show that a child used his vocabulary indiscriminately. Rather, it showed that this sequence was ambiguous and should be assigned different representations according to the situation. Her argument on this point is similar to McNeill's argument for the existence of grammatical relations given in the last section: If a child used words randomly, many different noun–noun relationships should appear. In fact, only those relationships that were listed above appeared. The limitation of a child's speech to five noun–noun relations constitutes grounds for inferring that those relations are present in child language. Further, since situational information helped specify those relations in general, it can legitimately be used to establish the grammatical relation of a specific sequence of words in a specific situation. This is Bloom's principal contribution to the application of transformational grammar to the study of child language.

Note that the five types of noun–noun relation listed above are described by a mixture of semantic terms (e.g., "possessor") and syntactic terms (e.g., "subject"). This inconsistency in Bloom's terminology seems to result from problems in trying to integrate semantic information into Chomsky's syntactic theory of transformational grammar and suggests possible inadequacy in the theory.

Bloom (1970) explicitly limits her expansions to specifying the relationships among the verbal elements of a child's sentences. Because a relationship must involve at least two elements, a constituent standing by itself can have no grammatical relations. This follows from her definition of a grammatical relation. As we saw previously, Chomsky (1965) defined grammatical relations between units that were at different levels of consitutent structure. By this definition, a noun phrase functions as *subject* if it is introduced by a rule which expands a sentence node in base structure. Chomsky explicitly denies that there is a relation "subject–object" and points out that the subject and object have no co-occurrence restrictions (pp. 73–74). Unlike Chomsky, Bloom takes grammatical relations to exist between elements that are not in a dominance relation. The relations that she uses are, then, compounds of the more elementary type of relations defined by Chomsky. For example, Bloom's relation "subject–object" can be decomposed into Chomsky's "subject of" (a sentence),

---

[5]A locative is a verbal expression of place.

"verb phrase of" (a sentence), and "object of" (a verb phrase). Bloom's treatment of grammatical relations obviously prevents the application of these concepts to single-word utterances.

Bloom wrote grammars for her subjects at different ages based on her evidence that some strings had different internal relationships from others. Although Bloom differed from McNeill in dealing with situational information and semantic relations, these relations were input to the grammar, not part of it. Like McNeill, Bloom used the framework of Chomsky's (1965) theory in formulating child grammars. An important difference between Bloom and McNeill, however, is that she explicitly recognizes the discrepancy between the power of the deep structure which she proposes and the shortness of the surface structure which appeared in the children's speech. Very few of the sentences for which she wrote grammars were more than two words long. Some of her grammers could, however, produce sentences of three words or more. For example, Bloom considers that a subject—object sentence must contain a verb at some level. She accounts for its absence by what she calls a reduction transformation, which can delete any major element in a three-word sentence.

Bloom observes two major criteria governing the operation of deletion. First, a node for which the child did not command the appropriate word, or for which the appropriate word is not completely specified in the lexicon, is apt to be deleted. For example, in the sentence *Jocelyn cheek*, the word *hurt* is missing. This might be because the child either did not know the word *hurt* or did not know that *hurt* could occur between two nouns (1970, pp. 165—166). Second, less productive or more recently acquired constructions are more likely to be deleted (1970, p. 167). Sentence subjects appeared relatively late, and were almost always deleted in negative sentences even after they were consistently present in affirmative sentences (1970, p. 154).

Bowerman (1973) used similar methods to study the acquisition of Finnish and has proposed a similar solution to the problem of missing verbs within the context of transformational grammar. In her data, subject—object strings are considered to result from the deletion of specific lexical items occupying the verb slot. Although this solution is supported by evidence from her particular subjects' speech samples, Bowerman recognizes that this solution, like the other possibilities she considers, is not perfect.

The psychological problem of deletion seems to be: How do we know that a grammatical category (Bloom's solution) or a lexical item (Bowerman's solution) was there in the first place? It seems to us that both Bloom and Bowerman were led to positing the underlying forms by the nature of the formal grammatical system they used. It is unconventional to generate a verbless sentence within the framework of transformational grammar. However, even if the grammatical system provides an essentially correct description of the competence of adult speakers (an assumption made by Bowerman), she herself points out that "the fact that deep structure elements are analyzed in a certain way in the adult language is not in itself sufficient reason for postulating the same constituent structure in children's utterances" (Bowerman, 1973, p. 93).

Treatment of deletion is important to any study of one-word speech that seeks to establish continuity with later grammatical development, since an analysis of single words in terms of deletion of every element but one is a reductio ad absurdum for a child who has yet to produce his first two-word combination. Brown (1973) recognizes the logic of a parallel situation when he points out that, if deletion rules are used to account for the early telegraphic stages of child speech, these rules must be dropped from the grammar as children's sentences get longer. The theorist is then in the untenable position of postulating a more complex stage before a simpler one. A more tenable position would hold that items that do not occur in early speech actually are not there. Such a solution would not require any deletion transformation nor would it confuse the process of development.

The recognition of semantic notions in child grammar makes treatment of single words a theoretical possibility. But if semantic notions must be coupled with deletion rules in order to explain the single word stage, such treatment becomes an absurdity. Principled objection to deletion rules in the two-word period, such as we have presented in the present section, opens the possibility of another approach to sentence length that will be as suitable for one-word speech as for the later stages of word combination. A tentative solution underlying the present study will be presented after considering Fillmore's case theory of transformational grammar and previous study of one-word speech.

A SEMANTIC APPROACH TO GRAMMAR

Whereas Bloom was the first to integrate situational information and semantic knowledge into a description of grammatical development, she did so within the theoretical framework of Chomskian (1965) transformational grammar. According to this theory, a base structure of the sort described earlier, through a series of grammatical transformations, yields the surface structure that ultimately becomes the actual spoken or heard sentence. Grammar is conceived by Chomsky as a system that relates sound and meaning: Base structure provides the input to a semantic (meaning) component, surface structure, the input to a phonological (sound) component. To give a simple illustrative example of one aspect of Chomsky's theory, let us compare *The boy hit the ball* with *The ball was hit by the boy*. Both surface forms are said to have a common base structure; each is derived from the base by a different process of transformation. Transformations must, in general, preserve meaning.

In contrast to this formulation, Schlesinger, a psychologist, suggested as early as 1967 (published in 1971a) that the deep structure level of grammar ought to be semantic rather than syntactic. His views and their relevance for explaining how grammar is learned were expanded in a second article (1971b).[6] Lakoff and Ross (1967), McCawley (1968), and Fillmore (1968), from the perspective of linguistics, and Olson (1970), from the perspective of psychology, made the same suggestion, although each of their proposals was somewhat different. Bowerman (1973) and Brown (1973) realized that Fillmore's proposal had unique possibilities for the description of language development, and set out to explore them with respect to their own data on the acquisition of Finnish and English. At the same time, Slobin (1970) noticed the suitability of Fillmore's case terminology for describing the seemingly universal semantic functions in two-word speech revealed by the Berkeley cross-cultural studies.

Before discussing the usefulness of Fillmore's case theory for describing the phenomena of language acquisition, we must set forth the basics of the theory itself. In the traditional linguistic treatment of case, nouns appear in various forms (e.g., case endings in Latin) that signal the place of a word in a construction. In this treatment, case is treated as a surface phenomenon of particular languages: Case categories are restricted to inflected languages; and even within these, the list of cases varies tremendously from language to language (Gleason, 1961). It had been realized that, on the one hand, case forms in languages like Finnish signal semantic, rather than purely grammatical, contrasts (e.g., *in* versus *out of*) and that, on the other hand, function words, like English prepositions, may serve the case function in some languages (Gleason, 1961). Fillmore proposed to treat case not as a surface phenomenon but as a semantic phenomenon of base structure. When a case like the Dative, usually defined as an indirect object, is taken as an underlying semantic concept, it becomes possible to talk about differing surface realizations both within and across languages. The English preposition *to* in the sentence *I gave the book to Mark* and the Latin inflection *-o* in *Marco librum dedi*, for example, constitute two different realizations (surface forms) of the same (Dative) case. A noun may be in the Dative case in the absence of any case marking, as in the sentence *I gave Mark the book*. Further, even the surface subject of a sentence may represent an underlying Dative case if the semantic relationship remains the same, as in *Mark received the book*. There is no underlying case for the subject of a sentence in Fillmore's analysis; the semantic relationship between the subject and the verb is determined jointly by the underlying case of the noun and the meaning

---

[6]Although Schlesinger was the first to suggest that base structure is semantic and to use this insight in the analysis of child speech, the formal characteristics of his system are less appropriate for one-word speech than Fillmore's linguistically motivated scheme. This point will be discussed later when we describe the rationale behind our data analysis. For a full discussion of the pros and cons of Schlesinger's system on theoretical grounds and in relation to two-word speech, the reader is referred to Brown (1973).

of the verb. The advantages of this conceptualization will become clearer after we lay out the main formal characteristics of the system.

The basic concepts are the case category (C), the proposition (P), the modality (M), and the sentence (S). The sentence is basically composed of a proposition and its modality:

(6) $$S \rightarrow M + P$$

The proposition "consists of a verb and one or more noun phrases, each associated with the verb in a particular case relationship" (Fillmore, 1968, p. 21). The modality component contains elements that modify the proposition as a whole, such as tense, negation, mode, aspect, and certain adverbial phrases.

The cognitive psychological nature of Fillmore's view of deep grammatical structure is clearly manifest in the following statement introducing his list of cases:

> The case notions comprise a set of universal, presumably innate, concepts which identify certain types of judgments human beings are capable of making about the events that are going on around them, judgments about such matters as who did it, who it happened to, and what got changed. The cases that appear to be needed include:
>
> *Agentive* (A), the case of the typically animate perceived instigator of the action identified by the verb.
>
> *Instrumental* (I), the case of the inanimate force or object causally involved in the action or state identified by the verb.
>
> *Dative* (D), the case of the animate being affected by the state or action identified by the verb.
>
> *Factitive* (F), the case of the object or being resulting from action or state identified by the verb, or understood as a part of the meaning of the verb.
>
> *Locative* (L), the case which identifies the location or spatial orientation of the state of action identified by the verb.
>
> *Objective* (O), the semantically most neutral case, the case of anything representable by a noun whose role in the action or state identified by the verb is identified by the semantic interpretation of the verb itself; conceivably the concept should be limited to things which are affected by the action or state identified by the verb. The term is not to be confused with the notion of direct object, nor with the name of the surface case synonymous with accusative [pp. 24–25].

The following two sentences with the cases of the nouns labeled illustrate the above categories in a simple way:

(7)   *The boy hit the ball with a bat.*
          A   O   I

(8)   *The architect built a house on the hill for his client.*
            A   F   L   D

Fillmore does not see his list as definitive, and we shall discuss needed modifications when we present our data.

Let us now compare a case analysis with the traditional transformational approach applied by most investigators of child language in the late 1960s. Whereas Chomsky distinguishes the grammatical relations of base structure from the surface means by which they are expressed, Fillmore separates semantic notions from grammatical ones. How this works in practice can be seen in the following set of examples:

(9) a. *John opened the door.*
     b. *The door was opened by John.*
     c. *The door opened.*

Fillmore and Chomsky would agree that sentences (9a) and (9b) have the same underlying relationships. *Door*, which is the grammatical object in sentence (9a), has become the surface subject of sentence (9b) by a passivization transformation. However, they would disagree in their analysis of sentence (9c). According to the traditional version of transformational grammar, *door* is the subject of sentence (9c) on both the underlying and surface levels. According to Fillmore's analysis, however, there are no underlying subjects: *John* is the underlying Agent, not underlying subject, of sentences (9a) and (9b), whereas *door* is the underlying Object in all three sentences. In sentences (9a) and (9b), the underlying Agent became the subject. In sentence (9c), *door* becomes the surface subject in the absence of an Agent. Thus, the case analysis captures the fact that the semantic relation between *door* and *open* is the same in all three sentences. In fact, although a given verb may occur with different sets of cases, the relationship between a noun in a given case and the verb remains the same. The verb *open* always occurs with an Objective case noun, but nouns in the Agentive and Instrumental cases may also occur optionally. Sentences (9a) and (9b) include both Objective and Agentive cases. Sentence (9c) includes only the obligatory Objective case. Some examples with Instrumental case nouns are:

(9) d. *The wind opened the door.*
          I   O

     e. *John opened the door with a chisel.*
          A   O   I

Arguing for the validity of his case theory of grammar from a linguistic rather than a psychological point of view, Fillmore shows that some grammatical transformations are governed by the semantic relations expressed by case categories. Thus, there is a principled reason for including semantics in general, and semantic relations in particular, in grammatical knowledge. The branch of transformational grammar known as generative semantics (e.g., McCawley, 1968) has presented many other arguments for a semantic base structure.

A case analysis gives formal recognition to semantic factors present in early speech (Bowerman, 1973; Brown, 1973). Bowerman (1973) has detailed the advantages of a case treatment for the analysis of beginning grammar in general and her Finnish subjects in particular. We briefly summarize them here.

At Stage 1 in the speech of Seppo, one of Bowerman's Finnish children, all subjects are, in fact, Agents. However, in English (and, presumably, Finnish) grammatical subjects are not restricted to semantic Agents, as Sentence (9c) illustrates. Therefore, it seems more accurate to attribute to Seppo the semantic concept Agent rather than the syntactic concept of a subject. As Bowerman points out, the concept of Agent is more powerful than selection restrictions on subjects in that it explains *why* animate nouns should be subjects. It seems to us, moreover, that the existence of an Agent case explains the one exception to the rule that subjects in the corpus of Seppo I had to be animate. Inanimate vehicles, such as *car*, could also function as subjects of his sentences because vehicles appear to instigate action, thus approximating the definition of an Agent. Thus, the case framework offers a better explanation of the data in this instance than does the framework of grammatical relations. Other advantages are more formal. For example, a case analysis does not impose the subject–predicate division on deep-structure elements. In discussing McNeill's use of grammatical relations, we noted that these relations are defined by a set of rules which define a sentence (S) as composed of a noun phrase (NP) subject and a verb phrase (VP) predicate, and a verb phrase as composed of a verb (V) and an optional noun phrase (NP) object. In graphic form:

(10)

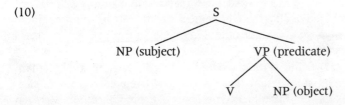

In adult language, there is empirical evidence that the verb phrase is a distinct constituent of the sentence. However, Bowerman (1973) points out that there is no empirical justification for attributing this structure to the child. The structure

(11)

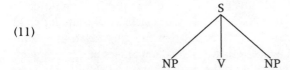

is equally justified by the data. Giving all noun phrases equal status in a sentence vis-à-vis the verb fits the developmental profile much better. The fact that S-O sentences often appear as early as the other two types indicates equal, not greater, complexity from a psychological point of view, contrary to the implications of the structure depicted in (10).

To the advantages Bowerman has noted, we might add some further ones: Case grammar allows one to refer to the role of a noun in a sentence without reference to other nouns in that sentence. For example, use of the Objective case facilitates recognition of the constant role of *record* in *I started the record and The record started.* Case terminology is, of course, ideally suited to one-word speech in which there is no sentence to which to relate a word. To call an isolated word an Agent is reasonable, provided that an action has occurred; to call it a subject is ludicrous. If we are to discover structure in, rather than to impose structure on, child language, it is useful to have a descriptive system which allows separate treatment of each element of the situation. In that way, we can trace the gradual development of a linguistic structure without assuming the presence of the total structure from the outset.

Finally, case grammar allows principled discussion of concrete semantic roles like Agent or Object independent of any particular vocabulary or syntactic structure. To discuss the use of nouns in child language, it is useful to have more categories than the number of nouns a verb can govern (three at most: subject, direct object, an indirect object), yet fewer categories than there are verbs. In a sense, each verb defines a different set of semantic functions: The properties of the subject of *see* are slightly different from the properties of the subject of *hear.* Most other semantically based theories of grammar (e.g. G. Lakoff, 1971) have too few categories to show their particular semantic similarity. Case grammar, however, allows us to treat them together in a simple and natural way: They are both Datives. It is this conreteness that makes case grammar more useful for child language than some other recent, semantically based versions of transformational grammar.

Bowerman (1973) found certain modifications necessary in applying Fillmore's theory to her data. These will be discussed with reference to our application of his system, for the psychological necessity of her modifications was even more compelling in the one-word stage. In addition, the problems identified by Bowerman relate to, and are consonant with, more basic theoretical modifications of Fillmore's model which are necessary if it is to be applied to the language acquisition process. However, she feels that the problems with a case analysis do not outweigh the advantages gained by rejecting certain basic assumptions of generative transformational grammar inappropriate for child speech. Brown (1973) agrees, but points out that the Chomskian or Bloom-type grammar has greater scope, especially for later stages of development, because Fillmore has concentrated on the deep structure of simple sentences. However, the transformational component of a case grammar in principle need be no different from that of a Chomskian grammar (Janet Fodor, personal communication, 1971).

In conclusion, a semantic approach to language which derives grammar from relations among perceived aspects of the real world opens the way to a theoretical treatment of one-word speech as structurally continuous with later grammatical development. Our formal analysis exploited this possibility, a possibility lacking to the earlier investigators of one-word speech, whose work will now be reviewed.

1.2 Earlier Studies of One-Word Speech

Studies of child language discussed so far were concerned almost exclusively with two-word and longer sentences, and slighted or ignored development during the one-word stage. However, a number of widely scattered observers of an earlier period wrote about one-word utterances on the basis of their own diary observations, often as part of longitudinal studies. Our historical review wll focus on earlier work from the point of view of the theoretical issues relevant to the present study, using specific authors as representative of points of view. A number of them, like Stern and Stern (1928), Leopold (1939—1949), and Werner and Kaplan (1963) have made more or less exhaustive reviews of the literature; this is not our purpose in the historical survey that follows.

STERN AND STERN

The extensive diary observations of Clara and Wilhelm Stern, first published in 1907, and revised for the last time in 1928, were a major influence on other studies of early language acquisition. Their work presents a rich store of detailed data on the language learning of three German children, integrating this material with the results of previously published child studies. In summarizing their major work, *Die Kindersprache*, Wilhelm Stern (1930) places major emphasis on the classification of vocabulary. The Sterns (1907; W. Stern, 1930) attempted to classify the child's words according to their class membership (part of speech) in adult language, and attempted to relate these classes to stages of semantic development. Thus, nouns are supposed to show their first appearance in Stage 1, the stage of substance; verbs are supposed to appear in Stage 2, the stage of action; and adjectives (as well as prepositions, adverbs, and numerals), in Stage 3, the stage of relations and attributes. Although we have found parallel stages of semantic development, the connection between grammatical class membership and semantic function did not hold up, and was rightly criticized by such contemporaries as K. Buhler (1926) and Guillaume (1927). The child often expresses a given semantic category by words that belong to more than one part of speech and often uses a given word differently from situation to situation.[7] Stern and Stern (1907) finally give up the classification

---

[7]Although we shall not attempt to treat her work, it should be noted that C. Buhler (1931) continued this German tradition of distinguishing various stages in very early speech. In her work, the very numerous stages were defined in terms of a potpourri of syntactic and semantic features.

of children's words into parts of speech saying: "The child's verbal units do not belong to any word class, because they are not words but sentences" (p. 164, by P.M.G. from Guillaume, 1927).

The theoretical problem plaguing Stern and Stern, as well as later investigators, appears to be the following: They noticed that the interesting aspects of the earliest language development are semantic, and felt that later grammar grows out of this stage, but they were unable to relate semantic and grammatical structure. The only grammatical concepts they had that could be related to child language and that might have some semantic function were the parts of speech. However, these categories were inadequate for the job.

BLOCH

After observing the language development of his own children, Bloch (1921) set forth two generally remarked properties of single-word utterances. One is the flexibility (and idiosyncrasy) of the meanings of children's words. For example, one child used *chaud* (hot) to mean not only cold and hot but painful as well (p. 707). *Ouvi* (*ouvrir*: open) was said when requesting that the father remove a scarf, while pulling on the head of a cane, while trying to remove a ball from behind a bed, while holding a knife and a piece of bread, and when trying to remove a coat (p. 708). Bloch also noted that the meanings of children's words often change. For example, *ada* (*soldat*: soldier) was used first by one child to mean only a particular toy of her brother's but later was extended to all toys (p. 709). Nevertheless, such changes only concern individual lexical items, and are not part of a general developmental pattern of the sort that we sought in our study.

Bloch distinguishes flexibility from a second type of broadness of meaning:

> Beyond the breadth and mobility of the meaning of words, the most remarkable trait of child language at its beginnings is the active value which all words are apt to receive. A substantive does not designate only an object, but all the actions with which it is related in the experience of the child [p. 700, translation by P.M.G.]

Many other writers have also observed this property (e.g., Dewey, 1894). For instance, Stevenson (1893) wrote

> In the infant's speech, these words are not nouns, but equivalent to whole sentences. When a very young child says "water," he is not using the word merely as the name of an object so designated by us, but with the value of an assertion, something like "I want water," or "there is water" [p. 120, quoted in Ingram, 1971].

These cases differ from Bloch's examples already cited in that the child does not extend the meaning of one word (e.g., *hot*) to include the meanings of what would be a number of semantically related words of the same part of speech

for adults (e.g., *cold, painful,* both adjectives). Rather, the child extends the meaning of one part of speech—a noun—to include the meaning of one or more
others—a verb, for example. Thus, Bloch's daughter said *lele* (*volet*: shutter)
to ask him to *open* the *window*. When she had *hurt* her *head* she said *atet* (*la
tête*: the head). In this view, shared by Preyer (1890), Stern and Stern (1907),
Paloma (1910), and K. Buhler (1926), these examples demonstrate that a single-
word utterence has essentially the meaning of a complete sentence. Such
single-word utterances are commonly called *holophrases.*

Although Bloch gives many interesting examples, like many investigators,
he blurs the basic distinction between the *referential* meaning of a word (what
the word alone denotes) and its *combinatorial* meaning (the meaning resulting
from the word in a specific combination with other elements). This mistake
is based on the assumption that, because words are uttered one at a time, there is
nothing for them to combine with; It leads to the conclusion that the entire
message is contained in the meaning of a word.

How might the distinction of referential and combinatorial meaning affect
Bloch's notion that child language differs from adult language in its flexibility and active value? The range of meaning of the word *hot*—both hot and
cold—must reflect a referential value different from the adult language. However, only the range of reference, not the type of reference, differs from adult
speech. The range of uses of the word *open*, in Bloch's previously mentioned
data, could result from the description of a *common action* applied to a variety
of objects in different situations rather than from changes in the referential
meaning of *open* itself. In this case, it would not be accurate to speak of the
meaning of *open* as more "flexible" or "Shifting" that in adult usage, since apparent changes of meaning are changes of combinatorial meaning, not referential
meaning. That is, the total message could result from *open* being combined
with a variety of objects. Thus, it is important to consider the nonverbal context
in which a word is used and with which the referential meaning of that word
may combine to yield combinatorial variants. Our study set out to investigate
the possibility that, if situational characteristics were taken into account, the
apparent "active value" of single-word utterances might be just another variety
of combinatorial meaning.

DE LAGUNA AND GUILLAUME

In contrast with Bloch's referential emphasis, de Laguna (1927) offers a theory
of the holophrase that is explicitly both structurally and developmentally
oriented. Although she accepts the view that single-word utterances are actually
complete sentences, she emphasizes the fact that single-word utterance are used
as a means of communication, and analyzes how these words are used in communication and how they are related to later, normal sentences.

De Laguna distinguishes naming behavior, which involves simply attaching a name to an object, from sentential holophrases, which develop later and make a statement about something (p. 86–87). She did not do any full-scale studies herself but uses examples from Bloch (1921) to support her analysis. For instance, when Bloch's daughter came crying to him saying *maman* (mama) because her mother had put her out of the kitchen, de Laguna says that she was making a statement about her mother rather than naming her.

In one aspect of her analysis of one-word utterances, de Laguna is confused and inconsistent. At several points, she states that one-word utterances are unitary and cannot be used where communication depends on analyzing the situation into separable elements (1963, pp. 86, 90, 91, 94), consistent with the idea that a single word "contains" a whole but undifferentiated sentence. Elsewhere, however, she points out that individual words are able to function as sentences because they are uttered in particular contexts (1963, pp. 90–91) and the missing linguistic elements are supplied by the situation. We might say that the word combines with elements of the total situation to produce a propositional message. For instance, de Laguna shows that analysis of the situation, in fact, is possible through the use of gestures (pp. 78, 99). In early proclamations, a property, *mm, no-no,* or *ca-ca* (dirty), is often predicated of an object whose existence is presumed or presupposed:

> This presumption may take the form of pointing to the thing in question, or perhaps of intently regarding it.... In such a case there is virtual or implicit predication; but the language form is rudimentary. The verbal utterance must be supplemented by some other form of bodily response, like pointing, which serves to indicate the object to which the verbal specification applies. But when so supplemented, it does serve to analyze the situation in a limited way [pp. 98, 99]

Similarly an object is distinguished from its properties when a child points to the object while verbally expressing a property, such as the name of its possessor (p. 99).

De Laguna notes that the communicative power of a child's speech increases with development. Whereas names can only control attention, sentential holophrases convey information about the situation in which they are uttered. After this stage, the child can substitute names for the original pointing gestures, changing from implicit predication, in which the object is presupposed by the verbal utterance, to explicit predication, in which the object is explicitly named in the utterance. According to de Laguna, this change from gestures to names allows statements about objects to be made in their absence (p. 100). Even though she may have underestimated the ability of single-word utterances to refer to absent referents, longer sentences, at the very least, facilitate communication about nonpresent objects and events.

An article by Guillaume appeared in French the same year (1927) as de Laguna's book in English. Apparently independent, their views, nonetheless, are amazingly similar. Like de Laguna, Guillaume stressed the communicative function of language: "A means of action of man on man." Guillaume talks of the *mot–phrase* (sentence-word) with global meaning, but, like de Laguna, gives some specific analyses which contradict this notion. For instance, he says that the objects of negation of early negative words are not expressed verbally at first. Thus, he implies that the negative word is combined with a situational element distinct from that word. In fact, he speaks of single-word utterances as predicates of the situation.

Guillaume notes that messages in which verbal and nonverbal elements are combined are the foundation for word combinations in the next stage of development. He reports that one child first used the word *encore* (*again* or *more*) alone to ask for the repetition of an act or thing, but later used *encore* with verbal complements. (Cohen [1952], a French linguist working 25 years later, presents additional evidence of this sort.) Guillaume also notes a progression from the use of a single verbal element, say a verb, in one particular situation, to its use in a variety of situations, with a variety of actors, objects, and circumstances but a constant common element, the action in the case of a verb. The ability to combine a single word with various situational elements is a step toward the dissociation of action, person, and object necessary for multiword sentences. Thus, Guillaume shows that child language is productive in that one verbal element occurs in combination with a variety of nonverbal elements. Our study makes explicit Guillaume's implicit notion of productivity and subjects it to a quantitative test not possible with diary observations alone.

Finally, Guillaume anticipates to an amazing degree our point of view concerning the most basic process of grammar acquisition: "The child does not invent grammatical categories: he finds these tools already made, but he must learn the use of them by the direct relation of the sentence to the concrete situation" (p. 25) He recognizes a number of different functions expressed by single words, for example, recognition, localization, object of demand, object of intended action. Grégoire (1937), writing 10 years later, echoes this idea, albeit in an uncertain manner, while specifically distinguishing syntactic from semantic structure: "Grammatical categories are not yet distinguished; however, one establishes the existence of fugitive intentions to mark a quality (adjective value), an action (verbal value), a negation, a designation (demonstrative value)" (p. 271, translation by P.M.G.). Operational specification of these "intentions" was quite lacking in the diary studies on which such conceptualizations were based. Nor did either Guillaume or Grégoire observe any developmental progression in the emergence of these semantic functions. The present study sought both operational definition of the relation between word and situation and systematic developmental change.

PIAGET AND SINCLAIR

Piaget (1951) amasses examples from his own children to stress the active quality of meanings in the single-word stage which Bloch noted: "It is clear that these words, far from denoting merely singular classes and being proper names — really represent complex schemas of action, either related to the subject or partly objective" (1951, p. 219).[8] Like Bloch, Piaget notes "the disconcerting mobility of the symbol" (p. 220). However, because he fails to distinguish between referential and combinatorial meaning, his examples of change and fluidity are a potpourri of clear lexical development and combinations of a constant word with a variety of situational elements. An example that shows clear lexical development—that is, change in the referential meaning of a word— is the following:

> L., at 1;3(4), said *ha* to a real cat and then to a toy elephant, but not to a hen or a horse. But at 1;3(19) *ha* was applied to the horse as well as to her toys. At 1;6(25) *ha* had become *hehe* and referred to all animals except the cat and the rabbit, to all kinds of people and even to her sister [p. 217].

An example from his daughter Jacqueline that, in our opinion, shows differences in combinatorial meaning rather than lexical development is:

> At about 1;6 the word *papeu* was used to mean *gone away* and was applied to people going out of the room, vehicles going away, matches that were blown out. At 1;6(11) she even used it of her own tongue which she had put out and then put in again [p. 217].

Our point is that *papeu* appears to have no more fluid meaning than the term *gone away* used by mature speakers in a set of sentences corresponding to the aforementioned examples:

(12)   a. *The people have* **gone away**.
                b. *The cars have* **gone away**.
                c. *The flame has* **gone away**.
                d. *My tongue has* **gone away**.

It is just these combinatorial possibilities of word and situation that seemed to us to be a possible basis for learning the combinatorial possibilities of words in the later acquisition of syntax.

Piaget insists that earliest speech is egocentric. This is, the child takes his own perspective on a situation or problem for granted without adequately taking into

---

[8]A similar view was expressed by Lewis (1951), who saw the single-word utterance as embracing a comparatively wide situation, including affective as well as conational (action) factors.

account the external situation or the perspective of other people. Egocentrism in small children derives both from the association of early speech with the child's own action and from the lack of stable denotation required by the conventionalized speech of a social group. Piaget seems to see no decentration (development away from egocentrism) during the period of early speech, even into the stage of two-word combinations. Furthermore, he believes that, to the extent that speech is still egocentric, it fails to communicate. This viewpoint is opposed to that of de Laguna who stresses the extraordinarily communicative quality of child language at its outset. There is no logically necessary connection between a word's relation to the speaker (degree of egocentrism) and its communicative power. We shall have occasion in this study to observe whether or not early speech communicates effectively and whether or not decentration occurs during the one-word stage.

Piaget also claims that "the first use of language is mainly in the form of orders and expressions of desire" (p. 222). This statement is curious in the light of the fact that his own examples do not support it (pp. 216–217). Yet, this idea has an ancient history, as Leopold (1939–1949) points out: Moreover, it has been taken up by other theoreticians of child language such as Jakobson (1969); we shall therefore subject it to empirical test.

Piaget's notions concerning the relation between action and language appear rather vague and inaccurate when applied to the analysis of language per se. Of greater value is his more basic theoretical tenet that symbolic representation in general and language in particular grow out of the sensorimotor developments of preceding stages of cognitive growth. The sensorimotor basis for representation is the *index* or *signal*, in which a part of the object or action stands for the whole. For instance, the infant stops crying when she hears her mother's footsteps: Footsteps signify the event of being fed. Differentiation of signifier and signified (referent) increases as representational development proceeds. The next stage is the *symbol*, in which an image stands for something it resembles. The child represents the referential situation by imitating it in its absence. For example, Piaget's child Laurent produced his first symbolic representation at 12(0) when he pretended to go to sleep, holding an imaginary pillow to his head. Conventional language becomes possible at the following stage, that of the *sign*. A sign differs from a symbol in that it has an arbitrary relation to what it signifies; that is, the sign need bear no resemblance to its referent. For this reason, the sign must also be a conventionalized form. The earliest signs are words.

The notion of the sensorimotor origins of language is, in its spirit, very much in accord with a semantic approach to the acquisition of grammatical structure, as Brown (1973) has noted. Sinclair (1969, 1970, 1971), a member of Piaget's Geneva group, has explicitly recognized that language acquisition must have a cognitive basis:

Our contention would be ... that the infant brings to his language acquisition task not a set of innate linguistic universals, but innate cognitive functions which will ultimately result in universal structures of thought ... since intelligence exists phylogenetically and ontogenetically before language, and since the acquisition of linguistic structures is a cognitive activity, cognitive structures should be used to explain language acquisition rather than vice versa [1971, p. 123].

In a more detailed theoretical statement, she relates concepts from Piaget's analysis of sensorimotor development to linguistic concepts from Chomsky's analysis of language abilities:

Speaking in a general and theoretical way, it is possible to show the similarity between Piaget's descriptions of sensori—motor structure and Chomsky's description (1965) of deep structure. The child at this stage can order, temporally and spatially; he can classify in action, that is to say, he can use a whole category of objects for the same action, or apply a whole category of action—schemes to one object; and he can relate objects and actions to actions. The linguistic equivalents of these structures are concatenation, categorization, i.e., the major categories (S, NP, VP, etc.) and functional grammatical relations (subject of, object of, etc.). These are the main operations of the base of the syntactic component which characterizes a highly restricted set of elementary structures from which actual sentences are constructed by transformational rules. Finally, these base rules have a particular formal property, namely that they may introduce the initial symbol S (sentence) into a line of derivation, so that phrase-markers can be inserted into other base phrase-markers. A psychological parallel to this so-called recursive property of the base can be found in the embedding of action—schemes one into the other, when the child can put one action-pattern into another pattern. This can be traced back to the simple circular reactions of a much earlier stage [1971, p. 126].

Thus, Sinclair draws specific lines of connection between sensorimotor accomplishments and later-developing grammatical categories and relations (which she conceives of in a strictly Chomskian framework). She also draws a parallel between embedding in action and grammar.

LEOPOLD

Leopold's four-volume diary (1939—1949), *Speech Development of a Bilingual Child*, offers an extremely rich source of empirical data from the one-word period of an English-speaking (albeit bilingual) child. Here, however, we shall be concerned with his theoretical orientation rather than with the data itself. Like de Laguna and Guillaume, but in contrast to Piaget, Leopold (1949) recognizes the communicativeness of one-word utterances and states that "since the child's environment is well-equipped to understand the intention of such utterances with the help of the concrete situation which is at that stage always involved, this primitive mode of expression satisfies the needs of communication for an extended period" (p. 3).

Leopold follows the Sterns in classifying children's words by adult part of speech, and is led to the conclusion that one-word speech is "unorganized" (1949, p. 173). Nevertheless, he recognizes that children express a number of semantic functions, such as action, object, negative, locus, and possession, and modes with their one-word utterances. Many of his observations are amazingly astute. For instance, Leopold distinguished between the action of an object and the action of a person. As an example of action of an object, at 20 months, Leopold's child says *away*, preparing to put a cart away. As an example of "person" action, at 23 months, she said *blow*, interpreted by Leopold as "You blow up my balloon." As the reader will see, we observed the appearance of these same semantic functions in the present study. In fact, we observed every semantic function described by Leopold, often under very similar circumstances. Leopold divides utterances into two categories on the basis of mode: emotional utterances, corresponding to volitional utterances in our study, and statements of fact, corresponding to indicative utterances in the present study. Lewis (1951) makes a parallel distinction. Like ourselves, Leopold observes that children use both intonation and gesture to express the mode of an utterance. Because he treats mode, like structure, in terms of adult grammar, he feels puzzled that a given word can occur in two modes; for instance, *up* could occur at one time to express a wish, at another to express a statement of fact. Apparently, Leopold feels that since the child at this stage cannot use syntax or morphology to distinguish the imperative from the indicative, she ought to do so by means of vocabulary. Lukens, writing in 1896 (quoted in Ingram, 1971), made a more productive assessment of the continuity between earlier and later speech when he wrote that "in the early stages of sentence formation where one or two words are used as a rudimentary sentence, tone and gesture perform the function of grammatical inflection and syntax, marking distinctions of thought long before they are represented in words" (p. 437).

Like Guillaume and de Laguna, Leopold (1949) sees a structural connection between one-word and two-word utterances. For instance, Leopold recognizes that a negative wish, such as *no X* consists of "a word to indicate the wish and a word to specify its domain. In this respect they represent a step forward from the one-word stage, in which either the wish or the specification had to be inferred from the situation" (p. 22). Leopold's analysis of the relations present in two-word utterances is often similar to the most recent semantic treatments (e.g., Bloom, 1970; Bowerman, 1973; Brown, 1973; Slobin, 1970; Schlesinger, 1971a,b). For instance, Leopold analyzes the sentence *I bye-bye* as including subject (*I*) and action (*bye-bye*). He goes on to describe still other two-word structures identified by these more recent workers:

> Another category of two-word statements consisted of verb and object. The omitted subject was supplied by the situation: (the cat) *drinks milk* 1;10, (she) *picks flowers* 1;11, (I) *bite Papa* 1;11, (the cat, who had just been mentioned) *bites me* 1;11.

> The lack of a third word was a serious syntactic deficiency when the verb was omitted because the child had the desire to express both subject and object. The complete predicate had to be inferred from the situation [p. 29].

Thus, not only did Leopold formulate the major structural types of two-word utterances, he also notices special difficulty in interpreting noun—noun combinations, a key point in Bloom's argument for the necessity of semantic information to determine the structure of two-word utterances.

WERNER AND KAPLAN

Werner and Kaplan (1963) presaged to a considerable degree the underlying theoretical notions and findings of our study in their unifying analysis of earlier diary studies of language development, including those of Bloch and Leopold. Most central, they had the idea of a developmental sequence of types of predication, of which each has origins in the one-word stage. Olson (1968) first called attention to their formulation, although he expressed doubt as to its validity. Here is an outline of the developmental sequence presented by Werner and Kaplan:

1. *Identifying predications.* In its explicit verbal manifestation, judgments of identification (identifying predications) take the form "This [pointing] is a B" or "A is a B."

> Identifying predications are evident in the earliest monoremic utterances of the child, for example, *tick-tock, wau-wau, fff,* especially when these are accompanied by deictic gestures, such as turning toward the presented content or pointing to it. At the two-vocable level, one finds that the deixis is represented by demonstrative vocal forms, for example *da* or *ta . . . .*

> Gradually, in early childhood, conventional forms replace the infantile demonstratives and names. For English-speaking children, the identifying predication in concrete situations takes the form "that is a ———." Subsequently, at stages beyond those considered in this chapter, identifying predications subserve class inclusion and exclusion: one asserts that "A is a B" or "A is not a B" [pp. 161–162, *Symbol Formation,* H. Werner & B. Kaplan, Copyright © 1963 John Wiley & Sons, Inc. Reprinted by permission of John Wiley & Sons, Inc].

2. *Predications of action.* The genesis of explicit verbal predication of action requires two things: (*1*) the establishment of agent (person or thing) vocables and (*2*) activity or state vocables. (Werner and Kaplan use the term "vocable" to refer to morphemes before the child is able to combine morphemes; they use the term "monoreme" approximately as others have used the word "holophrase." Also they used the term "agent" in a less strict sense than Fillmore's Agent—it seems to cover all entities animate and inanimate.)

Since the predication of action involves a connection between two terms, a thing (person) and an action, one might logically expect that the formation of predications of action requires, at a minimum, two-vocable utterances. Even a cursory perusal of observations reported in the literature indicates that this is not true. The beginnings of predications of action are found in situations in which one member of the relation is not linguistically articulated; rather it is present only as perceptual object or implied in gestural activity. Leopold's observation ... on the predicative use of the vocable *away* illustrates this point rather well: [The child said *away* after putting her toy away] only one member of the predicative statement (*away*) was linguistically expressed; the other member (*toy*) was non-linguistically given in the pragmatic—perceptual context [p. 165, *Symbol Formation*, H. Werner & B. Kaplan, Copyright © 1963, John Wiley & Sons, Inc. Reprinted by permission of John Wiley & Sons, Inc.].

3. *Predication of attributes.* Vocables stipulating a "quality" of an object are the early precursors of the predication of attributes. For example, Leopold (1939, I, p. 121) noticed that from 1;11 on, Hildegard used *pooh* "to predicate the attribute 'dirty' of various objects" (1963, p. 167).

Just as, in children of Indo-European linguistic cultures, true predications of actions and, correlatively, true verbs come into existence with the adoption and systematic use of morphological devices, so too do true predicate adjectives come into being with the adoption of syntactic means such as copula forms [p. 168, *Symbol Formation*, H. Werner & B. Kaplan, Copyright © 1963, John Wiley & Sons, Inc. Reprinted by permission of John Willey & Sons, Inc.].

This formulation manifests a large degree of convergence with the theoretical foundations and data of our study. At the same time, it joins a number of theoretical features that appeared only separately earlier formulations of one-word speech. First, Werner and Kaplan make a clear distinction between semantic relations and their syntactic realization which allows them to trace basic semantic relations back to one-word speech and see development during this stage. Second, they clearly differentiate substages within the stage of one-word speech. Third, they see a structural continuity between one-word utterances and later word combinations.

Unfortunately, these insights tend to get lost because they do not appear in the chapters of the book devoted to one-word speech but in a later chapter entitled "Early Stages in the Development of Predicative Sentences." In the earlier sections, Werner and Kaplan state that "the referents of early vocables remain relatively global in character, that is, total situations in which agent, action, and object are totally fused" (1963, p. 116). This analysis contradicts their later opinion that a single word has a *specific referent* and *combines* with situational features to form a total message. Their self-contradiction reflects the same underlying confusion that we saw in the work of others between the referential meaning and the combinatorial or structural meaning of a word. They attempt to resolve this internal contradiction by positing a developmental progression from global to specific predicative usage:

It is particularly during the later months of the monoremic stage that the child's vocal expressions seem, at least implicitly, to indicate a differentiation among various components of the situation referred to. Though, to be sure, monoremes characteristically refer to total happenings and never to precisely delimited components such as action per se or thing per se, the beginnings of such an implicit "categorization" of events through vocal expression seem to form [p. 137, *Symbol Formation*, H. Werner & B. Kaplan, copyright © 1963 John Wiley & Sons, Inc. Reprinted by permission of John Wiley & Sons, Inc.].

But it seems doubtful that their data could support the existence of such a developmental progression.

Werner and Kaplan distinguish two major aspects of a message:

One concerns the *attitudinal mode*. Various main attitudes are expressed through vocal forms: one is the attitude toward making social contact; it appears in expression of greeting, of saying good-bye, of communicating one's affection; other attitudes are those of *wish* or *command*, of *declaration*, of *questioning*, etc. The second aspect of a message is *reference*; that is, reference to a state of affairs articulated in terms of its components, e.g., self, other, object of discourse [p. 132, *Symbol Formation*, H. Werner & B. Kaplan, copyright © 1963 John Wiley & Sons, Inc. Reprinted by permission of John Wiley & Sons, Inc.].

This distinction is the semantic analog to Fillmore's (1968) division of the sentence into modality and proposition; this same semantic distinction has been utilized in our scheme for analyzing the messages conveyed in one-word speech.

1.3 Origins of This Study

Some informal observations on Lauren Greenfield (Greenfield 1968) led to the notion that semantic–grammatical relations develop during one-word speech. It was observed that, if one looked at the way in which single words *combined* with nonlinguistic elements, referential meanings were, in fact, neither so idiosyncratic nor so flexible as Bloch (1921) had claimed, nor so global as Werner and Kaplan (1963) had thought. When a child used a word in varying situational contexts, the adult's interpretation of the word varied in definable ways. Although it could be objected (as many did object) that such combinations were figments of the adult's imagination, it seemed to Lauren's interpreter (P.M.G.) that children's words could not be interpreted so readily unless *the individual words were being systematically combined with nonverbal cues*, unless each word occupied a specific position in a definite situational structure. For instance, when Lauren at 15 months, 5 days, said *Baba* (Barbara) upon hearing footsteps upstairs where Barbara (her babysitter) lived, it seemed that she was communicating information about the source of the noise. *Examples such as these led to the attempt, pursued in this study, to specify the cues underlying adult*

*interpretations of one-word utterances and their interrelationships—the semantic
structure of a concrete situation*

Earlier approaches to one-word speech seemed to have erred in not distinguishing the referential from the combinatorial aspects of meaning. The term
holophrase expresses this error, for it implies that a word somehow "contains"
a whole sentence. To earlier observers, a word appeared global or holophrastic
because they failed to see that this "sentential" meaning did not inhere in the
word itself, but resulted from the word being systematically combined with
nonlinguistic elements. Of course, the "meaning" of this combination of word
and situational elements differs from the referential meaning of the single word,
but the nature of this difference parallels the contrast between the "meaning" of
a whole sentence and the referent of a single, component word. Clearly, interpreting the referential meaning of single words to include nonverbal elements
with which they are combined will lead to the erroneous notion that early
words are more shifting, flexible, or idiosyncratic in meaning than the words of
an adult lexicon. If each combination of a verbal element with nonverbal
elements is taken to show a different meaning of the verbal elements, then its
referential meaning will, of course, appear to be wildly flexible—exactly as the
referential meaning of *chair* would shift wildly (and, in fact, infinitely) if it were
defined by the sentences in which it appeared in adult speech. *While the distinction between referential and sentential meaning is obvious in the case of sentences,
a major thrust of this work is to show that the distinction is equally basic, albeit more
subtle, for one-word speech.*

Two main aspects of the preliminary observations suggested that development within the one-word stage might have something to do with the basic
structural aspects of language and its acquisition. One was the fact that not all
usages appeared at once. For instance, simple naming appeared before use of a
word to indicate the object of a demand. Also, Lauren named important people
before she named any inanimate objects, but did not use a person's name in a
context where that person was the Agent of an action until considerably later.
There is no explanation for these delays on utilitarian grounds: It should be to
a child's advantage to use every new word in as many ways as possible. More
specifically, if developmental order were being governed by utilitarian value, the
child should name things she wants before using names simply to identify or
point out something, but this was not the case. It was the anti-intuitive nature of
these observations which suggested that structural constraints might be guiding
development during the period of one-word speech.

The grammatical studies previously cited indicated that semantic structure
could be traced in early two-word speech. Parallel to Ervin-Tripp (1971), we
surmised that the same semantic functions might be expressed by single words
in earlier speech, and that the development to two-word speech might consist
in expressing elements that formerly were implicit in the situation.

Another striking aspect of these preliminary observations was the appearance during this period of a form of dialogue that looked like a two person sentence. Lauren's words were not global responses to her mother's speech, but combined with it in very specific ways.

For instance, at 15 months, 7 days, Lauren's mother pointed to the sun on a three-dimensional wall plaque and said *sun*; Lauren responded *hot*. In this example, the adult supplied a verbal topic, and the child, a verbal comment of an attributive nature. Earlier, Lauren had been observed to point at an object and say *hot*; later, she combined both topic and comment in a two-word sentence in parallel situations. Thus, there was a progression in the role of gestures, verbal cues, and word combinations in Lauren's verbal production.

These observations suggested that children might use the context of real-world events as a structured framework which could be gradually filled in with verbal forms. If the child is signaling semantic relations, one element at a time, before she has the ability to combine words, this is evidence that nonverbal events—the child's actions and perceptions—are being structured in terms of the semantic functions of Agent, Object, Location, etc. and that words are being used in such a cognitive–perceptual–action framework from the outset. Thus, knowledge of the semantic relations of referents in a concrete context could be used by a child to learn *how* those relations are expressed in the child's particular language.

The two-person sentence also suggested the possibility of a structural role of dialogue in the language acquisition process. Thus, our monograph is concerned not only with the development of structure in the one-word period, but also with the two-way communication process which underlies the discovery of this structure and influences its progressive development.

chapter 2

A Longitudinal Study of
Two Children:
Its Theory and Method

2.1 The Children and the Study

THE CHILDREN

T he study follows two children, Matthew Greenfield and Nicholas Thompson, from the emergence of their first meaningful word through the one-word stage to the establishment of word combinations. The data reported in this volume end at a point where single-word utterances were in the minority for the first time.

Matthew is the second child of one of the authors. Nicky is the first (and, during the period of the study, only) child of Dorothy Thompson, who collaborated with the authors in collecting data on Nicky's speech development. Matthew and Nicky had a partially shared social and linguistic environment, for the Thompsons lived in an apartment downstairs from the Greenfields, and the two boys had known each other since the Thompsons' arrival in Boston from England when Matthew was 1 month old and Nicky was 6 months old. Dorothy Thompson cared for Matthew and his older sister Lauren for part of the day when their mother and father were both working, and the two families developed a close relationship. While Matthew and Nicky are, therefore, not two "independent" subjects of study, this situation made research collaboration with Nicky's mother much easier and more effective. Matthew's mother

(P.M.G.) is a psychologist, his father a physician. A sister, Lauren, is 2 years older than Matthew. Nicky's mother is a former language teacher, his father a biochemist.

DIARIES

The plan of the study was to combine diary observations and formal observation sessions to obtain a complete record of the children's speech. Jakobson (1969) has pointed out that diaries have the advantage of being able to record the exact temporal relation and interaction of different stages of linguistic development. At the beginning of language development, diaries have the additional advantage that they can capture and condense the child's infrequent use of language. Thus, diaries are complementary to formal observation sessions, which necessarily involve a limited time span. Even after speech production becomes more frequent and varied, it was thought that diaries could be used to report infrequent word usages and to document the onset of various structures in relation to their productive occurrence in an observation session.

Because the underlying concept of the study was to use naturally occurring expansions as a key to structure, and because it was not known in advance exactly what would be the most useful form of data, there was no attempt to shape the diaries into a standard format. D. Thompson was told that the study was about "grammar" in the one-word period, and she was instructed to keep track of new meanings in Nicky's speech. She was told that this involved not only acquiring new vocabulary, but also using old words in new ways. She was instructed to record the situational context of all utterances recorded in the diary. Her way of organizing the diary was to record together all the new usages that occurred over a span of time. The length of this interval varied from a single day to a month. The typical interval was a week long. Nicky's diary began at 8 (19) (8 months, 19 days) and ended at 21 (8).

Matthew's diary was organized somewhat differently. Critical events generally were recorded the day they happened. Only occasionally was a new development characterized as belonging to a more extended interval of time. The first observation was recorded at 7(22), the last observation at 22(0). Thompson's method of summarizing intervals led to relatively more information on the *frequency* of different types of speech event; Greenfield's emphasis on critical events produced fuller description of the *situational context* of particular utterances.

FORMAL SESSIONS

The diaries provide a relatively continuous record of many important events in the children's development. They contain, however, no check on the mother's reliability or completeness. The formal observation sessions provide a complementary source of data, which help to form a more accurate and complete picture of the children's development.

The procedure for the formal sessions was as follows: Each session took place at home and included three people—observer, child, and mother. In addition, Matthew was present throughout one of Nicky's sessions (VIII) and Lauren, Matthew's older sister, was present throughout the last session of Matthew (IX). Lauren also was present for parts of Matthew IV, Matthew VII, and Matthew VIII, and for parts of Nicky III, Nicky VII, and Nicky VIII. Matthew was present for parts of Nicky VI and Nicky VII. At the very beginning of Matthew IX, Matthew was in the care of a babysitter rather than his mother. There were also visitors from time to time; formal observation sessions were a sample from normal life.

As far as the children were concerned, the observer tried to stay in the background; she did, however, interact naturally with the mothers. The children went through normal activities of playing, eating, going to bed, or changing diapers as these naturally occurred; no activities were scheduled especially for the observations. For each utterance of the child, the observer wrote down a broad transcription, all relevant preceding verbal context, an expansion or interpretation, and the situational cues on which it was based. To give an example of this technique, at Session VI—22(21), Nicky uttered the word *dance*. His mother's interpretive expansion is *That one's dancing*. The ensemble of situational cues on which this is based is that Nicky is pointing to a picture of a bear dancing. The utterance *dance* was, in this case, later classified as Action or State of an Agent (the bear). Everything the child said, except nonlanguage sounds, was transcribed. In cases where the child was echoing or responding to what someone else had said, this preceding verbal context also was transcribed. The sessions were taperecorded with a portable Uher tape recorder to allow later completion and correction of the record. Situational information was recorded in approximately sentential form. The observer was instructed to pay special attention to the gestures and tone of voice of the child and the temporal relation of his utterance to surrounding actions. Of course, different aspects of the situation were relevant for the interpretation of each utterance.

Expansions and interpretations were given in several forms. When a mother's response to her child implied an interpretation of the child's sentence, the observer recorded that response, sometimes adding remarks of her own. When the mother directly told the observer what she thought the child was saying, the observer recorded that interpretation. In the remaining cases, the observer supplied the interpretation herself. There was a residual class of utterances that no one could interpret. Table 1 gives an example of how the observer recorded information.

Table 1
Sample of Observer's Notes: Nicky III—19(29)

Previous comments and questions	Utterance	Interpretation	Situation
	hurray	*Hurray.*	Finished building the whole tower.
	down	*You took it down.*	Took a cup from the tower and put it down.
	Oh	*Oh they all fell down.*	The cups fell down.
	dop (dropped)		Pointed to cups that had dropped on the floor.
	record 2 +	*You want the record now?*	Pointed to record player (no record on).
	no record, no recor	*That's a tape recorder. It doesn't go anyplace?*	
What's that?	*nut*	*Nut. That's right.*	Playing with nuts.
	gone	*Gone? He must have thought it was gone.*	Put nut into a cup. Looked up at me and said *gone.*
Stir with it?	*cracker*	*What? Caca? Is that a cracker?*	Playing with nuts and cups.
	poon		
	back, back	*Do you want me to put it back? There.*	Handed plate to mother.
Gone, yes.	*spoon*	*Yeah, that's a spoon.*	Picked up spoon again and looks at me.
	gone		
	ball	*What? Ball? Is one a ball? To observer: Might be talking about round hazel nuts.*	Looking at nuts (some round) and showing to mother.

34

Table 2
Schedule of Nicky's Observation Sessions

Period	Age	Duration	Total number of utterances
I	18(4)	2:00	126
II	18(27)	2:40	193
III	19(29)	2:35	222
IV	20(23)	2:15	359
V	21(17)	1:50	233
VI	22(21)	3:00	347
VII	23(21)	2:55	439
VIII	24(23)	3:45	495

Schedule of Sessions

At first, the observation sessions, each of which was to capture a complete cycle of waking activity, were to be scheduled at moments when significant change was observed by the mothers. Later, the schedule stabilized to one session per month. Short sessions, terminated by a child's irritable or unhappy state, were supplemented by another day's session. These supplementary sessions were considered part of the same observation period (indicated by Roman numerals). Although a complete sampling of major types of waking activity often could be captured in about 2 hours, rate of speech was another determinant of length of session. Thus, Matthew, the more laconic of the two, generally was observed for longer periods of time. The complete schedule of observations is shown in Tables 2 and 3.

Table 3
Schedule of Matthew's Observation Sessions

Period	Age	Duration	Total number of utterances
I	12(15)	1:15	
	12(22)	3:15	
		4:30	34
II	14(10)	1:15	
	14(18)	2:00	
		3:15	37
III	15(5)	1:30	
	15(17)	3:05	
		4:35	73
IV	16(2)	2:55	103
V	17(13)	4:15	137
VI	18(18)	2:45	217
VII	19(21)	3:15	253
VIII	20(26)	3:35	310
IX	22(1)	3:20	170

Matthew's formal sessions began before his one-word utterances were fluent (Table 3). Because of practical circumstances, Nicky's began after this point, as the number of utterances produced in I (Table 2) shows. Thus, we must rely relatively more on his diary for the earliest period. As noted earlier, the study ends at the point at which one-word utterances are in the minority for the first time for each boy.

2.2 Overview of Data

The children's utterances during the observation sessions are summarized in Table 4, where each child's total verbal production is broken down according to interpretability and reliability. As will become apparent from Table 5, Table 4 is arranged so that sessions with similar proportions of single-word utterances are in similar positions. As is customary in studies of child language, it was necessary to remove some utterances from consideration to allow analysis of the data.

Three major types of utterances were excluded from the data. First were the unintelligible utterances, utternaces and exclamations whose phonetic shape was not sufficiently close to an adult word to allow any interpretation. These utterances generally were not recorded and so are not included in the total numbers of utterances. Second are the uninterpretable utterances, isolated words that were produced "out of the blue," with no discernable link to the surrounding context, either situational or verbal. Third are imitations of preceding statement with no nonverbal evidence of comprehension.

The proportion of excluded utterances started high and quickly declined over the first three observation periods as children's comprehensible approximations to the adult language increased. The residue of uninterpretable utterances, rising and falling from period to period, probably stems from the fact that, as rate of speaking increased with development, it became increasingly difficult to observe and record all the relevant situational information. (At the time of our study, portable video equipment was unavailable in a practical format.) When this situational information was not recorded, interpretable utterances were not usable. This unavoidable selection process was a random one; hence, it should not bias the data in terms of particular semantic functions.

Table 4 also indicates that some utterances were included in the data but could not be interpreted with certainty. Because question—answer dialogue was of particular interest, questions answered by imitating a part of the question without any nonverbal signs of comprehension have been left in but have been marked as having insufficient context for interpretation. Imitations with some nonverbal evidence of comprehension are included, but the insufficiency of the nonverbal context is noted. Insufficient context also can

Table 4
Breakdown of the Children's Verbal Productions

Nicky

	I 18(4)	II 18(27)	III 19(29)	IV 20(23)	V 21(17)	VI 22(21)	VII 23(21)	VIII 24(23)
Total	126	193	222	359	233	347	439	494
Excluded from corpus	36.5% (46)	16.1% (31)	9.0% (20)	14.5% (52)	12.9% (30)	8.6% (30)	10.2% (45)	10.7% (53)
Included in corpus								
Sufficient context	49.2% (62)	67.4% (130)	75.2% (167)	64.6% (232)	73.8% (172)	73.5% (255)	62.9% (276)	75.3% (372)
Insufficient context	14.3% (18)	16.5% (32)	15.8% (35)	20.9% (75)	13.3% (31)	17.9% (62)	26.9% (118)	14.0% (69)

Matthew

	I 12(15) 12(22)	II 14(10) 14(18)	III 15(5) 15(17)	IV 16(2)	V 17(13)	VI 18(18)	VII 19(21)	VIII 20(26)	IX 22(1)
Total	34	37	73	103	137	217	253	310	170
Excluded from corpus	61.8% (21)	18.9% (7)	1.4% (1)	11.7% (12)	13.1% (18)	6.5% (14)	3.6% (9)	8.1% (25)	6.5% (11)
Included in corpus									
Sufficient context	29.4% (10)	59.5% (22)	84.9% (62)	68.9% (71)	65.0% (89)	71.9% (156)	75.9% (192)	82.2% (255)	85.3% (145)
Insufficient context	8.8% (3)	21.6% (8)	13.7% (10)	19.4% (20)	21.9% (30)	21.6% (47)	20.5% (52)	9.7% (30)	8.2% (14)

Table 5
Percentage of Different Utterance Types in the Two Children's Speech

	Observation period and age							
Nicky	I 18(4)	II 18(27)	III 19(29)	IV 20(23)	V 21(17)	VI 22(21)	VII 23(21)	VIII 24(23)
Single words								
Isolated	82.5%	78.8%	47.5%	31.9%	58.1%	53.6%	30.2%	9.5%
	(66)	(130)	(96)	(98)	(118)	(170)	(119)	(42)
Sequences[a]	15.0%	17.0%	27.7%	48.9%	27.1%	20.8%	35.0%	17.0%
	(12)	(25)	(56)	(150)	(55)	(66)	(138)	(75)
Repetitive	2.5%	0%	6.0%	5.5%	1.0%	0.3%	4.6%	.7%
sequences	(2)	(0)	(12)	(17)	(2)	(1)	(18)	(3)
Multimorpheme	0%	4.2%	18.8%	13.7%	13.8%	25.3%	30.2%	72.8%
utterances[a]	(0)	(7)	(38)	(42)	(28)	(80)	(119)	(321)
Total	80	162	202	307	203	317	394	441

Observation period and age

	I	II	III	IV	V	VI	VII	VIII	IX
Matthew	12(15)	14(10)	15(5)	16(2)	17(13)	18(18)	19(21)	20(26)	22(1)
	12(22)	14(18)	15(17)						
Single words									
Isolated	100.0%	83.3%	91.7%	83.5%	69.7%	48.8%	37.3%	37.9%	20.1%
	(13)	(25)	(66)	(76)	(83)	(99)	(91)	(108)	(32)
Sequences[a]	0%	6.7%	0%	5.5%	20.2%	33.5%	49.2%	36.1%	23.9%
	(0)	(2)	(0)	(5)	(24)	(68)	(120)	(103)	(38)
Repetitive sequences	0%	10.0%	8.3%	11.0%	10.1%	11.8%	6.5%	0.7%	1.3%
	(0)	(3)	(6)	(10)	(12)	(24)	(16)	(2)	(2)
Multimorpheme utterances[a]	0%	0%	0%	0%	0%	5.9%	7.0%	25.3%	54.7%
	(0)	(0)	(0)	(0)	(0)	(12)	(17)	(72)	(87)
Total	13	30	72	91	119	203	244	285	159

Note: Observation periods for the two boys have been placed according to total proportion of single words (including both isolated single words and sequences). In terms of the percentages presented in the table, observation periods are therefore placed according to proportion of multimorpheme utterances. By this criterion, Nicky I matches Matthew I, II, III, IV, and V. Nicky I was placed above Matthew III because of its distance midway between Matthew II and IV, both of which match Nicky I most closely in terms of proportion of the subcategory, isolated one-word utterances.

[a] There also existed a kind of sequence, termed *complex*, in which single-word and multimorpheme utterances were said in response to a single situation or were conversationally connected. The single-word members of such a sequence were counted under "sequences," the multimorpheme members were counted under "multimorpheme utterances."

39

mean that there was ambiguity in decoding the adult word or words the child was aiming for. Finally, in some cases, there is insufficient context to classify unambiguously the semantic function of the utterance. The proportion of utterances marked as having insufficient context in a particular session depends on a number of factors, such as the amount of imitation and the accuracy of the child's phonetic realizations. Because they involve more verbal material, sequences and multiword utterances (to be described later) were less likely to have insufficient context for interpretation. Utterances have been broken down in this way so that major analyses will not be affected by the less reliable data. Unless otherwise noted, only utterances having sufficient context for interpretation were used in the results to be reported.

Table 5 presents a quantitative description of the corpus in terms of utterance type and length. To facilitate comparison with previous studies of language development, the data are analyzed in terms of morphemes in this one table. The category "multimorpheme utterances" includes multiword utterances (e.g., *byebye car*) and single-word utterances that can be analyzed into several morphemes (e.g., *cars*). For a word to be analyzed into two morphemes, at least one of the component morphemes had to be used alone or in another combination by the child. For example, *airplane* was counted as two morphemes for Nicky, who previously was observed to use the word *plane* in isolation, whereas this same word was counted as a single morpheme for Matthew, who had never used either component alone or in another combination. Thus, for the purposes of this table, "single word" means "single unanalyzed word". Diminutive endings like *y* in *mommy* were not counted as morphemes. Sets like *ma, mama,* and *mommy* were treated as variants of a single morpheme. Repeated words generally were counted only once, unless someone else spoke between two repetitions of the child's word.

Table 5 breaks the interpretable utterances of a child into three broad categories: isolated single-word utterances, sequences, and multimorpheme utterances. Multimorpheme and isolated single-word utterances both are pronounced with a single intonation contour for the whole utterance. Multimorpheme utterances consist of two or more morphemes of which at least one occurs alone or in another combination. Sometimes children use several words in series but give each a separate intonation contour (symbolized by a semicolon). We called these series *sequences* and counted each word as a separate utterance, except in the case of repetitions without intervening adult verbalization. Sometimes a response by the mother occurs between the members of a series. When two *identical* words were separated by a comment from the mother, we call this a *repetitive sequence*, to distinguish it from a more interesting true sequence. The onsets of the words of a sequence always were separated by at least 1.1 seconds. With one exception, the maximum separation between consecutive words was 4.0 seconds. In contrast, the onsets of words constituting a two-word utterance were never separated by more than 1.5 seconds. Between 1.1 and 1.5 seconds, it was necessary to refer to intonation in order to decide whether a series of words should be classified as a sequence or a sentence.

A nonrepetitive sequence is composed of two or more successive remarks on a single topic or event. An example occurs in Matthew VII—19(21), in which Matthew says *ice* followed by *mommy* when his mother gives him some ice from her glass. Thus, he successively names an Object and Animate Being associated with the Object in the situation. A second type of sequence is the *conversational sequence* in which an adult response ties together two successive utterances. That is, the adult's response to one utterance becomes a stimulus to the second utterance. Because verbal, rather than situational, context forms the necessary link between utterances, the nonverbal context may shift slightly. Here is an illustration from the previously quoted conversational sequence as it continues. After saying *ice; mommy*, Matthew's mother responds *Is that mommy's ice?*; Matthew then points to his mother's empty glass and says *gone*.

It is clear from Table 5 that a developmental trend toward more long utterances is preceded by a developmental trend toward more sequences with increasing age. These trends reflect the development of utterance length on the one hand and discourse length on the other. A number of earlier observers of child speech (e.g., Guillaume, 1927; Stern, 1930; Leopold, 1949; and Cohen, 1952) have noticed the occurrence of sequences of single-word utterances as a later stage within one-word speech.

A sample of the information that the observer recorded was presented in Table 1 and discussed in Section 2.1; however, some remarks are in order concerning the form in which the data will be presented in the rest of this book. Table 6 shows the way in which the situational context and the child's utterances have been organized for purposes of analysis and presentation. The message has been divided into two major components, modality and event. The event corresponds to Fillmore's proposition, but may be represented wholly or in part by nonverbal elements. Just as Fillmore's proposition consists of a verb and one or more noun phrases, the simple event consists of a relation and one or more entities. Sometimes, as in the second example in Table 6, the relation is implicit—the bike's state of existing in a given location. The modality component corresponds to Fillmore's modality but may be expressed nonverbally. It includes all elements that modify the event as a whole. The most important and frequent modality element is the child's relation to the event; this is the mode or pragmatic function of the utterance. In the first example, from observation period I—12(15,22), Matthew said *down*. The observer noted

Table 6
Examples of Different Types of Situational Structure from Matthew's Corpus

Observation period and age		Examples			
	Preceding context	Modality		Event	
I 12(15)			M	getting down	
12(22)				*down*	
VII 19(21)		M pointing to	bike		
			bike		
	Lauren is up on cover.	M whining	M	*up*	
VIII 20(26)	*Where did Ismenia go?*			*bye-bye*	
	Can I wash your face?	M turns away whining			
				no	
			M	about to put	cup in sink
					sink
			M	picks up	crib
					sleep

Note: Broken horizontal lines separate utterances that were not part of connected discourse. Solid horizontal lines separate utterances from different observation periods.

"getting down from mother's lap." The relevant section of the observer's record is aligned directly above Matthew's utterance to show exactly what aspect of the event Matthew is encoding verbally. When necessary, the child (M) was supplied as part of the context. There is no overt indication of modality (except normal Indicative intonation) so the space under "modality" is left blank. Utterances with unmarked modality may be assumed to be in the Indicative mode. We generally have segmented the situational structure, by separating people and things from actions and states, to allow easy comparison of different utterances. (For instance, "M" and "getting down" are placed in different columns in the first example.) We will justify this procedure from a theoretical standpoint in Section 2.6.

In the tables, event follows modality on the same line for ease of reading; however, the event is actually cognitively embedded in (subordinate to) the modality.

The temporal relation between the utterance and the situational elements to which it is related is indicated by the tense of the verb. The present progressive tense indicates that an event was taking place simultaneously with the utterance. The present perfect tense (Matthew has (just) ...) indicates that the word was said upon completion of an action. A future indication (Matthew is about to ...) shows a statement of some future action. The simple present indicates an indeterminate temporal relation between word and context within the present situation. Horizontal lines separate utterances which are not connected discourse.

The second example, from Period VII, offers a case of marked declarative mode. Matthew says *bike*, and the observer records "pointing to bike." Here, the action of pointing is the nonverbal expression of the Indicative mode and is placed in the modality section. The agent of "pointing," Matthew, is supplied from the context. The child may express elements of either modality or event by intonation or gestures, or these may be implicit in the situation. When we are dealing with one-word speech, it is impossible for the child verbally to identify more than one item. This example also shows how the modality component is composed of two parts, speaker and relation to the event. Speaker is the left-head column of the "Modality" section of the table, relation occupies the right-hand column. In this example, M (Matthew) is the speaker and his relation to the event ("bike") is "pointing to" it.

In the third example, also from Period VII, Matthew whines and says *up*. The observer recorded "Lauren up on a cover." Whining is the intonation used to express the volitional mode and is recorded as the relational aspect of "Modality". Intonation as an aspect of linguistic expression is placed on the same line with the utterance. The situation to which Matthew is referring is not the actual one of his sister's presence on the cover but a potential one in which he, too, will be *up*. Thus, we do not place the observer's comment with Matthew's utterance, but count it as preceding context. The relations of Matthew and *up* to the potential event are similar to those of Matthew and *down* in the first example. However, the absence of any situational element above *up* shows that the event is potential rather than actual.

Sometimes, preceding verbal material provides the contextual structure on which an interpretation is based. In the fourth example, from Period VIII—20(26), Matthew's mother asks him *Where did Ismenia go?* and he answers *bye-bye*. Now *bye-bye* has a function similar to *up*, but Ismenia, the Agent of *bye-bye* is not present in the situation, as shown by the absence of anything corresponding to M of the preceding example. This item must be inferred from the context of the question. Dialogue in general is treated as a semantic structure created by two people together. Where the child's word relates to verbal context, the specific semantic function of his word is often more interpretable than otherwise would be the case in the same nonverbal situation. (In the rare cases where verbal and nonverbal context each led to different semantic interpretations of a word, the nonverbal context was given precedence.)

The next example, also from Matthew VIII—20(26), illustrates an utterance that is related both to preceding verbal context and to an ongoing nonverbal event. In this case, the nonverbal event is described on the same line as the preceding verbal context and the child's linguistic production is placed beneath the element it encodes, with intonation placed over word. In this example, negative volition is represented on three levels: action (turning away), intonation (whining), and word (*no*).

In some situational contexts, one event relation is embedded in another, thereby exceeding the limitations of our format. In such a case, the appropriate column will contain two elements with different functions. In the sixth example in Table 6, also from Matthew VIII—20(26), the cup is an Object and the sink is a Location. Naturally, Matthew's utterance corresponds to only one of these elements, as is shown by its position. In the last example, from Period VIII—20(26), Matthew's utterance *sleep* stands next to, rather than under, some part of the situation because it does not represent any element of the concrete situation, but stands in relation to one of them, the crib. This relation between crib and *sleep* is embedded in the act of picking up.

2.3 Expansion and Semantic Relations

THE METHOD OF EXPANSION

Our basic method for discovering the cognitive structure of one-word speech was the expansion of the child's single words by an adult. At first glance, this procedure may appear hopelessly subjective. However, we will show that it is not at all arbitrary and will argue that it has firm theoretical support.

When a child uses a word, he uses it within a very definite situational context. Likewise, an adult attempting to interpret the child's speech relies on cues from that context to arrive at his or her interpretation. The cues upon which an expansion is based include the child's gestures, orientation, and intonation, and the logical relation between the child's word and the context. By means of these cues, the adult isolates some elements of the environment which, together with the child's word, form a structure that can be represented by a sentence in adult speech. That sentence is an expansion. If a child whines, points to a fan that is turned off, and says *on*, the expansion *I want the fan on* relates all these elements.

Five basic assumptions are necessary for the expansion to reflect a valid interpretation. First, we assume that the child distinguishes entities and relations. Entities are "point-at-ables," or things; relations are actions and states that cannot be pointed at but can be predicated of entities. Thus, we assume that the child can distinguish a fan from its surroundings and knows that it is a point-at-able. Further, we assume that, with the word *on* the child is referring to an Action or State.

Second, we assume that the child distinguishes animate from inanimate entities. This assumption is involved in distinguishing an Object from an Agent, for instance. If, for example *on* were predicated of a cat jumping on a fence rather than a fan, *on* would be classified as an Action or State of an Agent rather than of an Object. These and other semantic functions will be described and justified in Section 2.4. In Secion 2.6, we present some psychological evidence to support these first two assumptions.

Third, we assume that the child's gestures and orientation, particularly pointing and reaching, indicate important elements of the situation. In the example given, we assume that, if a child is pointing to a fan, the fan is an element of the message the child wishes to convey, even though the child may not use the word *fan*. Further, we assume that other behavior of the child, such as whining, indicates the mode, or how he intends the message. A wide spectrum of linguistic and nonlinguistic behavior, from repetition to whining and reaching, is relevant here. The interpretation of this behavior is simplified by the fact that only two major categories—indication and volition—usually are being signaled, albeit with different intensities.

Fourth, we assume that the adult's experience with a given child's particular phonological system—his repertory of phonemes and pattern of sound substitutions—can help the adult to make a valid judgment of what word the child is attempting to say. For instance, the fact that a child never used final consonants and substituted *d* for *th* could be relevant knowledge in interpreting a child's *da* as "that" under appropriate circumstances.[1] Although we do not have any evidence on this point, it seems likely that the child's immediate imitations of adult speech develop the adult's notions concerning the child's emergent phonological system.

Fifth, we assume that an element that phonetically resembles an adult vocabulary item also semantically resembles it. In our example, we assume that the meaning of the child's word *on* is somehow connected with 'on'.[2] That is, *on* refers to a state, not an object, and that state is one which can appropriately be predicated of fans. Of course, the range of reference of a child's words is rarely identical to that of an adult. Children's words often are overgeneralized or idiosyncratic, as well as mispronounced. In a given situation,

---

[1] This assumption receives support from Bloch's (1921) study of the acquisition of French. Bloch noted that the characteristics of the child's early phonological system are such as to result in a large number of homonyms, but that homonyms never cause communication problems. The implication is that the hearer uses contextual information to disambiguate the message, just as he does when homonyms occur in adult speech.

[2] Single quotation marks indicate situational elements rather than words.

however, the referent usually will be clear enough to categorize the utterance in terms of semantic function. For example, if the fan had been on instead of off, but the child had still whined and said *on*, the whining would make it likely that the child wanted a change of state. This interpretation would be validated if the whining ceased when the fan was turned off. In practice, when they make their interpretations, parents also take into account whether or not their child knows the word *off* and how he has used *on* in the past, just as they take into account the fact that a child can't say *th* and says *d* instead. The important point for our purposes is that, although the child may be using *on* where an adult would say *off*, the situational context makes it clear that the child is encoding an Action or State of an Object. (This and other semantic functions will be described in greater detail in the next section.) Hence, the reliability of classifying by semantic function need not be compromised by this type of referential overgeneralization. For an expansion to reflect a valid semantic interpretation of an utterance, it is *not* necessary to assume complete identity of child and adult minds; all that is required is some sort of topological or relational correspondence between the two views of an event.

When two expansions differ in the inclusion or exclusion of an element, the elements common to both generally preserve the same relationships among themselves. When a child says *break* as his mother breaks some eggs, as occurred in Nicky VII—23(21), one might hesitate between *the eggs break* and *mommy breaks the eggs*. Both expansions, however, preserve the same relationship between the child's word, *break*, and the situational element, 'eggs': In Fillmore's terms, 'eggs' is the Object of *break* in both sentences. From adult usage and on logical grounds, we know that *break* obligatorily occurs with an Object: It is impossible to conceive of the action of the verb *break* without an Object. However, the expansions show that an Agent (mommy) is optional. The semantic categories of case grammar allow us to capture what is necessary in an expansion and common to all expansions of a given utterance while ignoring disagreements that do not bear on the basic semantic relationship.

Regardless of whether or not the interpreter takes note of the Agent in this situation, we have no way of knowing if the child does. But our assignment of the utterance to a particular semantic function is independent of this questionable sort of judgment. What we are doing is assigning the minimal semantic structure necessary to account for the utterance and its interpretive context. While the child must have, in some sense, the total framework implied by the various aspects of a speech event, he need not have explicitly articulated all the parts: We are specifying the relation of the one part he has analyzed, the verbal part, to the whole by describing its point and mode of connection with the situational structure as a totality. Thus, from the point of view of the classification process, the rule is always to make the minimal possible inference.

PREVIOUS USE OF EXPANSION

Many writers (e.g., Bloom, 1970; Brown, 1973) have expressed reluctance to interpret or expand child speech, and consider word order to be of overriding importance in validating what Brown calls the method of "rich interpretation." However, this confidence in word order is misplaced. Although the order of a sequence of words in a child's sentence helps to determine what construction they are in, word order alone is not sufficient to assign a unique base structure to a string (Chomsky, 1957, 1965). Otherwise, child grammars based on distributional facts alone, such as pivot grammars, would not have failed. Although we agree that word order is important in establishing the presence of *syntax*, it is not necessary to establish the presence of underlying *semantic structure*. In much recent work on grammar, including Fillmore's, underlying semantic structure is the base structure of grammar. In other words, semantic relations are a more fundamental component of grammar than are syntactic relations. Thus, early semantic relations could *both* lack syntax *and* still be fundamental to the acquisition of grammar. This is, in fact, our position.

In her study of early speech, Bloom claims to be concerned with syntactic, rather than semantic, relations. In English, syntactic relations naturally involve questions of word order in multiword utterances. However, word order by itself is not sufficient to determine the construction of each utterance. For example, as Bloom notes, an utterance like *mommy sock* is ambiguous between possessive and subject-object interpretation. To determine which construction is present in a given utterance, it is necessary to have recourse to semantic information. To see this, let us consider how an observer responds when he sees a mother putting on her child's socks and hears the child say *mommy sock*. The observer sees the mother putting on the sock, covertly assigns the mother the role Agent, notes that an Agent should be the subject of a sentence, and calls *mommy* the subject of the child's utterance. If the observer did not assume that the situation had a semantic structure, there would be no basis for assigning a role to *mommy*. Thus, Bloom implicitly assumes that semantic relations hold between situational elements; the grammatical relations that Bloom discovered in two-word speech have a thoroughly semantic basis. Further, since she deduces the child's grammatical relations from the adult's semantic reading, she implicitly assumes that child and adult have similar structures. However, she did not recognize these assumptions and so makes no attempt to justify them. In fact, Bloom contrasts semantic interpretation (what she does in her study) and expansion (what mothers do in real life). In her own words:

> Expanding the utterance "Mommy sock" would consist of supplying missing, but predictable, elements in a linear sequence and could conceivably continue indefinitely:

(i) *Mommy* puts on my *sock,*
(ii) *Mommy* is putting on my *sock* now.
(iii) I see that *Mommy* is putting on my *sock* . . .

> In contrast, imposing a semantic interpretation on the utterance would seek to account for only as much of the relationship between the elements of the utterance that actually occur, that is, between "Mommy" and "sock," as can be justified by what is known about the referent—that Mommy is the agent and sock the single object goal of an ongoing event. The grammatical relationship that holds between "Mommy" and "sock" in this case is that of subject–object, with a dummy element having features specifying the temporal immediacy of the event linking the two in the abstract underlying representation of the sentence [p. 13, Reprinted by permission of MIT Press].

Bloom sees that there are no logical limits to an expansion, and concludes from this that the two modes of interpretation are qualitatively different. What Bloom fails to note, however, is the large area of overlap between the two modes of interpretation. Every expansion, regardless of how elaborate or simple, includes the same underlying semantic relations contained in the corresponding semantic interpretation. In her own example, *mommy* fills the role of Agent, *sock* is the Object in all three expansions. The restriction of semantic interpretation to the occurring verbal elements is an artificial one which inhibits analysis of one-word speech without conferring any increased accuracy on the interpretation of longer sentences. In either case, the interpretation of the child's speech ultimately depends on the specification by an adult of a semantic relation among elements in the situational context. In Bloom's method, the child's words are used to locate at least two situational elements, whereas, in our method, the child's single word specifies only a single nonverbal element; so the observer must use the child's gestures or other cues to locate at least one element, a minimum of two elements being necessary for a semantic relation. In both methods, moreover, elements of the situation are referred to that are not direct referents of the child's words. In the *mommy sock* example, Bloom's assignment of the semantic role of Agent to the mother implies an ongoing action, without which her interpretation would not be tenable.

The exceptional circumstances under which Bloom is willing to assign semantic functions to single words illustrate how this restriction works in practice. Consider the following example, which she presents (pp. 12–13, Reprinted by permission of MIT Press):

ADULT	CHILD
	[Eric watching the tape-recorder reels through the window in the tape-recorder lid]
Window.	*see.*
See.	*window.*
Window. Close it up.	
Close it up.	
[Investigator trying to	

ADULT   CHILD
cover tape-recorder lid]   — — — —
hm? What?

[Eric looking at tape-recorder
reels through window in lid]
——— ——— *see.*
See.   *see. window.*
Window.

Because the child ultimately connects the single words *see* and *window* into a sequence of two single-word utterances (*see. window.*), Bloom is willing to interpret their earlier occurrences. Two overt linguistic elements must be present in the message for her to consider semantic interpretation. However, it is easy to imagine the same dialogue without any final summing up on the part of the child. In that case, it is not the child's words that have changed in meaning, but Bloom's willingness to interpret them. A further inconsistency in her treatment of single-word speech is that she shows no hesitation in interpreting single-word negatives. Thus, we believe that our method is the more natural of the two, in that it is not arbitrary in its selection of interpretable utterances.

2.4 Semantic Functions in Child Language

The utterances in the corpus were classified according to the semantic functions of their verbally encoded elements. The notion of semantic function is based on the concept of a semantic relation. A semantic relation describes the relationship between two elements in an event, for example, the relation between Agent and Action. Each element plays a role or has a function in the event. In the Agent–Action relation, one function is that of Agent, the other is that of Action; clearly, neither function could exist without the other; each presupposes the total relation. While both elements of a relation must, therefore, be represented in the total structure of the speech event, the child himself encodes only one element at the single-word stage. Our term "semantic function" refers to the role of this one expressed word. The use of the word "encode" for verbal production is not intended to imply that the child does not communicate more than he can "encode." It will become abundantly clear that that children can express much through intonation and gesture or action. However, it is useful to have a term for the verbal production exclusive of these additional elements. The way in which different semantic functions are verbally encoded can be seen in the following: If the child says *run* when his mother begins to run, *run* can be classified as Action of Agent. If, on the other hand, a similar event stimulates the child to say *mommy*, his utterance can be classified as expressing the Agent of Action. In each case, a different semantic function is expressed, but each is part of the same underlying relation perceived in the situational structure. In two-word speech, of course, both elements in a relation can receive overt linguistic expression, for example, in the sentence *mommy run.*

The semantic functions that were used are roughly those of Fillmore (1968). However, we did not wish to attribute to the child more linguistic intention than we could reliably extract from his speech, so we deliberately recast Fillmore's scheme into situational terms that could be operationally defined.

Brown (1973) points out that there is a problem in deciding how finely semantic categories should be distinguished. Three criteria for deciding whether or not two theoretically distinguishable, but closely related, semantic functions should be treated together or separately underlie the definitions and descriptions of semantic relations that follow. The first is clear operational definition in the behavior of the child. If two usages cannot be operationally distinguished, they are treated as a single semantic function even though they may be distinct in adult grammar. When, for instance, a child (Nicky II–18(27)) says *gone* after having put a nut in a cup, is he referring to the Action of making it disappear or to the present State of absence of the nut? Because there is no observable criterion for distinguishing these two possibilities, Action and State are treated as a single semantic function.

The second is productivity: If a semantic function does not achieve productivity in one-word speech, it cannot be a separate category. The function of Instrument, derived from Fillmore's Instrumental case, falls in this category. While each boy did upon occasion name an inanimate object causally involved in an action, it occurred too infrequently to be termed "productive." These instances are discussed, therefore, as special cases of Object involved in an Action or State.

The third criterion is more formal: A function must be independent of specific vocabulary. A semantic function cannot be defined in terms of a single lexical item, for this would call into question its structural status. All three of these criteria work against proliferation of categories; the resultant simplicity has advantages from both a theoretical and psychological point of view. In what follows, we define the functional categories according to which we classified the children's utterances. In Chapter 3, we discuss the precise order of their appearance and the type of development within each function.

Performatives are utterances that occur as part of a child's actions. For instance, the word *bye-bye* is at first coupled to the action of waving, and has no meaning (or use) separate from it. The notion of Performative is not found in Fillmore (1968) but is taken from Austin (1962). Austin makes a distinction between performative and declarative verbs. Performative verbs are complete when they are spoken, whereas declarative verbs can be used either truely or falsely, and depend on the extralinguistic context for their truth value. Austin's performative verbs include *declare, promise,* and *demand* which, when used in the first person and in the present tense, do not make a statement but constitute an act. A sentence beginning with *I promise that* may be spoken in bad faith, but cannot be false, since use of the sentence constitutes an act of promising. A child saying *bye-bye* as a greeting is far removed from a person making a promise. However, the similarities are sufficient to justify an extension of Austin's term: There is no way a child's use of *bye-bye* can be false; it can be merely inappropriate. Saying *bye-bye* to bid farewell is performing an act. We also regard as Performatives some verbal acts that are part of interpersonal routines. For example, when Nicky's mother is singing "Pop goes the Weasel" and Nicky says *weasel, weasel* is a Performative. It is an act without informational content. Instances of Performatives like these differ from Austin's verb in that they have no propositional complement, not even a nonverbal event. For this reason, it probably is more accurate to call them *pure* Performatives. In any case, we regard them as the ontogenetic basis of later Performatives.

The idea of applying this concept to child language comes from Gruber (1973), who used it to analyze the earliest two-word utterances. Following Werner and Kaplan (1963), who consider greetings like *hi* to be expressions of the attitudinal mode rather than the referential situation, we consider performatives elements of modality rather than of the event.

Pure Performatives are on the borderline between nonlinguistic and linguistic behavior. The earliest examples—like Nicky's *dada* to accompany a variety of actions—have the characteristics of Piaget's index, the most ontogenetically primitive form of representation, for the sound pattern is *part* of a total event; it does not represent something apart from itself. The index contrasts with the sign, Piaget's final stage of representational development and the hallmark of language proper: The sign stands for something apart from itself and does not resemble its referent in form. The earliest signs are Indicative Objects, to be described shortly.

Volition is a particular kind of Performative. Its basic function is to obtain some desired response from the person addressed. The most common examples of this category are *mama*, used to request something, and *no*, used to reject something. This category is the semantic basis of what later becomes the imperative mode, and includes words to encode the performative element of positive and negative demands. Like Austin's verbs, expressions of Volition have a complement, but it is expressed nonverbally, rather than verbally. For example, if a child reaches toward an object and says *mama*, the reach indicates which object is desired.

Volitional utterances are distinguished from Indicative ones by standardized intonation and gestures. Tonkova-Yampol'skaya (1969) has found that, between the second and seventh month, infants develop an intonation pattern like the adult indicative; around the seventh month, they acquire an intonation structurally similar to the adult's emotional request. Menyuk and Bernholtz (1969) have shown that adults can reliably distinguish indicative, emphatic, and interrogative intonation patterns for single-word utterances. Spectrographic analysis revealed that the objective basis for these distinctions was a difference of fundamental frequency contours. Sylva (1971) did a similar spectrographic analysis of some data from Matthew at 22 months of age, when single-word utterances were still frequent, and 30 months of age, when multiword utterances were the rule. She found that Matthew used the same two intonation patterns to express imperative (Volition) and Indicative at both points in time. For instance, two-word Indicative utterances from 30 months of age had the same overall pattern as one-word Indicatives, but the pattern was spread over both words. Demand intonation most frequently took the form of whining. Volitional utterances often are repeated until the desired response is obtained. Standardized Volitional gestures include reaching and motion toward an object. Leopold (1949) also reports handclapping as a standardized Volitional gesture for Hildegard.

The first two functions we have discussed are similar in that only the mode, that is, a modality element, is encoded. When the child learns to use names, the expression of mode is relegated to intonation and nonlinguistic means, and aspects of the event are encoded.

Indicative Object is a word that refers to the object of some indicative act. If a child pointed to a dog and said *doggie, doggie* would be an Indicative Object. The function of the child's utterance is roughly to call our attention to the expressed object. We already have mentioned the role of intonation in distinguishing indicative utterances. Gestures used to indicate the object include explicit ones, such as pointing and holding out, and implicit ones, such as touching and visual orientation. Leopold (1949) gives emphasis to the child's early use of pointing to clarify his message.

Werner and Kaplan (1963) have pointed out the intimate relation between looking and pointing. They note that, although grasping might appear to be the precursor of pointing, it is not, in that it serves to incorporate, whereas pointing is directed outward. Like looking, pointing constitutes a gestural acknowledgment of objects located at a distance from the self. Werner and Kaplan go on to suggest that referential behavior emerges through the shared contemplation of objects in an interpersonal context.

In this type of situation, the name represents the entity being touched, looked at, or pointed to. This representational relationship between word and referent is presupposed, both logically and psychologically in more complex messages. Werner and Kaplan (1963) view naming as the fundamental cognitive activity that makes possible all later types of linguistic predication.

Indicative Objects, like other semantic functions, can form part of a sequence. Often the indicative relation embeds another semantic relation as a sequence progresses. For instance, at II—18(27), Nicky says *akakoo* (record) pointing to a still record player, followed by *on*. If *akakoo* had been an isolated one-word utterance, in the same situation, it would have been called an Indicative Object. In relation to *on*, however, it is an Object of an Action. The best way to conceptualize this state of affairs is to view the relation between Object and Action as psychologically or cognitively embedded in, or subordinate to, the relation of indication. Yet, in a sequence, words relate to each other through their individual relations to a single situation; they do not yet have a syntactic relation, as in a two-word utterance. Sinclair talks about "the embedding of action-schemes one into the other, when the child can put one action-pattern into another pattern" (1971, p. 126) as a psychological parallel to the recursive property of linguistic structure. In this example of embedding, we have a developmentally intermediate form: Part of the embedded structure exists in verbal form, part in nonverbal.

A *Volitional Object* is a word that refers to the object of a demand. If a child whines and says *(ba)nana* while reaching for some bananas, *(ba)nana* is a Volitional Object. The intonation and gestures associated with Volitional Objects are the same as those associated with simple Volitional utterances. However, whereas Volitional utterances encode the mode of the sentence, these utterances encode the Object desired. A Volitional Object thus represents a combination of Volitional Modality with an Object in the event.

We have included both animate and inanimate Objects of Volition in this category just as we did in the case of Indicative Objects. Implicit in an animate Object of Volition is its function as Agent of some Action, if only moving toward the child, while implicit in an inanimate Object of Volition is its function as Object of some Action (for example, eating in the case of edible Objects). However, the child's awareness of Agent and Action is not expressed behaviorally in these Volitional situations, so we have preferred to classify them simply in terms of the behaviorally manifest Volition.

Early animate Volitional Objects are the developmental origin of the mature Vocative. Whereas in the earliest uses the child usually wants someone to come, in later uses, the child may only want that person's attention prior to addressing some statement to him. Thus, all Vocatives have been counted as animate Volitional Objects.

Indicative and Volitional Objects might be classed together as *Objects of Performatives*, since the difference between them is only one of mode. These utterances do not refer to a complete event, but only to a single entity. In this, they contrast with later, more complex, semantic functions, which often are combined with explicit indicators of modality. For instance, during Session III—15(5,17), Matthew repeatedly whined *down* while trying to get down from a couch. His Action, or State, encoded by *down*, is combined with the indicators of Volition, whining and repetition. From a semantic point of view, it is reasonable to regard his Action as embedded in a Volitional state. However, once the simple modality types were established, there was no apparent restriction on the combination of newly learned semantic functions with the existing modality signs For this reason, mode was not taken into account in classifying later-developing semantic functions.

This analysis of one volitional use of *down* is related closely to Ross's (1970) analysis of the role of performatives in adult speech. He observed various syntactic phenomena that suggested that declarative sentences, such as *John sings*, actually are embedded beneath performative verbs, as in *I report that John sings*. This led him to propose that all sentences actually contain a performative verb. He suggested that the characteristics of a sentence as a statement, question, or demand were dependent on the performative verb it contained. As an alternative to his performative analysis, Ross proposes and dismisses the pragmatic analysis. This view would claim "that certain elements are present in the context of a speech act, and that syntactic processes can refer to such elements" (Ross, 1970, p. 251). He dismisses this alternative because of the logical necessity that the situational elements utilized in the pragmatic analysis "not merely from an unstructured set. Rather, they must be assumed to be hierarchically grouped to form a structure which is exactly the same as that of a normal clause in deep structure" (Ross, 1970, p. 255). Ironically, this is precisely our claim—that situations are structured like sentences on a cognitive level. Thus, the Performative element in Volitional and Indicative Objects is expressed through nonverbal aspects of behavior. We suspect that this is true of adult sentences as well: that higher performative verbs in sentences like *John sings* are not deleted elements of linguistic structure, but unrealized parts of behavioral or conceptual structure.

A recently developed semantic relation often was embedded in an event structure, some aspect of which had earlier been encoded. As a hypothetical example, consider a message in which the child points to a man's coat and says *coat*. Coat is the Indicative Object in the situation. At some later point in time, the child points to the same coat and says *daddy*. The relation between *daddy* and coat is now embedded in the same speaker—action—object (child pointing at coat) relation of the first utterance. Such free combination of new semantic functions with old situational structures seemed to characterize word usage. Only by ignoring these combinations in categorizing semantic types could regularities in the sequence of development be discovered.

An *Agent* is "the typically animate perceived instigator" of an action (Fillmore 1968, p. 24). To avoid mistaking animate Indicative Objects for Agents, we classify a person as an Agent only if he or she is decisively connected with an action or change of state. If a child points at his father sitting in a chair and says *dada*, *dada* is classified as an Indicative Object, not an Agent. Although it is possible that the child wishes to call attention to his father as an Agent, who is sitting, there is room for reasonable doubt. On the other hand, if a child hears someone coming and says *dada*, *dada* is an Agent. There is a new defined Action present in the situation and the child's utterance is a clear response to that Action, so it is justified to classify *dada* as an Agent in relation to that Action. Because the child takes the Agent for granted under most circumstances, he usually encodes an event in terms of its Action, not its Agent, so examples of Agent as isolated single-word utterances are relatively rare.

It is not always possible to tell whether the child regards a person as the instigator of, or passive participant in, a particular event. For instance, if the child says that someone is crying, does he regard that action as voluntary or involuntary? Unfortunately, no researchers have studied the conditions under which children view action as voluntary. To avoid arbitrary and inconsistent interpretations of children's utterances, we have chosen to regard all actions of animate beings as instigated, and, therefore, always classify them as Agents. Conversely, we have restricted the definition of Agent to animate beings. Some experimental support for this decision is presented in Section 2.6. The resulting assignments are not always felicitous, but we have been unable to find another principled definition. Pictures of animate beings regularly are taken to re-present those beings and are considered animate. After some hesitation, we decided to classify body parts as animate, since it seems that, in some cases, the child does perceive them as such. In the situations where a child named a body part that appeared to be the instigator of an action, that body part was classified an Agent. Some frequency figures, but no orders of acquisition, would have to be changed if this decision were reversed.

In discussing actions and states, we distinguish the *Action or State of an Agent* from the *Action or State of an Object*. This cognitive distinction on the level of the event corresponds to Fillmore's linguistic distinction between verbs that require an agent and those that do not.[3] If a child's word refers to an Action that requires an animate Agent, it is so classified. However, if an Agent is only optionally part of the action, and there is an inanimate Object present, the word is classified as an Action or State of an Object. If a child says *eat* while pointing to food, *eat* refers to the Action or State of an Agent since eating is something done by a person rather than by food, on the level of event structure. This is the perceptual or behavioral equivalent of saying that *eat* requires an Agent on the level of grammatical structure. If a child says *down* while climbing off a chair, this is likewise an Action or State of an Agent, since he, himself, is animate. However, if he says *down* upon throwing a ball down, this is an Action or State of an Object, since it is the inanimate ball rather than the child that is going *down*. If he says *on* when a record starts playing, this would be classified similarly. It is possible that, in some cases, the child may mean to include the Agent in his communication, but we can find no objective criterion

---

[3]We deal further with the classification of verbs in our discussion of Chafe (1970) in Chapter 5.

for determining this. Again, our principle has been to make the minimal interpretation.

In classifying Actions and States, it is important to remember that the operational criterion for Agency is animateness. Thus, a constant State of an animate being is classified as instigated by an Agent. Such cases, however, are discussed separately.

The distinction between Actions and States in early speech is surprisingly difficult and was not attempted in any systematic manner. Some words, such as *jump*, refer unambiguously to actions, and others, such as *dirty*, refer unambiguously to states; however, *broke* may refer either to a past action, or a present state ('broken'), while *down* may refer to an action ('getting down'), a change of state, or the present condition. Perhaps careful experimental work could determine which meanings children intend.

Object in Fillmore's (1968) terms is "anything representable by a noun whose role in the action or state identified by the verb is identified by the semantic interpretation of the verb itself" (p. 25). He goes on to say that "conceivably the concept should be limited to things which are affected by the action or state identified by the verb" (p. 25). It is important to avoid mistaking Indicative Objects for true Objects. We classified a word as an Object only if it was decisively involved in an action that changed its state, or otherwise directly affected it. If a child looked at a ball and said *ball*, this was classified as an Indicative Object. On the other hand, if he said *ball* upon throwing one, this was counted as a true Object. In keeping with Fillmore's definition, inanimate objects that could be expanded as subjects of intransitive sentences were classified as Objects. If a child said *record* upon hearing a record beginning to play (which might be expanded as *The record went on*), this was counted as an Object. All Objects are inanimate. The reader should remember that, if an animate being is actively involved in an action, we have chosen to regard its animateness as crucial and have classified it as an Agent. If an animate being is the object of an action instigated by an Agent, it is classified as a Dative.

The *Dative* case is "the case of the animate being affected by the state or action identified by the verb" (Fillmore, 1968, p. 24), that is, the case of the animate being who experiences, rather than instigates, an action. The Dative case long has created problems for students of child language, since it is rare (Bloom, 1970) and encompasses a number of functions (cf. Brown, 1973). While Fillmore (1968) has provided a unified and principled semantic definition of the Dative case, there is room for serious doubt about whether or not the case has cognitive unity. Some of the different distinguishable functions that have been lumped together in the Dative case at one time or other include: recipient of an object (*John gave the ball to* **Bill**); beneficiary of an action (*John bought the ball for* **Bill**); possessor of an object (**Bill** *owns the car*, **Bill's** *car*); experiencer of a perception (**Bill** *sees John, John looks tall to* **Bill**); and animate correlates to the objective case (*John killed* **Bill**, **Bill** *died*).

The first function to appear in one-word speech is typically the recipient: A child gives a ball to his father and says *dada*. The beneficiary role appears later: Matthew asks for a cookie, saying *wawa* (Lauren); he subsequently takes the cookie to her. We have chosen to treat early examples of possession in a later, separate section. The Dative as experiencer of a perception arose only once in our corpus, in the two-word sentence *I see*, which joins the Dative *I* with the Indicative *see*. Interpretation of the other functions is complicated by the difficulty of deciding when an animate being is an instigator. Our decision, explained in connection with the Agent function, was to consider an animate being the Agent unless the action already had an Agent (as when one person gives something to another and names the recipient). A number of cases of Dative result from our decision to classify body parts as animate.

Some cases of the dative function, such as the example involving *dada*, may also seem to serve a vocative function. A vocative is an animate object of Volition. Like other semantic functions, the Dative may occur in either the Indicative or Volitional mode.

The Dative is, in a sense, a hybrid, in that it combines animateness with passivity. The *Instrumental* is a hybrid in the opposite way, combining activity with inanimateness. The relationship among the four semantic functions of entities involved in action can be seen in Figure 1. We did not obtain enough examples of Instruments to justify categorizing them separately (although the figures might change somewhat if body parts were reclassified). The relative rarity of both these hybrid functions supports the notion presented in Section 2.6 that young children associate animateness with activity and instigation, inanimateness with passivity.

An *Object Associated with another Object or Location* involves naming an object that is often *not* present in connection with an object or location that *is* present. Utterances in this category state general truths about the world and do not relate to specific actions. Three major subtypes can be distinguished. The first involves locations: When Nicky was being changed, he put his hand on his bottom and said *poo* (feces), although he had not had a bowel movement. The second is a type of attribution: Matthew had been playing with some thread and later said *kite*. Unlike the first type, this type has an analogue in later speech in attributive noun phrases (e.g., *kite string*). Cases in which animate nouns seemed to be used with attributive instead of possessive force (e.g., *bear book* 'a book about bears') were placed in this category. The third subtype

	animate	inanimate
active	AGENT	INSTRUMENT
passive	DATIVE	OBJECT

Figure 1 Relationship among four semantic functions.

involves metaphors: Nicky put his diaper on his head and said *hat*. This example is not a case of overgeneralization, since Nicky had a word in his vocabulary for diaper. Since no one of these subtypes achieved productivity individually, we did not distinguish them for purposes of classification.

An *Animate Being Associated with an Object or Location* involves naming an animate being, usually a person, in connection with an indicated object or location. Many examples seem to involve possession: Nicky says *daddy*, *mommy*, and so on, while touching clothes in the closet. However, when Nicky sees Lauren's empty bed and says *Lara*, it is difficult to tell whether he is referring to a present state of possession (*'Lauren's* bed'), a past action (*'Lauren* slept here'), or an habitual action (*"Lauren* sleeps here"). Actually, these same possibilities exist for *all* instances of this function, although some may seem, to an adult, relatively less likely in a given situation. For this reason, we have not attempted to classify into Agents and Datives the names of animate beings used in this way.

Fillmore (1968) defines the Locative as "the case which identifies the location or spatial orientation of the state or action" (p. 25). It is somewhat more difficult to arrive at an operational criterion for recognizing *Location* in child language. First, we exclude cases in which the location is not clearly distinct from the state or action. If a child drops a block and says *down*, that is an Action or State, not a Locative. Likewise, if he points to a ball outside on the grass and says *outside*, it is not clear that the child recognizes 'the outside' as an entity, and it is classified as a State. *Grass*, however, would be a Location in the same context. Second, we exclude objects that might be considered Objects of Actions. If a child says *chair* after an adult has sat in a chair, we do not consider this necessarily a Location, since it might equally well be an Object. The definition we have adopted in the interest of operationalizability might be called Location of an Object: If a child places a toy on a chair and says *chair*, *chair* is considered a Location. The situation is made unambiguous by the presence of two non-Agent entities in the situation. (cf. the example concerning *grass*)[4].

The differentiated specification of Locus develops relatively late in the one-word period. According to a linguistic analysis by E. Clark (1970), locatives and possessives have a common structure: A possessor is a location, too, but an animate one. In light of this analysis, it is interesting that Animate Beings Associated with Objects, and Locations of Objects, emerge one after the other in both Nicky and Matthew. More evidence for their cognitive relatedness is the fact that the order of emergence *within* the pair of semantic functions is different in each boy, a fact that could indicate a kind of "free variation" in the development of the two semantic functions.

[4]This case corresponds to Chafe's (1970) definition of Locative as the spatial position or orientation of the Object (cf. Edwards, 1974).

A final category, *Modification of an Event*, involves a word that modifies an entire event rather than a single element. When Matthew says *again* to mean that he wants his mechanical train wound again, he is referring to an entire potential event, nut just one element of it. In Fillmore's system, such adverbials are a part of the modality, not the proposition, of a sentence. The implication of this is that they modify the whole proposition, analogous to our event. Hence, our analysis of Modification of Event parallels Fillmore's concept of adverbials very closely. Modification of an Event involving time, manner, and quantity falls into this semantic category.

These, then, are the semantic functions that a child expresses with his one-word utterances. The clearest way to explain further the various semantic functions and to show how contextual material has been used to distinguish one semantic function from another is to give an example of a single word that entered into a number of different semantic relations. These instances are taken from Matthew's diary and formal observation sessions. At 17(23), Matthew says *Yaya*, his word for his sister Lauren, while pouring cereal for her. (It is preceded by *pou(r)* in a sequence of single-word utterances.) The act of giving her the cereal demonstrates that *Yaya* is the animate recipient of the cereal, and *Yaya* therefore would be classified as filling the semantic role of Dative. The same word enters into a second semantic relation at 18(18) (Matthew VI) when Matthew says *Yaya*, pointing to Lauren's toy. His pointing gesture shows that he is communicating a message about the toy. Because Lauren is not present, his utterance shows recognition of some sort of habitual relationship between Lauren and toy. This utterance would be classified as serving the function of an animate Being associated with Object or Location. At 19(21) (Matthew VII), Matthew uses the same word to serve a third semantic function. He says *Yaya* upon hearing her make sounds outside. Here, the word is stimulated by the act of making sounds and *Yaya* is therefore classified as serving the function of Agent of Action.

2.5 Classification and Reliability

Maternal expansions or interpretations were used to locate the situational cues on which they were based. They often gave information about which aspects of the situation were relevant to the child in connection with his utterance. Utterances then were classified in terms of their relations to these situational cues. Thus, the classification of utterances is based entirely on object-ively specifiable and observable cues rather than directly on the mothers' interpretations. If, moreover, the mother's interpretation was incomplete (perhaps limited to identifying the vocabulary item), the classification of the utterance could be based on additional situational cues that were identified by the observer. In fact, the roles of observer and mother *both* contributed to the description of the situation critical to classifying the utterances by semantic function. Similarly, the situational information in the diaries was used to classify the utterances by semantic function, although, in that case, it is provided only by the mother.

There are two major requirements for a method for interpreting child language. One is that it be consistent and reliable. Although all semantic classifications were made by the first author, interobserver reliability was tested by having a second person, trained in the system, independently classify a set of 194 isolated single-word utterances by semantic function on the basis of the observer's record. All utterances had sufficient context for interpretation; they were drawn from every observation period of both boys. Within these sampling constraints, utterances were randomly selected. This sample constituted 15% of the total corpus of isolated one-word utterances with sufficient context for interpretation. Comparison of the independent sets of semantic classifications made by Greenfield and another judge yielded the percentage of agreement figures shown in Table 7. For certain semantic functions, initial training of this judge was inadequate to get satisfactory reliability. Because the sample of utterances available to test reliability was limited, a different person had to be trained and a new reliability test run on these semantic functions. The reliabilities based on the second judge are indicated in the table. Again the comparison is between the classifications made by Greenfield

Table 7
Percentage Agreement in Semantic Classification of One-Word Utterances

Performative	81.8
Volition	94.4
Indicative Object	89.6*
Volitional Object	81.8
Agent	66.6*
Action or State of Agent	96.4
Action or State of Object	90.4
Object	90.0
Dative	87.5*
Object Associated with Another Object or Location	83.3
Animate Being Associated with an Object or Location	90.0
Location	100.0
Modification of Event	87.5

Note: No asterisk indicates comparison between Greenfield and the first judge. Asterisk indicates comparison between Greenfield and second judge. (See text for explanation.)

and another judge. The overall reliability is quite high: average reliability is 87.6%; for six categories, the agreement is 90% or better; for only one, Agent of Action, does it fall below 80%. (This one low reliability probably results from the fact that Agents were relatively rare in isolated single-word utterances rather than from any intrinsic unreliability of the category.) Thus, assigning semantic functions to one-word utterances does not have to be subjective and unreliable; the connections between word and context defining each semantic role can be specified in such a way that another person understands the same utterance as expressing the same semantic function. If we define communication at this stage as consisting, at least in part, of transmitting information about semantic relationships, then the high degree of reliability indicates that a child's communicative skill at the one-word stage may be less idiosyncratic and more general than previously imagined.

A second requirement for a method of interpretation is that it allow insights into the structure of child language. In Chapter 3, we present evidence of a constant sequence of changes in semantic interpretations over time across different children. Such a constant sequence would constitute evidence that semantic interpretations correspond to something in the child and not merely to adult fantasy. One can still posit the existence of the development of *systematic errors* in adult interpretation, but this position would seem to violate what we know about the centrality of communication in human evolution.

2.6 The Structure of Experience as the Basis for Learning Grammar

The fact that different observers can agree on interpretations of children's utterances suggests that the semantic functions we have proposed have some reality. Further evidence for their reality comes from experimental work on the perceptual world of infants. In this section, we present evidence that preverbal children already possess the ability to make the basic distinctions on which our proposed semantic functions are based. We shall return to this topic in Chapter 4.

Our empirical problem was the following. Given the arguments for assigning semantic structure to one-word utterances and given the arguments for using verbal expansions as a tool for getting at this structure, how does one describe the common conceptual base that every possible expansion of a given one-word utterance in context has? Our solution, presented in an earlier section, was to cast the *situational cues* on which the expansions were based into a structured framework composed of *entities* and *relations*. An entity is conceived as any point-at-able object; a relation is any action, operation, or state that an entity may undergo.

The distinction between entity and relation is the most basic distinction to which the grammatical categories of noun and verb can be related. While this is an a priori way to characterize a basic aspect of the way very young children structure events, there is abundant evidence that such categories have reality for the child, even at the very beginnings of life. Even newborns are sensitive to visual qualities that are crucial to object perception—the vertices of a triangle, for example (Salapatek and Kessen, 1966). More specifically, young infants segregate their environment into units corresponding to objects or entities. Bower (1965, 1967) has shown that, by 6 weeks of age, infants use the Gestalt object properties of common fate and good continuation to define a perceptual unit. Newborns also respond differently to stationary and moving things (Haith, 1966), indicating some form of the object—action or entity—relation distinction. By 22 weeks of age, babies are able to dissociate an entity from its movement in their definition of an object (Bower, 1966).

Much more evidence on infant perception could be cited to show that children have the basic cognitive—perceptual capacity to make the entity—relation distinction; the critical point is that the cognitive—perceptual basis for this way of structuring events does, in fact, exist in the child at the time he begins to learn to speak. The existence of such capacities makes more plausible the idea that the entity—relation distinction made by an adult observer may correspond to some distinction in the child's head. The entities in an event structure can be conceptualized as fulfilling the various semantic functions parallel to Fillmore's cases—Agent, Object, Dative, and so forth. The *relation* in an event structure, an Action or a State, can be thought of as fulfilling the semantic function of the verb.

Experimental evidence also suggests that young children can identify and differentiate the situational roles of Agent, Object, Location, Action, and so forth on a cognitive—perceptual level. Bower (1971) has shown that, during the second half of the first year, the infant begins to perceive animate entities (people) as Agents—instigating their own movement and able to act on inanimate objects—while perceiving inanimate entities as passive Objects, unable to move of their own volition. Bower reports that "an inexplicable disappearance of an inanimate object is thus likely to provoke an assault on the experimenter, whereas a similar disappearance of an animate object will produce searching" (pp. 124—25). Thus, the perceptual prerequisites for differentiating Agents from Objects of Action are present before the child's first word. Similarly, Bower (1966) has demonstrated that the infant differentiates an object from its location by 22 weeks of age. Hence, the perceptual prerequisites for expressing one object as the location of another are present long before the infant can express this concept in his or her speech. A distinction between noticing something and wanting it—relevant to our proposed contrast between Indicative and Volitional modes—is clearly present in the infant's behavior from the first days of life.

While we are far from doing justice to the literature on infant development, these results suggest that our semantic categories may fit facts concerning the nature of the infant's world. Much more work, however, is needed on the cognitive—perceptual or sensorimotor analogs to those aspects of semantic structure relevant to language acquisition. Piaget's observations on the sensori-motor period extending to about age two are, of course, relevant, as Sinclair (1971) points out. There seems to be widespread agreement that the basic cognitive prerequisites exist by the time syntax first appears (Bloom, 1970; Brown, 1973; Sinclair, 1970; Donaldson, 1970). Yet, the earlier forms of these mental structures in perception are of particular importance to our argument because we are talking about language development occurring *during* the sensorimotor stage, not after it.

While cognitive prerequisites logically must precede the verbal structures that presuppose them, the relevant processes of cognitive development cannot be complete when the first words appear. Rather, this development must be a continuing process. This, essentially, is MacNamara's (1972) conclusion in his article, "The Cognitive Basis of Language Learning in Infants."

At this point, a skeptic might argue that semantic development during the one-word stage consists entirely in the development of general cognitive capaci-ties and involves nothing specifically linguistic. However, many relevant cognitive capacities are present long before the appearance of the corresponding linguistic expression, even in single-word form. Harris (1971) notes the poverty of linguistic structures in comparison with cognitive—perceptual capacities during infancy. In Chapter 4, we discuss a number of cases in which linguistic expression of a distinction did not occur until long after that distinction was cognitively possible.

Our scheme for dealing with the structure of one-word speech in relation to the cognitive structure of nonverbal events solves a major theoretical problem of earlier investigations—the problem of deletion discussed in the last chapter. Essentially, the problem is that the formulations of Bloom (1970) and McNeill (1970a,b) yield base structures that are richer than any surface string actually uttered by the child at that stage. Instead, we propose that, at the outset of language development, the base structure is not composed of words but consists of a structured perception of real (or imagined) entities and relations. The surface string may be thought of as a partial verbal realization of a nonverbal base. With this formulation, we need not be bothered by the fact that two-word utterances describing the Action of an Agent upon an Object sometimes encode the Agent and Action, sometimes the Action and Object, and sometimes the Agent and Object, but never all three, as Bloom (1970) and others report. If the base structure is a perceptual—cognitive structure of ongoing events, then the base will not be *linguistically* more complex than the surface, although it may be *cognitively* more complex. The verbal realization of the base may, of course, affect the nonverbal framework by endowing its different components with greater articulation. This theoretical solution was not available to Bloom (1970) because she made the implicit assumption that linguistic knowledge was the only possible source of structure for the child.

This formulation is identical in spirit with that proposed by Schlesinger (1971b) and applied to two-word speech, except that Schlesinger did not face the deletion problem. As Brown (1973) points out, Schlesinger would say that *mommy* was perceived as the Agent, *sock* as the Object when *mommy sock* was uttered as mother removed Katherine's sock. For Schlesinger, moreover, these semantic relations would replace Chomsky's level of deep structure. But "he has not indicated how he would represent the action of 'putting on' which does not appear in the surface sentence" (Brown, 1973, p. 115). We are postulating that the situation is structured as a whole, even if all the parts are not individually articulated. Schlesinger was not forced to come to terms with the problem of missing elements because he always had at least two overt elements that could be translated into a semantic base.

Within this framework, it is possible to think of the development of uterance length as an *accretion* process whereby progressively more of the base structure is given verbal realization. One possible line of empirical evidence in favor of this hypothesis is a common situational context underlying the earliest expression of given semantic relations in one-word and two-word form at the appropriate points in development. We shall look for evidence of this sort in our data. Moreover, the choice of *which* entities and relations to encode, given a developmental limit on sentence length, then becomes a cognitive problem rather than a matter of linguistic structure. We shall test the hypothesis that, given the possibility of encoding a number of different semantic aspects of an event by single words, the child chooses the most informative aspect. Here, informative is used in the information theory sense—the child encodes that aspect of an event where he sees alternatives, where there is uncertainty in terms of the situational structure. This hypothesis can be stated in terms of presupposition: The child will not express verbally the presupposed element in the situation. In Chapter 4, we shall see whether this hypothesis can explain the particular entity or relation given verbal expression in a particular context.

Another theoretical problem solved, at least in principle, by this approach is how children learn particular languages. The "child as grammar machine," an approach derived from Chomsky's work, is not a viable approach to language learning if the essence of child grammar does not lie in its distributional features. Schlesinger (1971a) was perhaps the first of the modern developmental psycholinguists to point out difficulties with this conception. He saw an innately structured way of viewing the world as the key to specific language learning. We have extended this type of theoretical formulation in the following way.

The child begins by combining words with nonverbal aspects of an event; adults understand the total message and often respond by expanding the single verbal element into a sentence. The child already knows the situational relations the adult is going to express and he also knows the referents of one or more words; when he hears the adult sentence, he can learn something about syntax: how to order and modify words when they enter into those particular semantic relations. Slobin (1970), Ervin-Tripp (1971), and McNamara (1972) have made a general argument of the same type, the latter two asserting that the child must already know the meaning of the adult sentence in order to learn anything about syntax from it. If our approach to analysis of the structure of one-word speech does work, this theoretical problem will be essentially solved; still, it remains to discover how this operates in practice. We will try to use our data on adult–child dialogue as a beginning step.

In conclusion, we are in a position of attempting to prove wrong the pessimistic pronouncement made in 1963 by the semantic theoreticians Katz and Fodor, that the knowledge of the world that speakers share is not capable of being systematized and, hence, any theory relying on it is not a serious model of semantics (cited by Olson, 1970).

chapter 3

The Emergence of Semantic Relations

3.1 The Evidence for Combinatorial Structure in One-Word Speech

T he results of our study indicate that semantic functions do play a role in the development of one-word speech. An analysis of samples of children's speech recorded at different stages in their development reveals that children are constrained in the number of semantic functions they can express at any given time and that this number changes with time. However, within the confines of these constraints, children use words freely. In other words, semantic functions combine freely with available vocabulary to produce the variety of observed utterances. This combination of constraint and productivity indicates that semantic functions have structural status in one-word speech: Children learning to speak already possess the equivalent of combinatorial rules that can generate a potentially infinite number of situationally distinct messages. In this chapter, we shall first summarize the evidence for such structural status and then discuss the emergence and use of each function in detail.

A LIMITED NUMBER OF SEMANTIC FUNCTIONS

The most general argument for structure in one-word speech follows the lines of McNeill's (1970a,b) and Bloom's (1970) arguments for the existence of structure in later speech. If there were no structure to single-word utterances, one would not expect to find a constraint in the usage of newly acquired words. Yet, the child clearly is constrained in the combinatorial possibilities of using his lexicon since new words generally take on only a very limited set of usages. For example, at about 14 months of age, Nicky could use a new inanimate-object name to serve only one function—to indicate it. Similarly, before 18 months of age, he could use people's names only to name them, ask for them, or express them as Agents. However, during his nineteenth month, he began to use names in connection with objects associated with a given person. For example, he used *dada* not just to name his father, but also in reference to his father's coat. By the time he was 21 months old, he had extended this new usage to cover most of the names in his vocabulary. A given word can be used in more ways as a child's command of language increases, but there is always a definite limit to the total number of types of uses of a given word. Not just any semantic function appeared in one-word speech, but only the thirteen semantic functions already described. Every one of these functions has its counterpart in later two-word speech, where rule-boundedness is not in question (Bowerman, 1973; Brown, 1973; Schlesinger, 1971b).

DEVELOPMENTAL SEQUENCE

A well-defined developmental sequence is a constraint on random productivity. As Brown (1973) points out, if there were no rules, all possible utterances would appear at once. However, this does not happen. Instead, the development follows a generally consistent, definite order.

The assessment of order of acquisition is somewhat problematical. How do you know exactly when a child "has" a given semantic function? Although we could use a productivity measure as the criterion for acquisition, this is not entirely satisfactory for several reasons. One is that both boys used many semantic relations before the first formal observation session, and it is difficult to measure productivity from diary observations, our only source of data for this period. A second is that frequency of occurrence, one aspect of productivity, is very much affected by situational structure, and some semantic functions are used only in relatively rare situations. Thus, measured productivity is a function of the context and, therefore, does not directly measure children's linguistic abilities. There are a number of semantic functions (e.g., Nicky's Agent) that occur in single instances during observation sessions well before they achieve productivity.

A third reason is that children's linguistic production is sensitive to the strangeness of the environment, so the strangeness of an observation session inhibits a child's use of newly acquired relations. For example, Matthew's first Indicative Object is reported in his diary at 8(12), yet no reliable spontaneous instance occurred in a formal session until Matthew II—14(10, 18).

Although the diary observations offer no quantitative measure of productivity, they are much better suited to catching the rarer types of utterance. This is shown by the fact that all of Matthew's semantic functions and all except two of Nicky's were noted first in the diaries. For this reason, we decided to use the first recorded example of each semantic function to establish and compare orders of development for the two boys. This method allows us to include data from both diary and formal observation. Even though single examples can be flukes, as Brown (personal communication, 1970) has pointed out, the first recorded appearance does seem more likely to get at underlying capacity or competence than does a quantitative measure. All of the relations that were recorded in diaries also occurred during a formal session from a few days to a few months later. This pattern confirms the usefulness and reliability of diary data for the study of early speech.

Tables 8 and 9 show the ages at which different semantic functions first occurred in diary and formal-session data for both boys, and describe the first

Table 8
Onset of Semantic Functions: Order and First Occurrence for Nicky[a]

Semantic function	Age	Instance
Performative	8(19)	*dada*, to accompany every action
Performative Object	9(8)	*dada*, looking at father
Volition	11(28)	*na, na*, crawling to forbidden bookcase
Agent	13(3)	*dada*, hearing someone come in
Action or State of Agent	14(21)–15(18)	*do(wn)*, when he sits or steps down
Object	16(19–25)	*bar* (fan), demanding fan to be turned on or off
Action or State of Object	18(1–8)	*down*, shutting cabinet door
Dative	18(4)[b]	*mama*, when he gives book to mother
Object Associated with Another Object or Location	18(8–16)	*poo*, putting his hand on bottom while being changed, usually after a bowel movement
Animate Being Associated with Object or Location	18(19–25)	*lara* (Lauren), upon seeing her empty bed
Location	18(19–25)	*bap* (diaper), to indicate location of feces
Modification of Event	19(29)[b]	*more[c] record*, pointing to record playing

[a] Bracketed examples were considered simultaneous.
[b] Occurred in formal observation session. All other examples are from Nicky's diary.
[c] First example occurred in context of two-word utterance.

Table 9
Onset of Semantic Functions: Order and First Occurrence for Matthew

Semantic function	Age	Instance
Performative	7(22)	*hi*, as accompaniment to waving
Performative Object	8(12)	*dada*, looking at father
Volition	11(24)	*nana*, turning away from stairs in response to mother's *no*[a]
Dative	11(28)	*dada*, offering bottle to father
Object	13(0)	*ba(ll)*, having just thrown ball
Agent	13(3)	*daddy*, hearing father come in door and start up steps
Action or State of Agent	13(16)	*up*, reaching up, in answer to question *Do you want to get up?*[a]
Action or State of Object	14(6)	*down*, having just thrown something down
Object Associated with Another Object or Location	14(29)	*caca* (cracker, cookie), pointing to door to next room, where cookies are kept
Location	15(20)	*bo(x)*, putting crayon in box
Animate Being Associated with Object or Location	15(29)	*fishy*, pointing to empty fish tank
Modification of Event	ca. 18(1)	*again*, when he wants someone to do something for him again

[a]These imitative examples are used because of clear behavioral evidence of comprehension; none of the other examples in this table are imitative.

recorded example of each function.[1] The development within each function after its first appearance will be examined in the sections that follow. In comparing the development of the two boys, sequence is much more important than age. Thus, we do not compare the ages of acquisition of a given function, but compare its position in the developmental sequences. Such emphasis on sequence and de-emphasis of chronological age is consistent with current thinking in developmental psychology (e.g., Piaget, 1966).

The order of appearance of the different functions is substantially similar for the two boys. The Kendall rank order correlation between the order of first appearance of each semantic function for the two boys is .83, significant at the .0001 level (l-tailed test). It is possible that the true correlation could be even

[1]*Ba(ll)* in Table 9 illustrates a convention used throughout the text. The letters in parentheses indicate a sound or sounds omitted by the child in pronouncing the total adult word. This way of depicting the child's word also means that the part uttered by the child was pronounced as that component is pronounced in the full adult word. Because this was a semantic rather than a phonological study, we were interested in what adult word the child was attempting to approximate, rather than in the phonological nature of the approximation itself.

higher, since the largest reduction results from a diary example involving an ambiguous vocabulary item. This is Matthew's first expression of Dative, when he hands his father a bottle while saying *dada*, at 11(28). Earlier, he had been using a similar syllable, *dat*,[2] as a Performative to accompany many actions; it is difficult to distinguish the two usages in this example.

If we segregate the functions into the larger categories indicated by the groupings in the tables, the agreement of orders of appearance is perfect. The order is: performative functions, functions involving a relation between an entity and an action, relations between two entities, and modification of events.

The similarity of the developmental sequences of the two boys cannot be attributed to the influence of expectations, as Nicky's mother was not aware of any hypotheses about order of development. The parallel development of semantic functions in the two boys reflects a parallel sequence of semantic interpretation in the two mothers, and thus constitutes evidence that one-word utterances are, in fact, systematic in their communicative effect. These results militate against the idea that early language, being egocentric, fails to communicate.

This developmental sequence also belies the idea that the first use of language is to express orders and desires. Performatives certainly do not express desire, although they may not be language either. If one considers that Performative Objects are the first example of language proper, it is clear from Tables 8 and 9 that the first instances are Indicative rather than Volitional. Volitional Objects occur later for both boys. The first example of a Volitional Object noted for Matthew occurs at 9(16), when he says *mamama*, gesturing that he wants mother 1 month after the first instance of naming an Indicative Object. For Nicky, the first clear-cut example occurs between 14(12) and 14(18) when he says *Do(t)?* (mother's name), looking for her. The expression of Volition itself occurs after the first Indicative Objects, as Tables 8 and 9 show.

The sequence shown in Tables 8 and 9 agrees with the less detailed sequence noted by Werner and Kaplan (1963). "Identifying predications," the first stage in Werner and Kaplan's scheme, corresponds to our Indicative type of Performative Object. "Predications of action," the second stage in their scheme, corresponds to our two Action or State categories. "Predications of attribution," their third stage, corresponds to our two categories that involve Association. In fact, Werner and Kaplan present an example of a "Predication of attribution" that is almost identical to Nicky's first expression of Object Associated with Another Object or Location, shown in Table 8.

Tables 8 and 9 also show that every semantic function made its first appear-

---

[2]Imperfect phonological productions are interpreted by a combination of phonological and situational cues. The latter often enable the differentiation of potential homonyms (e.g., *dada* [daddy] and *dada* [doggie]).

ance in single-word form, except Nicky's Modification of Event, the last function to develop. Comparison with Table 5 shows that this developmental sequence of semantic functions in one-word form was essentially complete for both boys before two-word utterances occurred in formal sessions. Nicky's Modification of Event, the one seeming exception, is not actually inconsistent, for it appears *after* Nicky has used two-word utterances in a formal session.

PRODUCTIVITY OF SEMANTIC FUNCTIONS

To demonstrate that the semantic functions we have defined have structural status in early speech, it is desirable to show that they all are used productively. This can be done by measuring the variety and frequency of their use during the observation sessions. Tables 10 and 11 show the number of examples of each semantic function in isolated one-word utterances produced during each formal observation period.[3] Because examples with insufficient contextual information could not be interpreted reliably and because multimorpheme single-word utterances were counted (e.g., *cars*), the total production recorded for a session may differ from that reported in Table 5. Within a session, instances of a given relation are broken down according to whether they are unique examples or identical to some other utterance during that session. During a session, if a child used the same word in the same way, combined with the same general contextual elements, more than once, then only one such instance was added to the first figure for that session (the columns of Tables 10 and 11 "dif." for "different"); the remainder were added to the second figure (the columns labeled "same"). The first figure thus represents the combinatorial productivity of a particular semantic function at a particular period.

If we define the achievement of productivity by a function as the occurrence of three nonrepetitive instances during a single session, then all but three functions achieved productivity in the speech of both boys during the observation period. Modification of an Event was never used extensively by Nicky. Performatives were never recorded in great number for Matthew (although this lack was more apparent than real as Section 3.3 explains); Animate Beings Associated with an Object or Location were also rare for Matthew. During the last observation period, the productivity of one-word semantic functions declines, as functions originally expressed by means of a single word gain expression in multiword sentences.

---

[3]Tables 10 and 11 (like Table 7) show more functions than Tables 8 and 9 because they distinguish Indicative and Volitional Objects, whereas the latter do not. As we pointed out in Chapter 2, differences of Modality are significant for development within a function, but not for comparison between functions.

PRODUCTIVITY OF INDIVIDUAL WORDS AND
GESTURES WITHIN A SINGLE SEMANTIC RELATION

The productivity of child language can perhaps be appreciated better by considering how a given word can be used in a variety of situations while the semantic function remains constant. This phenomenon was noted by Guillaume (1927). During VI—18(18), Matthew used *gone* in relation to six different inanimate objects—everything from juice, to pieces missing from a toy, to an airplane. Illustrations of the various combinations are presented in Table 12. Within the confines of a given relation, Action or State of an Object, this word achieves great productivity through combination with varying but appropriate situational elements.

Like individual words, individual gestures and actions have a generative or productive aspect. For example, the pointing gesture functions as an indicator. Each child could point to and name a seemingly unlimited number of objects. Performative gestures, like reaching or pointing, become virtually as conventionalized as words and, undoubtedly, combine with more situational and verbal elements than any single word.

SINGLE WORDS, MULTIPLE FUNCTIONS:
SEMANTIC DEVELOPMENT IN INDIVIDUAL VOCABULARY

As a final illustration of productivity at the one-word stage, we shall give some examples of the use of a single word in several semantic functions. One such example was Matthew's use of *yaya* (Lauren), presented in Section 2.4. As a second example, consider his use of *dada*. Here, we give the earliest recorded instances of its use in different functions.

At 8(12), Matthew says *dada* while looking at his father. Here, *dada* is an Indicative Object. At 11(28), he says *dada* while offering a bottle to his father. *Dada* is a Dative in this situation. At 13(3), he says *daddy* upon hearing his father come in the door and start up the steps. *Daddy* is an Agent in this context. At At 17(15), Matthew says *daddy*, pointing to a cup that belongs to his father. *Daddy* here represents an Animate Being Associated with an Object or Location. At 18(11), *daddy* functions as an Agent in response to the question, *Who went bye-bye*? Whereas Matthew previously had expressed Agents in reaction to perceived events, here, he is responding to a verbally presented situation. The event is brought to his attention by the question *Who went bye-bye*? This example illustrates another developmental theme of our findings: In general, each function first appears in relation to perceived situational elements, and only later in relation to a linguistic representation of those elements.

At 20(3), Matthew uses *daddy* in a Comitative sense in reply to the question: *Do you want to go with mommy*? The Comitative is tentatively proposed by Fill-

Table 10
Frequency of Semantic Functions Expressed As Isolated Single-Word Utterances at Different Periods in Nicky's Development

| | Period I | | | Period II | | | Period III | | | Period IV | | |
| | 18(4) | | | 18(27) | | | 19(29) | | | 20(23) | | |
Semantic function	Dif.	Same	Total	Dif.	Same	Total	Dif.	Same	Total	Dif.	Same	Total
Performative	2	5	7	1	5	6	3	1	4	1	—	1
Object of Performative Action Indication	10	—	10	37	11	48	18	—	18	25	3	28
Volition	22	1	23	3	—	3	3	—	3	2	—	2
Object of Performative Action Volition	4	—	4	3	—	3	7	—	7	5	1	6
Agent	1	—	1	1	—	1	4	—	4	1	—	1
Action or State of Agent	2	—	2	7	11	18	6	—	6	3	—	3
Object	2	—	2	8	2	10	14	—	14	9	—	9
Action or State of Object	—	—	0	8	5	13	10	—	10	16	1	17
Dative	2	—	2	—	—	0	4	—	4	3	—	3
Object Associated with Another Object or Location	—	—	0	2	—	2	11	—	11	4	1	5
Animate Being Associated with Object or Location	—	—	0	2	—	2	1	—	1	7	—	7
Location	—	—	0	—	—	0	—	—	0	1	—	1
Modification of Event	—	—	0	—	—	0	—	—	0	—	—	0

74

	Period V		21(17)	Period VI		22(21)	Period VII		23(21)	Period VIII		24(23)
	Dif.	Same	Total	Dif.	Same	Total	Dif.	Same	Total	Dif.	Same	Total
Performative	3	—	3	—	—	0	1	—	1	3	—	3
Object of Performative Action Indication	21	4	25	27	1	28	20	1	21	16	—	16
Volition	10	—	10	2	—	2	3	—	3	2	—	2
Object of Performative Action Volition	7	—	7	5	—	5	10	—	10	5	—	5
Agent	1	—	1	4	—	4	3	—	3	—	—	0
Action or State of Agent	8	2	10	23	2	25	13	—	13	3	—	3
Object	14	1	14	28	1	29	28	—	28	5	—	5
Action or State of Object	24	1	25	28	4	32	22	—	22	5	—	5
Dative	3	—	4	6	—	6	1	—	1	—	—	0
Object Associated with Another Object or Location	1	—	1	8	1	9	3	—	3	1	—	1
Animate Being Associated with Object of Location	1	—	1	1	—	1	3	—	4	2	—	2
Location	6	1	7	2	—	2	1	—	1	—	—	0
Modification of Event	—	—	0	1	—	1	1	—	1	2	—	2

Table 11

Frequency of Semantic Functions Expressed as Isolated Single-Word Utterances at Different Periods in Matthew's Development

Semantic function	Period I 12(15) 12(22)			Period II 14(10) 14(18)			Period III 15(5) 15(17)			Period IV 16(2)			Period V 17(13)		
	Dif.	Same	Total	Dif.	Same	Total	Dif.	Same	Total	Dif.	Same	Total	Dif.	Same	Total
Performative	—	—	0	1	—	1	1	—	1	1	—	1	1	—	1
Object of Performative Action:Indication	—	—	0	10	—	10	13	1	14	9	—	9	3	—	3
Volition	8	—	8	—	—	0	10	—	10	—	—	0	9	—	9
Object of Performative Action:Volition	2	—	2	—	—	0	8	1	9	4	—	4	18	1	19
Agent	—	—	0	—	—	0	—	—	0	—	—	0	—	—	0
Action or State of Agent	—	—	0	4	1	5	12	2	14	18	2	20	16	1	17
Object	—	—	0	2	—	2	5	—	5	18	1	19	5	—	5
Action or State of Object	—	—	0	1	—	1	—	—	0	7	—	7	6	—	6
Dative	—	—	0	—	—	0	—	—	0	1	—	1	1	—	1
Object Associated with Another Object or Location	—	—	0	—	—	0	4	—	4	6	—	6	3	—	3
Animate Being Associated with Object or Location	—	—	0	—	—	0	—	—	0	1	—	1	1	—	1
Location	—	—	0	—	—	0	—	—	0	—	—	0	—	—	0
Modification of Event	—	—	0	—	—	0	—	—	0	—	—	0	—	—	0

76

Semantic function	Period VI 18(18) Dif.	Same	Total	Period VII 19(21) Dif.	Same	Total	Period VIII 20(26) Dif.	Same	Total	Period IX 22(1) Dif.	Same	Total
Performative	1	—	1	—	—	0	—	—	0	—	—	0
Object of Performative Action:Indication	16	2	18	10	—	10	7	—	7	9	—	9
Volition	7	—	7	10	—	10	15	—	15	3	—	3
Object of Performative Action:Volition	5	—	5	11	—	11	8	1	9	2	—	2
Agent	—	—	0	3	—	3	3	—	3	—	—	0
Action or State of Agent	19	—	19	11	1	12	23	4	27	11	1	12
Object	5	—	5	14	1	15	6	—	6	1	—	1
Action or State of Object	21	—	21	16	2	18	17	—	17	6	1	7
Dative	—	—	0	2	—	2	3	1	4	—	—	0
Object Associated with Another Object or Location	1	—	1	2	—	2	—	—	0	—	—	0
Animate Being Associated with Object or Location	2	—	2	—	—	0	2	—	2	2	—	2
Location	—	—	0	2	—	2	4	—	4	1	—	1
Modification of Event	2	—	2	3	—	3	5	—	5	3	—	3

77

Table 12

Action or State of Inanimate Object: Examples of Single-Word Utterances Involving *Gone* at Matthew VI—18(18)

Preceding context	Modality			Event	
Milk carton has been empty (unaware now full).	M	looking into	container	empty *gone*	of juice
	M	pointing to	milk carton	gone	
				Has taken off gone	rings from toy
	M	looking at	M		
Gone. Yeah.				empty *gone, gone, gone*	record jacket *record*
Where's the record?				gone	
Gone.				no	
All gone? You know where				all gone	
The record is. It's up there.				gone	
It's gone cause it's up there.					
It's going round and round.				gone	
The record's going round and round.					
It's not gone. It's here.				gone	
Look. Here's the record.					
What is it?	M	looking	for spot of light	going around *round-n-round*	on ceiling
Huh?				*round-n-round*	
Round and round? What's going round and round?				*round-n-round*	
	M	points to	airplane (in sky) *airplane airplane*	gone	
Airplane. That's right.	M			gone	

Note. Broken horizontal rules separate context utterances that were not part of connected discourse.

more as the conjunction of two nouns (two things in situational terms), often signaled by the preposition *with*. It intrinsically involves a sequence of at least two nouns (e.g., a sequence of two Agents) and so was not treated as a separate semantic function in our analysis of one-word utterances. In this example, *daddy* implicitly replaces *mommy* as object of the preposition *with*, and thus constitutes an example of paradigmatic substitution.

That same day, Matthew's father asks the question *Who am I?* and Matthew answers *daddy*. Here, an early semantic function, Indicative Object, is expressed in relation to a *wh* question, implicitly filling the slot occupied by *Who* in the question. Thus, Matthew's word for father, the first adult word he acquires, is used successively in all semantic functions which an animate noun can fulfill.

As a third example, consider Matthew's use of *bye-bye*, an early relational word. *Bye-bye* is initially, at 13(26), a Performative, functioning as the verbal aspect of the act of waving. However, at 14(3), Matthew progresses to using *bye-bye* to represent his own Action or State of motion, saying *bye-bye* while riding his bike, for instance. At 14(29), he uses *bye-bye* while playing with his toy cars, thus encoding the Action or State of an Object. Not until 16(2) (Matthew VI) does Matthew use *bye-bye* to express the Action of an Agent other than himself: He says bye-bye to report that a visitor is about to leave. This example illustrates the more general developmental finding that children encode their *own* actions or states before the actions or states of *others*. The development of *bye-bye* again shows that new uses become possible for an old word as semantic development proceeds.

These examples show that the range of possible uses of a word at a given stage of a child's development is not solely dependent on the referential meaning of that word. Rather, it also depends on the semantic functions the child can express at that time. Thus, old vocabulary items are used in new ways as semantic development proceeds. The limited range of early speech is not merely a result of limited vocabulary; limitations on the number of semantic relations are just as important.

3.2 Developmental Change in the Expression of Semantic Relations: An Overview

In what follows, we shall give a more detailed picture of semantic relations from a developmental perspective, emphasizing regularities, but noting some differencies in the development of the two boys. Their development will be delineated with respect to a number of different aspects including the relevant situational cues and their structure.

First, we shall watch the development of the child's ability to use each semantic function in combination with verbal as well as situational context.

Children usually begin using a semantic function in isolated words and only later use that same function in single-word answers to questions and retorts to statements.

Second, we shall trace the development of the expression of each semantic relation from expression in single words, through expression in multiword sequences, to expression in two-word form. The differences between these types of utterances were noted in section 2.2. The role of verbal context in this progression will be observed. In particular, sequences with intervening adult responses—conversational sequences—will be distinguished from simple sequences.

Third, we shall look at the content of the utterances involving each semantic function in terms of the child's involvement in the situation to which his single word makes reference. We shall examine the evidence for a decentration process in which the child becomes increasingly able to encode events external to himself.[4]

Finally, we shall attempt to analyze the development of the range of expression of each semantic function, insofar as it is distinct from the other progressions we have noted.

The plan of the rest of the chapter is as follows: Semantic functions will be taken up one at a time in the order of their appearance in Nicky's speech (Table 9). (Volitional Objects, a part of the category Performative Objects in that table, will be discussed after Volition.) A short introduction to the nature of each function is given, but the reader should refer to Chapter 2 for more complete definition. In the section covering each semantic function, its development will be traced chronologically from its appearance in single-word form to its use in two-word sentences. Generally, Nicky's development is discussed first, and Matthew's is compared to it. A summary of their development is provided at the end of each section. Examples are selected to show the earliest instance of each function and other occurrences of interest. All of the first occurrences and many of the other examples are listed in Tables 39 and 40 at the end of this chapter, to allow the reader to compare development across functions. Tables 8 through 11 should also help the reader coordinate the development of different functions within a single temporal framework. The summaries at the end of each section and at the end of the chapter allow a general overview of Matthew and Nicky's development. Tables in the text present a representative sampling of different functions and forms. Because the focus of this study was one-word speech, examples of longer utterances are generally given only to illustrate the transition to more mature forms.

---

[4]Decentration is the process of development away from an egocentric perspective. When the child views something egocentrically, he is restricted to his own perspective. As decentration progresses he becomes increasingly able to view the phenomenon from a perspective outside himself. A child (or adult) is not either egocentric or not; decentration is a continual process throughout the lifespan, always being repeated on new levels and in new domains.

3.3 Performatives

Both children began speaking by using nonstandard sounds to accompany their actions. Later, they used easily recognizable words in similar ways. Some words are used first in a Performative sense and are later transferred to factual statements. This developmental sequence was noted by Grégoire (1937), who observed a child in whom the first significant word started out as a (Performative) train sound. The connection with action is less strong in later usage, but Performatives retain the characteristic of constituting an act.

NICKY

The first speech sounds Nicky used consistently were a nonreferential *dada*, 8(19), to accompany many actions for a period. Around 12(7), his mother reports that he says *ada* and similar sounds while pointing to things around the house "meaning a sort of 'eureka/there it is.' Does not appear to be attempting to communicate anything to anyone." The following week she writes, "N. points to things with one of the 'words' above—but predominantly *ada* (intonation of "What's that?") and seems to *expect* to be told the name. He then repeats the *intonation* of the name with one of the 'words' above." The first reported example of a Performative with a conventional word is at 13(8) when Nicky began to say *hi!* to other people. At 13(18), he waved and said *bye-bye* to say good night to his father. The following day, he repeated this when his father left for work. He had known how to wave for at least a month. Later, he learned to use *bye-bye* without the accompanying wave, thereby substituting the word for the action. Table 13 presents a sample of Performatives from Nicky's observation sessions. Since Performatives, by their nature, often are used in imitative responses (e.g., *hi*, *bye-bye*), imitated words have been included in the frequency count.

MATTHEW

Matthew's use of Performatives is analogous to Nicky's. From 7(22), he used *ah* (hi) to accompany a wave. At 8(6), he said *dat* (pat) to accompany clapping and while playing pat-a-cake. During the same period, he smiles and says *mm* while eating a cracker. Table 9 shows few cases of Performatives for Matthew because most of the examples were imitative and hence eliminated from the analysis. Table 14 includes imitations in the frequency count and presents some examples from Matthew's observation sessions.

CONCLUSION

The earliest Performatives are on the borderline of language proper. These examples lack complete separation of word and referent and are part of the

Table 13
Frequency and Examples of Performatives at Different Periods in Nicky's Development

Observation period and age	Frequency	Examples		
		Preceding context	Modality	Event
I 18(4)	8	*Bye bye.*	N going to *bye*	bed
II 18(27)	6		N finishes *(hurr)ay*	tower
III 19(29)	4		repeats *hurray*	N puts together two balls of play dough
IV 20(23)	2	camera is on. *Say "hi"*	N pointing to *hi*	camera
V 21(17)	4		N clapping *hurray*	
VI 22(21)	1	*Nightnight, Nicky.*	*night night*	
VII 23(21)	1	Mother singing song; about to sing "baby."	*baby*	
VIII 24(23)	3		N goes over to repeats *hi*	Lauren

Note: Solid horizontal rules separate utterances from different observation periods.

Table 14
Frequency and Examples of Performatives at Different Periods in Matthew's Development

Observation period and age		Frequency	Examples		
			Preceding context	Modality	Event
I	12(15) 12(22)	0			
II	14(10) 14(18)	1		M points to and tries to pick up *hi*	picture of telephone receiver
III	15(5) 15(17)	1		M waving out the window *bye*	
IV	16(2)	2	Bernice has entered the car.	M *hi*	
V	17(13)	4	*Say "bye"*	M talking into telephone *bye*	
VI	18(18)	4	M has put all the rings on his toy.	M *yay*	
VII	19(21)	1	*Can you say "bye?"*	*bye*	
VIII	20(26)	0			
IX	22(1)	0			

Note: Solid horizontal rules separate utterances from different observations periods.

child's own nonverbal action. With development, more language-like forms appear. These forms are more decentered and less tied to the child's own action: The word substitutes for an action rather than merely accompanying it. For example, the greeting *hi* is first part of the act of waving; later it functions as a greeting without a wave. This separation from the child's own actions is a form of decentration; egocentric speech is clearly not the "all-or-nothing" matter implied by Piaget (1923).

3.4 Indicative Objects

A child's next messages call attention to objects by naming them—the first instance of language proper. This order appears to be confirmed by the observations of Leopold (1949, pp. 5—6) and others (Werner and Kaplan, 1963).

NICKY

Nicky used *dada* at 9(8). Like Matthew, he was taught the meaning of *dada* as soon as he started focusing on this double syllable in his babbling, as part of a replication of another study (Greenfield, 1973). (This was the only instance of a deliberate attempt to influence language development in the course of the study.) *Mama* was first observed as an Indicative Object for Nicky at 12(7)

Whereas the performative modality element is implicit in the child's directed visual attention in these earliest instances of naming, it takes on the more explicit form of pointing as development proceeds. The indicative gesture of pointing is not joined with real naming in its developmental beginnings. Starting at 12(7), Nicky goes around the house saying different double syllables while pointing to various objects. These syllables have no stable referents, and therefore cannot be considered words, but the context shows clearly that their function is to call attention to objects. Nicky first labels an inanimate object, *ba(ll)*, at 13(9). In this example, Nicky says the name while looking at the referent. Later, pointing becomes joined with the stable names that are developing at the same time. (Because formal observation sessions were begun earlier for Matthew and because these furnish a more precise gestural record than the diaries, we shall use Matthew's data to examine the development of Indicative Action in more detail.)

Although Nicky names animate entities before inanimate, he names himself relatively late. Between 20(3) and 20(10), Nicky touches his head and says *nini* (Nicky), the first instance of self-indication. This accomplishment would seem to indicate decentration from an earlier stage in which the child took himself for granted and was unaware of himself as an entity to be named.

Sometime after being able to name Objects of Indicative Action, Nicky can answer *wh* questions. During Nicky I—18(4), he responds to the question *What is that?* by pointing and saying *baby*. Nicky would not, of course, have to understand the full question in order to respond, since comprehension of question intonation and the mother's pointing gesture would suffice to give a response. Indeed, it is probably the rule that adult verbal context is *added* to, and is not a substitute for gesture and other nonverbal elements in early dialogue. The fact that Nicky used the word *dat* (that) in his own pointing messages during the same session, shows that he could understand the word *that* in the question. Nicky's pointing gesture provides supporting evidence that he really is responding to the question. *Baby* may therefore be considered to fit into the structural framework provided by the question, and thus implies the message *That is baby*. Because both the demonstrative and the specific name refer to an entity that is the object of pointing, these two types are placed in the same semantic category. Implicit in this is the recognition that object existence and object place are not linguistically differentiated at this stage, for pointing simultaneously indicates both the location and the existence of something. The common origin of existence and location in pointing is consistent with—and, in an ontogenetic sense, perhaps explains—the fact that existential and locative constructions are closely related from a formal, linguistic point of view and have a common locative basis in many languages (cf. Lyons, 1967; H. Clark, 1970).

Sequences involving indication occur from Nicky I—18(4), where, for instance, he says *mommy; dat*, pointing to a picture. At Nicky IV—20(23), there is a conversational sequence in which Nicky names an Indicative Object, is corrected by his mother, and then imitates her correction. Here is the example:

MOTHER	NICKY
	[N pointing to picture of boat]
	bee
That's not a bee;	
that's a boat.	*boa*(t)

More interesting are conversational sequences in which Nicky creatively generates a list of Indicative Objects; this occurs for the first time at Nicky IV—20(23):

MOTHER	NICKY
	[N sees Lauren and Matthew through window]
	Lara (Lauren)
There's Lauren.	*mama* (Matthew)

This sequence looks very much like a situational analog to a paradigmatic word association, in which words filling the same syntactic function are associated. It contrasts with earlier sequences, analogous to syntagmatic associations, in which words filling complementary but dissimilar functions are uttered in sequence. An example of the latter type of sequence occurred at Nicky I—18(4), when Nicky said *mommy* followed by *dat* (that) while pointing to a picture. Here, *dat* is an Indicative Object, while *mommy* is a vocative. Thus, syntagmatic sequences precede paradigmatic ones, just as syntagmatic word associations precede paradigmatic ones (Brown and Berko, 1960; Ervin, 1961). These listlike paradigmatic sequences continue in Nicky's later speech.

Indication assumes multiword form for the first time at Nicky VIII—24(23). In asking the question *Who dat?*, he differentiates between object and name. During the same session, he explicitly differentiates between Object and Location in the three-word utterance *here it is*, which he says when he finds a number 6 under a lid. Whereas the act of pointing can refer to either an object or a place, in this sentence, *here* can refer only to the Location.

NEGATIVE INDICATION

One particular type of indication, the negative, must be treated separately. Although we originally treated negation (and affirmation) as a single category, it was semantically diverse and, unlike our other categories, was defined in terms of lexical items (*no* and *yes*). Consequently, we decided to categorize *no* according to the semantic scope of its negation. Of the early students of one-word speech, Grégoire (1937) was particularly astute in noting the semantic diversity single-word negation; he contrasts refusal with nonexistence, absence, or disappearance.

Negative Indication makes its first appearance at Nicky II—18(27) when Nicky says *no; no,* referring to the fact that there is no milk in a cup. This type of Negative Indication corresponds to Bloom's (1970) category of nonexistence. Negation was the one area in which Bloom (1970) was willing to assign semantic structure to single-word utterances; she, too, found examples of nonexistence expressed in single-word form. Nonexistence develops into two-word form in the next formal session, Nicky III—19(29): Nicky, who has been crying, says *no daddy* when his father is not at home.

A second type of Negative Indication is an instance of what Bloom (1970) terms denial and the McNeills (1968) call negation of truth: An object name is denied. It makes its first appearance at Nicky III when Nicky draws a picture of something that is not an eye and says *no eye*. Other examples of these two types of negative Indication occur in later sessions. It is interesting that the first two-word utterance expressing denial occurs at the same time as the first two-word utterance expressing nonexistence, although the latter had earlier been expressed in single-word form. Negative Volition (Bloom's rejection) and denial of an Action or State will be taken up later when the corresponding semantic functions are presented.

MATTHEW

Matthew's development of naming parallels Nicky's. Matthew used *dada* looking at his father at 8(12). At 8(26), he began to use the same double syllable *dada* for doggie,[5] probably because of his limited phonological system. At 8(30), Matthew answered his first *wh* question: His mother said *Who's that?*, pointing to a picture of a dog, and he answered *da* (dog). Thus, expression of the Object of Indicative Action occurs later developmentally in relation to verbal context than in relation to situational context alone.

Like Nicky, Matthew does not point at what he names until later. The first instance recorded in his diary is at 10(9) when he says *da* (dog), pointing to a dog going down the street. Matthew named the Object of his Indicative Action twice during the first formal observation period—his eye once and a bird once. In both cases, the label was instigated by his mother's mention of the word. Therefore, they were omitted from the productivity table even though each label was accompanied by an appropriate pointing gesture.

During the second observation period, at 14(10, 18), this semantic function achieves true productivity; there are 10 reliable occurrences with 5 different words. On four of these occasions, the name is a response to the question *What is that?* In 9 of 10 cases, naming is accompanied by pointing: thus, pointing is very much a part of this semantic function at the time it first achieves productivity. (This period in Nicky's development was recorded only by diary observation, so we lack data on the relationship between pointing and naming at this point.) The constant relation between naming and pointing at this stage suggests that the gesture is a fundamental aspect of the semantic structure. In other words, the performative element, in this case the Indicative gesture of pointing, is not just an incidental characteristic of early speech. In Matthew's later observation periods naming gradually is freed from the act of pointing, just as it was for Nicky. At Matthew VI—18(18), the point at which Objects of Indicative Action reach their highest frequency (Table 11), Matthew reliably names 6 different objects a total of 7 times while pointing at them, and 8 objects, a total of 11 times in combination with other Performative gestures like holding or looking at the named object. Where naming is accompanied by looking at the object named, the Performative element is, again, becoming relatively internal and implicit. The important developmental trend, however, is the diversification of Indicative Actions—the relative independence of naming from pointing in comparison with Matthew II, when this semantic function first became productive.

One type of name is somewhat problematical. Both Matthew and Nicky used animal sounds (e.g., *woof woof*) alternatively to name an animal and to describe what it does. Thus, if a child looks at a dog and says *woof woof*, his mother's reply might be either *Yes, that's a doggie*, or *Yes, a doggie goes woof woof*. If the child did not have another name for the animal (e.g., *dog*), the animal was silent, and the

[5]In either case, Matthew would be naming an animate Object, so the possible phonological confusion would not change the classification according to our system.

child used a clear Indicative gesture, then the occurrence was counted as an Object of Indicative Action. If, on the other hand, the animal was in the process of making sounds or sounds were implied by the previous question, then the utterance was classified as Action or State of Agent. Many instances of animal sounds, however, lacked these criteria, were considered ambiguous, and were therefore excluded from the reliable utterances tabulated in Tables 10 and 11. The use of animal sounds to name an animal is hard to evaluate; it may, in fact, be nothing more than an early form of onomatopoeia.

Unlike Nicky, Matthew often uses *yeah* to express assent or agreement. The earliest instances in connection with naming occur at Matthew VI—18(18):

MOTHER	MATTHEW
That's Bernice's pen.	*yeah*

Although interesting, *yeah* is ambiguous because it is impossible to know whether *yeah* affirms the identity of the pen or its possession by Bernice. Perhaps, however, additional situational information could clarify the scope of the affirmation in this type of situation. For example, if Matthew had been playing with the pen and his mother had asked him to stop, then we might infer that the pen's identity was presupposed and that Bernice's ownership was what was affirmed. On the other hand, if Matthew's mother had just pointed out Bernice's pencil, then we might infer that the object's identity as a pen was the affirmed relation.

Like Nicky, Matthew expresses negative Indication, although less frequently. An example involving a conversational sequence occurs at Matthew VIII—20(26):

MOTHER	MATTHEW
	[M points to bear]
	giraffe
Is that a giraffe?	*no*
What is it?	*bear*

One example of nonimitated negative indication in two-word form occurs for Matthew during the period under study. During the same session, Matthew's mother asks *Do you want to put the duck in?*, referring to an inlaid puzzle. Matthew puts the duck piece in the tree hole and says *no tree*, apparently denying that it is a tree.[6] Corresponding to Matthew's use of *yeah* in isolated single-word utterances to affirm the identity of something is his use of *yeah* in indicative sequences. The first example occurs at Matthew VIII—20(26):

---

[6]Since *tree* might be interpreted as a Location (i.e., the tree hole) rather than an Indication, this example is ambiguous. If this were true, this would be an example of denial of an action or state, analogous to *no fit.*

MOTHER	MATTHEW
	[Matthew picks up pot piece of puzzle]
What is that?	*pot*
Is that a pot?	*yeah*

This example also shows how, once Matthew acquires the affirmative word *yeah*, his mother uses it to check her interpretations of his speech. Such verbal confirmations of semantic interpretations are another piece of evidence in favor of correspondence between the basic semantic structure of child utterance and adult interpretation.

Like Nicky, Matthew forms sequences involving Objects of Indicative Action. The earliest example, at Matthew II—14(10, 18), is one in which Matthew names something, is corrected by his mother, and then imitates the correction:

MOTHER	MATTHEW
	[Matthew pointing to picture of mommy]
What's that?	*daddy*
That's a mommy.	*mama*

At Matthew III—15(5, 17), Indicative Objects occur in repetitive sequence in which Matthew repeats the same word at different points in the conversation. For example:

MOTHER	MATTHEW
	[Matthew looking at picture of door]
	door
	[Matthew pointing to picture of door]
Where's the door?	*door*

The significance of this sort of sequence seems to be that it provides an opportunity for repetitive practice and for the clarification of messages. Although repetitive sequences occur for a variety of semantic functions, they will not be mentioned in later sections because they appeared to be of less theoretical significance than nonrepetitive sequences.

Like Nicky, Matthew forms sequences in which an Indicative relation embeds another semantic relation as the sequence progresses. The earliest example is at Matthew V—17(13). When Matthew says *nany* (candy), his mother answers *What?*, and he responds *lara* (Lauren). His mother then queries *Does Lauren have candy?* and he nods affirmatively. *Nany* at first appears to be simply a name, but then turns out also to be something associated with his sister Lauren.

De Laguna (1927) and Werner and Kaplan (1963) among others have written of a developmental transition in which the pointing gesture is augmented or replaced by a demonstrative form (e.g., "this") to yield a two-word utterance like "this X." Brown (1973) refers to two-word identifications like "this X" as Nomination, and notes the universality of this operation of reference. As in the case of Nicky, two-word utterances of this sort develop late in the period under consideration, during Matthew's last three observation periods. An example from Matthew IX—22(1) occurs when Matthew picks up his sock and says *this one*.

SUMMARY

For both Matthew and Nicky, language proper begins by naming Indicative Objects. This developmental priority of Indication in the case of both boys constitutes counterevidence to the claim of Piaget (1951), Jakobson (1969), and others that the first use of language is to express orders and desire. From both a logical and psychological point of view, naming entities is basic to all semantic relations in which an entity is expressed. Once able to express Indicative Objects, the child has made the basic leap to language proper. He now has points of reference for the language—world correspondence.

Both children name people—animate objects—before inanimate objects, and name themselves only much later. The behavioral manifestation of Indication shows a developmental shift from looking to a pointing gesture to free use of a variety of means of Indication.

Pointing utterances differ from what we have termed "pure" Performatives in that pointing is the gestural representation of the Indicative Mode. Pointing can thus be considered the action translation of the semantic class of indicative verbs such as *show* and *indicate*, which Austin (1962) and Ross (1970) treated in their discussion of Performatives. Like linguistic Performatives, the pointing gesture takes a complement, in this case an entity; and the entity is encoded verbally with a label as well. Thus, pointing at something that is named constitutes a synthesis of two earlier developments—the "pure" Performative on the borderline of language proper, and the name. Hence, the Performative becomes part of the contextual framework, enacted by child and interpreted by adult, but is not given linguistic expression. The pointing gesture itself achieves productivity, for it becomes capable of being combined with an infinite number of objects.

Whereas, initially, the children use names only in response to objects themselves, they later do so in response to verbal context and questions such as *What's that?* Later developments of Indication include equative statements, such as *this bear*, and questions, such as *who dat?* Children also encode their own Indication with verbs such as *touch* and *have*; however, these utterances could be considered as constative rather than performative. Negative statements of non-existence and denial are made relatively late.

Naming is the basis for subsequence language use. Thus, Indicatives come to be incorporated into sequences and embedded within other functions.

3.5 Volition

Volitional utterances appear only after the Indicative is established. With the appearance of these utterances, the child has two modes the Indicative and the Volitional at his disposal. The two modes are generally differentiated by intonation or gesture. This contrast between Indication and Volition corresponds to Lewis' (1951) distinction between the declarative and manipulative functions of early words, the former used to draw attention, the latter to demand. It similarly corresponds to Leopold's (1949) distinction between statements of fact and emotional utterances. Because the children had three main words to express volition—*mama*, *no*, and *yes*—this section, unlike the others, will be organized mainly in terms of specific lexical items. All three words were used in other semantic functions as well; the present section deals only with their use in Volition.

MAMA

Mama is probably the single most confusing word that children use. It is often their first linguistic means for expression of desire or volition. *Mama* probably derives from the "call sounds" that Werner and Kaplan (1963) and others have noted in connection with straining movements of the child toward objects. They point out that because the child is directing itself toward a distant object while making them, call sounds are a step in the progression toward reference-making speech. Lewis (1951), on the other hand, has suggested that the use of the *mama* to express volition relates to the use of the name *mama* in distress cries. Another possibility is that *mama* represents a generalized agent in this context. (S. Braunwald, personal communication) The identity of *mama* to the word for "mother" does not seem critical, since Piaget (1923) cites an example of a child using his grandfather's name in demands. We have a number of examples in which a child uses *mama* to direct requests to people other than his mother.

In our treatment, we have distinguished the name *mama* from the Volitional marker *mama* on the basis of gestures and intonation. In an utterance with demand intonation, if the child reaches toward or otherwise gestures for his mother, *mama* is considered a Volitional Object, not a simple marker of Volition. On the other hand, if the child did not orient toward his mother but toward a desired object or location, *mama* is taken as a Volitional marker. In some later cases of *mama*, as a Volitional Object the child used *mama* with the intonation of adult Vocatives. More careful analysis of gestures and intonation, along with experimental work on the child's awareness of the role of agents in satisfying his demands, might allow a better definition of the uses of this word.[7]

Nicky

Nicky's use of *mama* to express Volition, beginning at 13(19), does not refer to his mother, since, by then, he no longer called his mother *mama*, but rather called her by name (*Do[t]*). He used *mama* even for requests to his father, although he already had the word *dada* in his vocabulary.

During his first formal observation session, at 18(4), Nicky produces a number of two-word sequences, the first member of which is *mommy*, to express the attitude of desire, and the second member of which is the name of an indicated or desired Object. Each element of the sequence had already developed in one-word speech: *mama* from 13(19) and Object words in Volitional contexts from 14(12–18).

All the Volitional *mommy* sequences from Nicky I are presented in Table 15. The function of *mommy* in the first example is somewhat ambiguous, but the next example is clearly Volitional: Nicky repeatedly calls because he wants the *showel* (shovel). Whether *mommy* refers specifically to mother as a Vocative or Object of Volition in these examples, or still functions as a generalized request is unclear from our data. In support of the Volitional interpretation, however, is the report from his diary that, as recently as the week before the first formal observation session, Nicky had been using *mommy* to his father in situations where he wanted something. In the period between 16(25) and 17(1), Nicky said *daddy; mommy; daddy* when he wanted his father to pick him up. In this sequence, *daddy* appears to be the term of address (Vocative), *mommy* the Volitional element. *Mama* as a volitional pivot ultimately drops out. Therefore, it seems best to think of *mama* and its variants as initially retaining an expressive quality characteristic of prelinguistic verbal communication, a kind of Performative with an unverbalized object. *Mama* is, thus, the first instance of the Volitional Mode.

Matthew

Beginning around 12(8), Matthew began to use *mama* to request specific objects or actions. This usage is already productive during the initial formal

[7]We are grateful to Edy Veneziano for making us aware of this problem.

Table 15
Volitional Sequences Involving *Mommy* **at Nicky I—18(4)**

Preceding context	Modality		Event			
Fan is off.						
What's that? Fan	N	banging	fan			
			ban			
		mommy				
	N	repeats				
		mommy				
What do you want?			*showel* (shovel)			
	M	whining				
		mommy				
What?	M	reaching for	piggy bank	to put in	penny	
		whining, repeats	*bappy* (bank)			
	M	reaching toward	drawers	on	dresser	
		whinning, repeats	*door*			
		mommy				
What do you want?	M	reaching for	clock			
			clock			

Note: Broken horizontal rules separate utterances that were not part of connected discourse.

observation period at 12(15, 22), when there are eight unambiguous instances. These examples are presented in Table 16. The fact that Matthew is whining every time he says *mama* makes clear the volitional intent.

Mommy is a component of Matthew's first sequence of two single words on a related topic. At 15(11), Matthew calls *mommy*; his mother answers *What?* and he replies *down*, which is interpreted as an Action request. Note that in this conversational sequence, *mommy* functions conversationally as an adult Vocative.

Around 16(4–18), *mommy* is extensively used as an initial-position Volitional marker in early two-word sentences. *Mommy* was combined with names of objects such as *ball* and *cookie*, and actions such as *down*. Between 16(7) and 16(13), Matthew forms the sequence *mommy; daddy; mommy* in order to express a desire for his father, who is absent. Here, *mommy* is used in a situation similar to the earlier single-word instances, but is now combined sequentially with *daddy* as the Object of Volition. About two months later, at Matthew V—17(13), *mommy* becomes the first word to be used productively in the formation of sequences. During this observation session, *mommy* enters into five sequences

Table 16
Uses of *Mama* at Matthew I—12(15) and 12(22)

Preceding context	Modality		Event	
	M	pointing to whining *ma*	microphone	
	M	reaching for whining, repeats *mama*	orange juice glass	
	M	looking at whining *mama*	bottle of milk	
Mother holding doll.		walks to whining *mama*	doll	
	N	reaching toward whining repeats *mama*	tape recorder	
With mother in room, sitting on rocking chair that he has stopped rocking.	M	whining, repeats *mama*		(to be taken off)
	N	holding whining *mama*	rocking horse	(to ride)
	N	pointing to whining *mama*	bell button	(to push)

Note: Situational descriptions in parentheses relate to later events which confirm the semantic interpretation. Broken horizontal rules separate utterances that were not part of connected discourse.

with a variety of other words. In several of these, *mommy* is used in situations parallel to earlier uses of *mommy* as a general request term. For example, Matthew's mother asks *Do you want some spaghettios?*, to which Matthew replies *spaghettios*, followed by multiple repetitions of *mommy* in a whining intonation. As in Nicky's case, each of the component semantic functions was well established in one-word form before occurring together in a sequence.

NO AND YEAH

No was first used to accompany the performance of desired, but forbidden, actions. However, its most common use in a volitional context was to reject objects or events. Leopold (1949) has pointed out that children often show some initial confusion between *no* and *yes*, and use *no* to give an affirmative answer to questions. *Yes* is only acquired much later in the course of linguistic developments (Leopold, 1949).

Nicky

At 11(28), Nicky says *na; na* (no; no) while crawling to a forbidden bookcase. At this early point in development, the expression of desire cannot be separated from the act of crawling toward the bookcase. Later, at 15(19), he says *no* when merely tempted to touch a forbidden object. Thus, the expression of desire has been separated from the action. However, it is still difficult to tell whether Nicky is expressing a negative prohibition or a positive desire to carry out the forbidden act.

At the time of Nicky's first observation session at 18(4), *no* is a productive word. All examples of his use of *no* in single-word, volitional utterances are presented in Table 17. The three instances of *no* that occur during the first session are all related to preceding verbal context. Thus, Nicky already has passed beyond the stage, recorded in his diary, at which *no* is only used in relation to situational context. Note that Nicky uses *no* to mean *yes* in response to the question *Do you want to go out in the backyard?* The affirmative nature of the reply is indicated by the fact that Nicky did not oppose going out and was, in fact, happy outside. Thus, although he earlier used *no* appropriately to signal rejection in relation to nonverbal context, when Nicky begins to respond to verbal queries, he uses *no* to signal both terms of the assent—refusal opposition. This confusion must be cleared up later, but our data do not throw light on the progression.

The next qualitative development in the volitional *no* is reported in Nicky's diary between 18(15) and 18(21). At this stage, Nicky uses *no* to express his will concerning the actions of others, not just himself; for instance, he says *no!* to tell other children not to touch his toy. Here, we have yet another example of a decentration process within the period of one-word speech. This usage of *no* is confirmed during the next formal observation sessions, Nicky II—18(27) and Nicky III—19(29), as the next example in Table 17 show.

According to diary observations, Nicky first used *no* in a two-word combination between 19(15) and 20(5). These combinations had single-sentence intonation and timing from their inception. The first such sentences used during a formal observation session occurred at Nicky III—19(29); they are given in

Table 17

Nicky's Use of *No* to Express Volition at Different Observation Periods

Observation period and age	Examples		
	Preceding context	Modality	Event
I 18(4)	*Do you want to go out in the backyard?*	*no*	N happily goes out to backyard
	Would you like some fruit now?	*no*	
	Have your banana, Nick?	*no*	
II 18(27)		whining *no*	N is playing peek-a-boo
		no	mother has pushed away block (N picks up block)
III 19(29)		N whining *no*	Lauren and Matthew go upstairs
	Do you want that?	*no*	
		no	N playing game with mother
IV 20(23)	*Push it back.*	*no*	
V 21(17)	*Let's go to the bathroom.*	*no*	

96

		Utterance	N	Action		Object		Situation
		whining / no	N	takes off	· (mother puts away)	cover of toy (his toy)		*Do you want to put them in the bag?*
		N hands / no	toy		puts away	to mother		
		N whining / no	mother	picking up		his toy		
		N running away with / no	plates					
		N shouting / no	cup	falling down				*Mother puts 'hi' record on. That's the 'hi' record. Should I take it off?*
		no						
VI	22(21)	no	N					*Can you go under?*
VII	23(21)	no	N	stops eating				*Are you getting full?*
VIII	24(23)	no, no	Mother	starts to sing				
			Matthew	pushing		table		

Note: Situational descriptions in parentheses relate to later events which confirm the semantic interpretation. Broken horizontal rules separate utterances that were not part of connected discourse; solid horizontal rules separate utterances from different observation periods.

97

Table 18. Note that, in the first example and in the complex sequence, Nicky is rejecting an Object. A number of earlier investigations (Guillaume, 1927; Leopold, 1949; and Cohen, 1952) also observed two-word utterances in which the object of the negative wish, previously unexpressed in single-word utterances, is added to the negative element. It is interesting that this sentence has no precedent in sequences. That is, no sequences occurred through Nicky III in which Nicky used *no* in a volitional context, followed by a word expressing a rejected Object or State. However, there is an interesting sequence at Nicky III in which a volitional *no* is followed by naming an object he is being denied.

Table 18

Uses of *No* to Express Volition in Two-Word Utterances at Nicky III—19(29)

Preceding context	Modality		Event		
	N	closes	book		
		no	*book*		
	N	takes	diaper		from mother
		no	*bapper*		
			Bernice	taking	apple from chair
		no			*apple*
	N	points to	tape recorder		
			record		
That's a tape recorder.	N	reaching toward	record player		*on*
It's on. Do you want to listen to it?	N	whining			
		no	*record*		
Do you want me to take it off?		*no*			
Record still on. *No record?*		*no*	*record*		
No record. Off.		*no*	*record*		
Baby?	N		is riding		his horse
		no	*bye-bye*		
	N				
		no	*nightnight*		
N climbs into box	N	shakes head			
		no	*nightnight*		
Do you want to dance?		*no*	*dance*		

Note: Broken horizontal rules separate utterances that were not part of connected discourse. The particular connected discourse in this table is an example of a complex *sequence*, including both single- and multiword utterances.

Nicky's mother, saying *Let's go down; let's get down*, takes him down from a chair from which he could watch the tape recorder. Nicky's response is *no!* followed by *cacor* to express the Object of a positive Volition.

The second and third examples in Table 18 superficially appear to involve rejection of an object. However, examination of the situational context reveals that Nicky probably is rejecting an action in which the object is involved. Thus, it appears that *no bappa*, far from indicating that Nicky doesn't want his diaper, indicates that he doesn't want his mother to do something to it. In the last four examples, he is rejecting an action in which he would be involved.

At Nicky IV—20(23), *no* is also productive in two-word utterances, occurring nine times in Volitional contexts, but there are a couple of new developments. One is that Nicky has been talking about his *hi cord* (record with word "hi" on it) and then rejects it with the words *no hi*. Here, he uses *no* in connection with a word used to describe an attribute or State of the thing he is rejecting. This seems like an added level of cognitive embedding. Another new event is that the word *don('t)* appears, a more adult form of *no* in the Volitional context, as when his mother says *I'm really going to put on the hi record. It's really going to be that one*; and Nicky answers *don('t)*. During this session, he also expresses the Volitional relation itself, saying *no wan(t)*, again with reference to the "hi" record.

Finally, the first example of a three-word Volitional utterance involving *no* occurs: Nicky's mother has put on the "hi" record, and he responds *no; no hi*. His mother answers *Yes hi. You asked for hi*; and Nicky says *no want it*. Thus, we see an orderly progression in the expression of negative volition, from one- to two- to three-word form; each step involves the addition of an element previously implicit in the situation. (Although other types of three-word utterances occurred in the period under study, we do not generally trace semantic relations into their three-word form in the context of this book.)

An interesting example involving *no* appears in a complex sequence during Session IV. In this example, Nicky whines *no record* and follows with *off*. Here *off* serves a as kind of paraphrase of his previous statement.

The next period, Nicky V—21(17), manifests one new development in the volitional use of *no*: Nicky's mother is putting bread in her mouth, and Nicky responds by whining *mouth; bread; no mouth*. Here, for the first time, Nicky rejects a Location rather than an Object or Action.

At Nicky VI—22(21), we find a new variant of a three-word volitional message: *no more (ba)nana*, as Nicky hands his mother a banana. Here, *more* is an attribute of banana and the phrase *more banana* is subordinate to the Modal element, *no*.

At Nicky VII—23(21), there are several new types of Volitional utterances involving *no*. One of these is *no* in combination with a vocative. For example, Nicky's mother says *Now leave the candle there*, to which Nicky responds *no mama!*

Another is *no* in a three-word utterance in which the Action is encoded in two words:

MOTHER	NICKY
Are you ready to run around?	*no run around*

At Nicky VIII—24(23), new variants of Volitional utterances with *no* appear. Nicky rejects an animate Object or Dative in the following complex sequence: Matthew is trying to get up on a stool, and Nicky responds, *no feet; no feet please; no feet Math*. He also uses *no* in several three-word utterances involving Agent's Action plus Object, as in *no push truck* when Matthew is about to push a truck. At the same time, *not* appears for the first time with a Volitional function: Nicky says *not on door* as Matthew is putting shapes on the door. Finally, *yeah* in a Volitional context makes its first appearance:

MOTHER	NICKY
You want to go downstairs now?	*yeah; bye bye*

Matthew

The development of the Volitional *no* in Matthew's speech is similar to its development in Nicky's. We shall discuss only those few aspects in which Matthew differed from Nicky or provided complementary information.

At Period III—15(5, 17), Matthew uses the Volitional *no* in three out of four cases to reject situational events rather than verbal propositions. During this same session, Matthew also encodes an Object of negative, rather than positive Volition when he says *(s)poon*, pushing away a spoon. Here he encodes the Object of rejection rather than the attitude of rejection itself. In Chapter 4, we shall show that informational and presuppositional structure explain why rejection is more frequently encoded than the rejected object. In later sessions, nonexistence similarly was signaled both by the word *no* and by naming the nonexistence referent.

Negative Volition is much less frequent for Matthew than for Nicky. Matthew's infrequent use of *no* is compensated by his frequent use of the affirmative word *yeah*, a word almost never used by Nicky. *Yeah* first appears in a conversational sequence at Matthew V—17(13): Matthew whines *fishy*, pointing in their direction; his mother responds *Do you want to see the fish?* and he answers *yeah*, thus expressing positive Volition or desire. Affirmation is from the beginning an operation on a linguistic, not a situational structure. From Matthew VI—18(18), *yeah* is frequently used simply to answer questions about his desires, both in sequences and independently. An example of this occurs when Matthew replies *yeah* to his mother's question *Do you want to sit down at your table?*

Yeah continues to be used in later sequences, where it affirms desired actions as well as objects. For instance, at Matthew VI, he says *pour*, whining and point-ing to a milk container. His mother responds *Do you want to pour?* and Matthew answers *yeah*. Whereas Matthew is affirming his own desired action here, he later uses *yeah* to affirm a desired act on the part of another person. At Matthew VII–19(21), the following sequence occurs: Matthew gives a spoon to his mother and says *cut*. She answers *Do you want me to cut?* and Matthew replies *yeah*. Thus, there is a process of decentration in Matthew's Volitional use of *yeah*, just as there is for both boys' Volitional use of *no*. Affirmative Volition is also used in sequence in relation to semantic functions other than Objects and Actions. For instance, at Matthew VIII–20(26), Matthew whines *mommy*, trying to put in a puzzle piece; she answers *Do you want me to help?* and Matthew answers *yeah*. Thus, he expresses a desire for his mother to act as Agent. In this way, connected discourse expands along with other developmental changes.

SUMMARY AND FURTHER DISCUSSION

Expression of the Volitional modality occurs only after the indicative has been established. The earliest examples of Volition involve using *no* to accom-pany forbidden actions. In later uses, Volition becomes an expression of mode separated from action and takes on an autonomous role.

Mama is used early by both boys as a general Volitional pivot to demand a wide variety of objects and actions. Although *mama* comes to be used in sequ-ences, it commonly is used only to initiate a sequence, not to respond to a mother's inquiry. In later speech, *mama* does not become incorporated into two-word sentences, but rather moves toward a more clearly Vocative role.

The initial appearance of *no* in an adult usage is for the rejection of objects or actions in nonverbal contexts. Rejection is expressed first with regard to actions that directly concern the child; later, the child expresses volition regarding the action of others. Subsequently, *no* comes to be used in response to verbal context, namely, to answer yes–no questions. However, a positive yes–no question presupposes that both responses are equally probable, so neither alternative is marked. Thus, *no* is used to encode either assent or refusal. This early experience of relating *no* to words, not just to things, through struc-tural combination of question and answer may explain why *no* is common in children's two-word speech. Chapter 4 will treat this issue further.

Yeah appears later than *no* and serves to encode assent to yes–no questions. Matthew acquired *yeah* sooner and used it more frequently than Nicky. As in adult speech, *yeah* is not used in response to nonverbal contexts, since some alternative must be suggested verbally before *yeah* is appropriate.

The fact that exactly the same situational context is the basis for assigning a given semantic structure and content to utterances, whether they be expressed in one-word, two-word or three-word form, is evidence for a common underlying semantic structure at each level of syntactic complexity. For example, during Nicky's first observation session, in which he made no two-word utterances, he answers the question *Would you like some fruit now?* with the single word *no*. During Nicky IV, he answers the question *Do you want a cracker?* with the two-word utterance *no cracker*. In each case, a similar preceding verbalized question is taken as the source of the proposition which Nicky is opposing. There seems to be no reason to accept the preceding question as evidence of semantic structure in the second case, but to reject it in the first. *No cracker* is no less ambiguous than *no* alone, since, as Bloom (1970) points out, an utterance like *no cracker* is, without context, ambiguous among the three alternative readings: negative Volition (I don't want a cracker), nonexistence (the cracker is gone), and denial (it's really a cookie). Structured situational context is equally necessary to a semantic interpretation in both singleword and multiword situations.

Jakobson (1969) has suggested that the progression from *no* to *yes* is an example of development from an unmarked to a marked form: *Yes* represents a new level of specificity or marking because affirmation (in the form of the simple proposition) has been assumed before the emergence of the affirmative word. The negative by contrast is not assumed, so negative marking must be used to signal the contrary of an event or proposition.

This formulation and our findings show a fascinating congruence with a theoretical formulation of adult processing of negatives by Wason (1971). Synthesizing a heretofore heterogeneous and confusing set of results from many experiments, Wason concludes that the natural function of a negative proposition is to signal a change in meaning, whereas the natural function of an affirmative proposition is to signal constancy of meaning. Before this, negative processing had been conceptualized in terms of grammatical and logical transformations necessary to bridge the gap between sentence and state of affairs. But this approach did not really work, as Wason shows. His conclusion fits perfectly with our results on the origins of negative and affirmative form and function in children. In its Volitional function, as well as other semantic functions described in other sections, *no* is used "to contradict or correct; to cancel a suggestion of one's own or another's," as Strawson (1952, in Wason, 1971), the philosopher, said. Wason states that negatives function in an affirmative context. The same holds true even when the context is nonverbal—both Nicky and Matthew begin by rejecting unwanted actions. Just like adults, they are not describing the present state of affairs, but negating it. Precisely the same holds true when negatives begin to relate to verbal context in a dialogue situation: *No* is used to contradict or correct someone else's verbal suggestion. Wason has shown how, even at adulthood, when the negative is part of one's own sentence, this is still the primary or natural function of the negative. Similarly, our data on the origins of *yes* show that affirmative marking arises to signal constant meaning.

When children begin to answer yes—no questions relating to Volition, their first response is the unmarked affirmative: Analysis of data from Matthew shows that he repeats the key word in the proposition. The earliest examples are at Matthew II—14(10, 18) as in this exchange:

MOTHER	MATTHEW
Do you want to get up?	*up*

This first stage is the most unmarked form, the simple affirmative proposition. Furthermore, it signals *constancy* of meaning in the most direct way possible— by repeating the key word in the proposition. The next stage is the marked negative, *no*. Here is an example from Matthew III—15(5, 17):

MOTHER	MATTHEW
[carrying Matthew upstairs]	[whining]
Can you walk upstairs?	*no; no*

No is marked relative to the simple affirmative proposition, repeated by the child at the earlier stage. It also differs from the earlier affirmative in signaling change or opposition to the proposition contained in the question. The final stage is the marked affirmative *yeah*, first appearing at Matthew VI—18(18), for instance:

MOTHER	MATTHEW
Do you want to pour?	*yeah*

Again, the affirmative signals constancy of meaning, even in its new marked form. Thus, there is a clear three-step progression toward the acquisition of increasingly marked forms, exactly in accord with Jakobson's concept of marking. At the same time, the earliest form of affirmation—repetition— dramatically concretize Wason's idea that the affirmative signals constancy of meaning, while the Volitional use of *no* indicates that negatives do, in fact, signal a change in meaning relative to a positive context.

Both Wason's and Jakobson's formulations are confirmed by the development of the child's responses to yes—no questions of a Volitional nature. The continuity between the origins of the negative and affirmative operations and their later use appears to be of great theoretical significance. It indicates that the structural origins of language in one-word speech are basic to mature adult linguistic competence and might even offer clues as to its nature.

3.6 Volitional Objects

Children ask for specific people or objects only after the naming function (Indicative Object) is firmly established. Guillaume (1927) pointed out the existence of such single-word utterances expressing the Object of a demand. Although we have chosen to separate Performative Objects according to mode—Indicative or Volitional—clearly, the distinction between animate and inanimate Objects also is important, for the vocative may be defined as an animate Volitional Object. We have refrained from organizing our material in terms of both distinctions for simplicity of presentation rather than for theoretical reasons.

NICKY

Nicky's first use of a Volitional Object is unique in involving interrogative intonation. Between 14(12) and 14(18), while his mother is hospitalized, he goes around the house saying *Do(t)?* while looking for her (e.g., under pillows). A second example occurs between 15(19) and 16(18), when he says *Ke(lly)*, trying to call a friend named Kelly.

Between 16(19) and 16(25), Nicky's diary first notes a demand in which an inanimate Object of Volition is given verbal expression—Nicky uses *maw* or *naw* (milk) to demand milk. Thus, expression of the Object of Volition emerges after expression of the Volitional attitude by *mama*. The delay is not due to lack of vocabulary, since a child often can label an object before he asks for it.

During Nicky's first observation session, there are a number of examples of the Vocative type of Volitional Object. For example, at one point he indicates a picture and says *mommy; dat*. Here, *mommy* seems to express a demand for attention. When the mother's attention is secured, Nicky follows with an Indication.

By the time of Nicky's first observation session at 18(4), he is already using inanimate Volitional Objects in response to verbal context. However, he continues to express objects of volition in combination with nonverbal elements throughout the period under study (cf. Table 10). During this first session, whining, reaching, and repetition all are used to indicate the Volitional mode. For example, on one occasion, Nicky says *mil(k)* while reaching for milk. On another, he answers the question *Any more milk?* by whining and saying *(ba)nana*. On a third, he answers the same question by repeating *(ba)nana, (ba)nana*. A child often will repeat a demand until he gets what he wants; the fact that the child stops his repetition validates the mother's interpretation of the child's utterance. Some idea of the variety and productivity of this function is given in Table 19, which presents all the reliable instances at Nicky VII—23(21)—the formal session at which this semantic function is used most

Table 19
Instances of Volitional Objects at Nicky VII—23(21)

Preceding context		Modality	Event
	N	going to get	diaper
			diaper
	N	whining	*cracker, cracker*
	N	reaching for	eggs
			eggs*
	N	reaching for	bread
			bread
	N	reaching for	lid
		repeats	*lid*
What are you looking for?	N	points to	picture of Doogle
			Doogle
	N	going over to	bike
		whining	*bike*
Where are you going to?			*library*
	N	looking for	letters
		whining, repeats	*C*
	N	looking for	something
		whining	*C*

Note: Asterisk (*) indicates two morphemes. Broken horizontal rules separate utterances that were not part of connected discourse.

frequently. Note that locomotion toward an object, as well as reaching for it, is considered an expression of the Volitional attitude. Functionally, the two appear identical; the only difference is that reaching involves only the hand, whereas locomotion toward an object involves the whole body.

The first use of a Volitional Object in a sequence occurs after isolated Volitional Objects are well established. Our first example is the *mommy; showel* (shovel) sequence at I—18(4) described in Section 3.5. In the course of the following session, Nicky II—18(27), Nicky used his first two-word sentences combining the expression of Volition with Object of Volition. One good example is *awa(nt) pretzel*, as he reaches for a pretzel. (*Awa* is treated as a single unanalyzed word rather than *I want* because neither *I* nor *want* had ever appeared alone or in another combination.) The situation is of exactly the same type as those in which single-word Volitional utterances have occurred previously.

MATTHEW

In his earliest use of *mama*, Matthew seemed to use *mama* as a vocative simply to ask his mother to come. This phenomenon was reported in his diary, at 9(16), when he greeted his mother with *mamama* while gesturing that he wanted her. Matthew's diary first mentions him reaching for an inanimate object which he names—*c(r)acke(r)*—at 12(23). Objects of Volition are produced by Matthew in every formal session except the second (Table 11). For Matthew, as for Nicky, the performative elements of reaching, whining, and repeating are used in combination with Object names. At 13(23), it was noted in Matthew's diary that he was starting to point at, rather than reach toward, Objects of Volition. At this point, it seems as though Matthew is able to rely on relatively more verbal cues—intonation and repetition—to express Volition. Table 20 presents all the reliable examples of Volitional Objects from Matthew V—17(13), the session in which he produced the largest number. These examples illustrate the productivity of this semantic function.

Matthew first uses a Volitional Object in a sequence between 16(7) and 16(13): the *mommy; daddy; mommy* example from the diary described in Section 3.5. At 17(11), he is reported to answer a question by expressing a Volitional Object of Performative Action. His mother asks *Where are you going?* and Matthew answers *(f)ishy* as he goes downstairs to the aquarium at the foot of the stairs. Remember that "moving towards" is considered a performative expression of Volition and note that this element is present in both his mother's question and Matthew's action.

At Matthew VIII—20(26), we find the first multiword utterance in which both Volition and its Object are expressed verbally. Reaching toward his mother's coffee, Matthew says *I wa(nt) some.* (Because *I* has already appeared in another context, this is considered a three-word utterance.) Note that the reaching gesture is present in the volitional situation just as it was in many earlier single-word utterances in which Object of Volition was the only element linguistically encoded.

SUMMARY

Volitional Objects have the same event structure as Indicative Objects, but involve different modality elements. Both boys produce their first Volitional Objects after Indicative Objects are established in their speech, and express animate Volitional Objects before inanimate ones.

Object of Volition is a very productive semantic relation for both boys, involving a wide variety of combinations of verbal and situational elements. The single-word Object of Volition is expressed first in isolation and is used later as a response in dialogue. It also comes to represent but one aspect of the

Table 20
Instances of Volitional Objects at Matthew V—17(13)

Preceding context		Modality	Event
	M	whining, repeats	*fishy*
	M	whining, repeats	*fishy*
	M	looking around for whining	bottle *bottle*
	M	whining	*bottle*
Bananas are on table	M	pointing to whining	bananas *(ba)nana*
	M	reaching for whining	banana *(ba)nana*
	M	reaching up towards	mother *mommy*
	M	whining, repeats	*(spaghett)io(s)*
Sitting on mother.	M	whining, repeats	*cookie*
	M	looking at mother whining, repeats	*cookie*
	M	running & pointing to whining	record player *cacord, cacord* (record)
Record player is off.	M	running to	record player *record*
	M	whining	*milk*
	M	pointing to whining	door *door*
	M	whining, repeats	*door*
Door is open.	M	whining	*door*
	M	reaching for whining	refrigerator door *door*
	M	reaching towards	drawer *drawer*

Note: Broken horizontal rules separate utterances that were not part of connected discourse.

situation encoded sequentially by several single-word utterances. Finally, Volition and its Object both are expressed together in two-word utterances, in situations having a nonverbal structure exactly like that which characterized earlier utterances. Once again we find a systematic progression from single words to syntax. During this progression, the child comes to use words in response to verbal context and to encode more than one aspect of a given event.

3.7 Agent

Agents are expressed infrequently by either boy as isolated single-word utterances, as Tables 10 and 11 show. Our explanation for this is that children usually do not express situational elements that can be taken for granted. Thus, an Agent will be expressed only where its identity cannot be assumed, that is, under conditions of uncertainty, in the information theory sense, where *from the point of view of the child* there are alternative Agents possible in the situation. Since the identity of an Agent usually can be taken for granted, Agents are expressed infrequently. This is especially likely in the case of the child's own actions. We explore this topic further in Chapter 4.

NICKY

In the earliest examples, a sound made by an absent person is identified by naming that person. In this situation, the Agent is not present, so his identity is maximally uncertain. For Nicky, an instance of this type is recorded in his diary at 13(3), when he goes to the door upon hearing someone coming in, and says *dada*. Because his father already is present in the room, this instance is somewhat ambiguous, but we do know from another study (Greenfield, unpublished data) that, at this time, Nicky referred to people other than his father as *dada*. A more clear-cut instance is reported in the diary around the time of the first formal observation. Between 18(1) and 18(8), Nicky says *auwen* (Lauren, Matthew's sister) upon hearing her voice outside. The name is an Agent in the sense that it answers the question *Who is making the noise?* A similar example occurs during the formal session itself. At 18(4), when asked the question *Did you hear them outside?*, Nicky answers *Ma(tthew)* upon hearing crying outside. Once again, the earliest nonimitative examples of a semantic function are stimulated by situational context alone; only later does verbal context become part of the stimulating situation. As in this case, verbal context often combines with, rather than replaces, the nonverbal structure of the situation.

The next example, from Nicky's diary between 18(19) and 18(25), involves an Agent who is present, but uncertain for other reasons. Nicky's mother had been playing "Ring around the Rosy" with Nicky and Matthew. Nicky wanted to play again, so his mother took his hands, ready to play. Nicky broke away and said *Ma(tthew)*, then was content when all three played together. In this example, Matthew had been excluded as active participant or Agent in the game, and Nicky was signaling a desired *change* of Agent. Thus, the function Agent is used here in a volitional context.

During the formal session that follows—II 18(27), Agents are expressed sequentially for the first time in the following conversation. The situation is like earlier ones in that absent Agents are involved.

MOTHER	NICKY
[Doorbell rings]	
There's someone coming in.	*wawa* (Lauren)
Mmm. That's Lauren out there.	*mama* (Matthew)
And Matthew too.	*ma* (tthew)
And Matthew too.	

Thus, we find once more an orderly progression from single-word utterance to sequence.

Note that in all the examples thus far, Nicky has not named himself as Agent. This is further confirmation that a role that is assumed or presupposed will be less likely to be linguistically encoded at an earlier stage. We would expect the decentration process, described in earlier sections, to lead to the expression of self as Agent at a later point in development. For Nicky, encoding his own body parts is apparently an intermediate stage in becoming aware of, and encoding himself as, Agent. At Nicky III—19(29), Nicky says *hand*, referring to his hand holding crayons. *Hand* is considered an Agent because it is the animate instigator of the holding action.

During this same session, a conversational sequence occurs in which, for the first time, Agent and Action are sequentially encoded in a series of single-word utterances. Nicky says *owl*, looking at a picture of an owl to which his mother is pointing. Mother echoes *That's an owl*, to which Nicky responds *tootoo*, thus expressing the owl's Action. (Because Nicky had just said the word *owl*, *tootoo* is considered to refer to the sound rather than to the bird itself). In this sequence, *owl* has a dual function. In relation to the situation, *owl* functions as Object of Indicative Action, but once Nicky has said *tootoo*, *owl* can be thought of as the Agent. The correspondence between word and thing embodied in Indicative Objects is intrinsic to the expression of more complex semantic functions. As has been the case for other sequences described up to now, each semantic function had been established earlier in isolated single-word form before appearing as a member of a sequence.

Not until Nicky VI—22(21) does Nicky name himself as Agent. On three occasions, he says *Nicky*—once going to get up on a chair; once trying to climb on the bed; and once chasing Matthew. (In the second instance, *Nicky* was repeated in a whining intonation.) At this point, the decentration of the Agent function is complete.

During this same session, we find the first Agent—Action two-word utterances: Nicky, waiting for Matthew to push a toy to him, says *Nicky catch*; Nicky, lying in bed, says to his mother, who is not in bed, *mommy sleep*. Thus, the progression from single-word utterance to sequence to sentence is completed for the Agent function.

MATTHEW

At 13(3), Matthew is reported to say *daddy* upon hearing his father come in the outside door and start up the steps to his apartment. Thus, Matthew, like Nicky, starts by expressing the absent Agent. This type of example is described several more times in the diary in the next month or so. Matthew's use of the Agent is so infrequent in the observation sessions (cf. Table 11) that we must rely on the diary to chart the development of Matthew's expression of Agent.

At 16(17), Matthew expresses Agent in a sequence when, addressing his mother, he says *mommy; daddy* as his father starts to sharpen a knife. In another example, at 19(14), Matthew has been trying unsuccessfully to cut his meat with a knife when he hands the knife, an instrument, to his mother, saying *mommy*. Here, the Agent case is again used to signal a desired *change* of actor. Another example illustrates the same point, but both alternative Agents are verbalized. At 20(10), Matthew's sister Lauren says *Let me do it*; Matthew answers *mommy*, explicitly replacing the Agent of the verbal context, *me*, with *mommy*. This type of contrast of one Agent with another, alternative Agent is frequent. Clearly, the children verbalize an Agent when it will be informative, in the information theory sense of partitioning alternatives. At 17(2), Matthew forms his first sequence involving an Agent and an Action: (*f*)*ishy; ea*(*t*) while watching the fish eat. Both component functions had appeared earlier in isolated single-word form. At 17(12), Matthew is reported to have formed his first Agent—Action (or State) two-word utterance: He says *daddy bye-bye*, after his father has left for work. (This occurs before the first two-word utterance in a formal session, as inspection of Table 5 shows.) Here we have the completion of the now familiar progression from single-word, to sequence, to multiword utterance.

The expression of an Agent in response to a verbal question is first reported at 18(3), long after the first instances involving situational context, but also after the onset of multiword utterances; this latter fact constitutes a small inconsistency in the data. The instance is part of a conversational sequence: Matthew says *gong* (gone) in the middle of dinner. His mother answers *Are the people gone?* Matthew replies *birdy*. In fact, the pet canary had died and been buried that day.

All the occurrences of Agent as an isolated single-word utterance are shown in Table 21. It can be seen that all are situations in which the Agent cannot be taken for granted: The Agent either is absent (first five examples) or his identity is in question (last example). It is, perhaps, because this situational requirement rarely is met that Agent is expressed in isolated single-word form with relative rarity. When a relatively long-absent person is named, it often is hard to tell what semantic role the child has in mind. Because such instances usually had to be eliminated for lack of context, the number of Agents may have been disproportionately reduced. This fact does not detract in any way from our analysis of the relatively clear-cut instances.

Matthew's first verbal expression of self as Agent is the final step in the Agent development, as it was for Nicky. Unlike Nicky, however, Matthew, at 19(3), takes this step in the context of a two-word utterance: He says *me (l)igh(t)* in a situation where he wants to turn the light on.

SUMMARY

The expression of Agent in single-word form is relatively infrequent for Matthew and Nicky. Especially at the early stages, it mainly seems limited to situations where the Agent cannot be taken for granted by the children. This state of affairs excludes the encoding of self as Agent; however, with

Table 21
Matthew's Expression of Agent at Different Periods

Period and age	Preceding context	Modality		Event
VII 19(21)			Lauren *Lara* (Lauren)	has left room
		M hears	someone *Yaya* (Lauren)	making sounds outside
		M hears	Dot *Dot*	talking
VIII 20(26)		M hears	Lauren *Yaya* (Lauren)	crying
		M hears	mother *mommy*	coming
		M sees	Natche *Natche*	coming from a distance.

Note: Broken horizontal rules separate utterances that were not part of connected discourse; solid horizontal rules separate utterances from different observation periods.

development, there is a decentration process such that both boys eventually name themselves as Agents.

The first examples for both boys involved identification of an absent person who can be heard. These examples are Indicative; later Volitional examples involve expression of a desire for a change of Agent. These findings were confirmed by Veneziano (1973) in a study of two children acquiring Italian. She found that verbalization of the Agent was relatively infrequent, and that it often was expressed in situations where change of Agency was involved or where there was evidence that the child was aware of alternative Agents.

The earliest nonimitative expression of Agents is a response to situational context; later, Agents also may be expressed in response to verbal context. There is, too, a regular progression from isolated one-word utterance to sequence to sentence in the verbal expression of the Agent function.

3.8 Action or State of an Agent

Children typically describe their own actions before they describe those of other Agents. As an ideal type, Action or State of an Agent differs from the earliest Performatives, on the border of language proper, in that there is a more clear-cut and language-like separation of word and act: The Action word *refers* to the act rather than being *part* of it. This separation, however, appears gradually, as Nicky's earliest example shows.

The first words used to encode Action or State often are not verbs. Leopold (1949, p. 52) observed that adult adverbs were used before verbs in both English and German. It was findings like these that led him to despair of using parts of speech as a framework for analyzing early language. Guillaume (1927) also observed that, in French, both verbs and other forms in adult syntax were used by children to encode the same action.

NICKY

Nicky first labels an Action at 13(30), when he says *do(wn)*, sitting down in the appropriate place in the "Ring around the Rosy" game. At this point, *down* still has characteristics of a "pure" Performative because it is part of a social routine. Between 14(21) and 15(18), he is reported to use this word *down* while going down steps or sitting down. This is the first proper instance of Action or State of an Agent. Between 16(25) and 17(1), Nicky begins to say *u(p)* while going up a step. Between 17(1) and 17(17), he uses the word *dag* (back) to describe his action as he walks backwards. At the time of the first formal observation, 18(4), Nicky says *up* while reaching up to the fan. The performative element of reaching indicates that the word *up*, which describes Nicky's

Table 22
Different Uses of *Down* to Express Action or State of Agent at Nicky II—18(27)

Preceding context	Modality	Event	
	N	sits down *down*	
	N	sits down *down*	
	N	sits down *down*	
	N	sitting down *down*	
	N	gets down *down*	
Where are you going?	N	gets down from *down*	chair
	N	gets down from *down*	chair
	N	getting down from *down*	table
	N	getting down from *down*	table
	N	has gotten down from *down*	table
	N	steps across to *down*	sofa
	N	trying to get up on *down*	sofa
	N	trying to get up on *down*	table
	N	has just gotten up on *down*	table
	N	gets up *down*	
	N	gets up *down*	
	N	gets up *down*	
	N	standing up *up*	

Note: Broken horizontal rules separate utterances that were not part of connected discourse.

113

intended action, is embedded in a volitional context. The Action or State word *up* is thus part of a more complicated cognitive structure involving both demand and description of action. During the same session, Nicky says *hot* while starting to eat hot soup. This type of usage has been classed as Action or State of Agent rather than Object because the child changes state to hot. If this were a description of the Object, it would represent a constant-State description, a development that occurs much later. At Period II—18(27), Action or State of an Agent is expressed spontaneously 18 times. *Down* is the principle vocabulary item, being used in a range of situations. Table 22 presents all the different usages of *down* at this time. One notable feature of the table is that it records Nicky using *down* when he is getting up, on six occasions. Because the child—speaker is always the Agent in these early expressions of instigated action, the degree of separation between word and act is hard to assess. Encoding his own Action or State can thus be seen as a transitional mechanism that helps the child separate word from act and ultimately leads to the generalized verbal encoding of Actions and States.

During this session, for the first time, Nicky encodes Action of Agent in a nonimitative response to verbal context. His mother asks *Where are you going?* and Nicky answers *down* as he gets down from a chair. Once again, the ability to express a given semantic function in relation to a verbal element follows the ability to express it in relation to a situational one.

A new semantic development is reported in Nicky's diary between 18(25) and 19(1): Nicky uses *down* when he wants someone else to pick him up or put him down. Here, *down* describes the Action or State of a Dative rather than an Agent. Because these instances are rare, they have not been placed in a separate category.

During the next formal session, III—19(29), Nicky first encodes the Action or State of an Agent other than himself. This happens in response to a question from his mother: *Do you want to hear the dog go woof woof?* Nicky responds *quack quack*. This utterance involves paradigmatic substitution—*quack quack* for *woof woof*—rather than the syntagmatic completion of the earlier dialogue. It is also the first example of encoding Action or State in a situation which involves a process rather than change of state. There are several other examples in this same session. One involves a more standard sort of verb: Nicky says *bay* (play) a number of times during an extended complex sequence in connection with playing in the water.

Between 20(3) and 20(10), a new type of usage appears. Semantically, it could perhaps best be categorized as what Fillmore (1968) terms the Factitive, the object or being resulting from an Action or State. Nicky says *dot* while drawing some dots; he also says *cr(oss)* when he wants his mother to draw a cross for him. These observations are confirmed by the next formal session, Nicky IV—20(23), when the following two examples occur:

1. Nicky, about to draw a cross, says *cro(ss)*.
2. Nicky's mother asks *What are you going to draw?* and Nicky answers *dot*, proceeding to draw some.

These examples are treated as a special type of Action or State of Agent because of their rarity. Although a case could be made for treating them as a special type of Object of Action, it probably is most revealing to think of them as a new type, combining features from both types of semantic function. Because *cro(ss)* and *dot* describe the child's movement as well as its result, these Factitives were placed with Action or State of Agent rather than with Objects of Action. It is interesting that the result of an action should first appear after the two more differentiated categories—Action or State of Agent and Object of Action— whose features it combines. This pattern is repeated by Instrument of Action, an amalgam of Agent and Object (cf. Figure 1), described later in this chapter.

During session V—21(17), Nicky first expresses a transitive action where both Agent and Object are communicated in a message. The examples all involve the word *touch*. In one example, Nicky points to the tape recorder and says *touch*. Here the tape recorder is implied as Object by the gesture of pointing, while the word *touch* implies Nicky as an Agent. This attainment involves a development from a one-place predicate (Agent *or* Object) to a two-place predicate (Agent *and* Object). Although one might posit an alternative inter-pretation of this usage as representing a development from *adverbial* (*up*, *down*) to *verbal* (*touch*) encoding of Action or State, such an interpretation is not supported by the facts, for Nicky had used the verb *dance* much earlier in an intransitive sense.

Nicky VI—22(21) represents the height of Nicky's productivity for Action or State of Agent. Table 23 presents all the examples of this function occurring in Nicky VI in isolated one-word form. The development of Nicky's ability to encode process where before he was limited to change of state is best illustrated by Nicky's use of *jump* when he is about to jump (Table 23). A few months earlier, he would most likely have communicated his intention with *down*. Table 23 includes the first example of the encoding of a constant state rather than change of state or process: Nicky points to a picture of a bear in bed and says *night night*. Since he has not seen the bear go to bed, it seems that he must be encoding the present constant state of the bear rather than process or change of state. Another similar, but more convincing, example occurs when Nicky says *rest* as he points to a picture of a bear resting.

Nicky VI also sees the appearance of the first two-word utterances encoding Agent plus Action. These have already been described in the preceding section on Agents. At the same time, there are also two-word utterances which encode the Action and resultant State, each by a separate word. An example occurs when Nicky, about to get down, says *get down*.

Table 23

Instances of Action or State of Agent at Nicky VI—22(21)

Preceding context	Modality	Agent	Event	
	whining	N	wants to be upside down on *down*	bar
		N	trying to get *up* on *up*	chair
		N	trying to get up on *up*	stool
		N	climbing on bed *nightnight*	
		N	climbing on bed *rightnight*	
		N	lying in bed *rightnight*	
picture of bear	N points to		in bed *nightnight*	
		N	about to jump *jump*	
		N	kicking in air *kick*	
father			getting ready for work *work*	
picture of bear	N pointing to		dancing *dance*	
picture of bear	N points to		playing *toot toot*	the flute

Context	Subject	Gesture / Action	Object	Description	Utterance	Referent
	N			is about to eat	*eat*	cheese
	N			is about to pull	*pull*	toilet handle
M knocking on window	N			is knocking on	*knockknock*	window
What am I doing?	mother			is changing	*change*	his diaper
	N			has sneezed	*sneezed*	
	N			making circular motion	*round-n-round*	
	father			getting ready to leave	*bye*	
Mother is sitting up. N is lying in bed.	N	repeats			*rest*	
	N	whining, repeats		resting	*rest*	
	N	points to	picture of bear	resting	*rest*	
	N	pointing to	picture of bear	resting	*rest*	
	N	pointing to	candle		*touch*	
	Matthew			whining	*crying**	
	Matthew			had banged	*bang*	head

Note: Asterisk (*) indicates two morphemes. Broken horizontal rules separate utterances that were not part of connected discourse.

117

MATTHEW

Matthew's development of Action or State of an Agent parallels Nicky's. The first example occurs at 13(16) in an imitative context: Matthew's mother asks *Do you want to get up?* and he reaches up and says *up.* The gesture indicates that he understood the question. The first nonimitative instance to be recorded in Matthew's diary occurred at 14(5) when he said *nigh(t) nigh(t)* while getting ready for bed. Action or State of an Agent also appears in Matthew II—14(10, 18). Action of an Agent is a productive relation, but it occurs nonimitatively only in connection with the word *down.* On three of these occasions, *down* is used in a situation in which an adult would use *up.*

During this same session, we find our first example of expression of Action or State of Agent in nonimitative response to verbal context. Matthew's mother asks *Do you want to get up?* and Matthew, about to climb up, answers *down.* These examples illustrate the verbal nondifferentiation of opposite poles of a dimension.

Again mirroring Nicky's developmental sequence, Matthew next embeds Action or State of Agent in the Volitional mode. This occurs a number of times at Matthew III—15(5, 17). A representative example occurs when Matthew whines *dow(n)* while trying to get up on a chair. During the same session, Matthew encodes an Action or State of which he is the Dative rather than the Agent. In this example, Matthew, standing on a chair, reaches to his mother and says *down.* Here, Matthew indicates his mother as Agent, himself as Dative.

Encoding the Action or State of another person emerges next for Matthew, as it did for Nicky. At Matthew IV—16(2), he uses *bye bye* on two occasions when two different people are preparing to leave the house. It is not addressed to the people who are leaving, but is, rather, a description of their Action or State change.

At this same time, Matthew, like Nicky, forms a sequence involving Action or State of an Agent, although the second word encodes Object or Location rather than Agent. In this example, a woman is going out the door and Matthew says *bye bye,* followed by *door.* The first example of the use of this function in a two-word sentence was at 16(5), when Matthew said *mommy down* when he wanted to get down from somewhere.

Transitive Action or State is the next development for Matthew. In the period from 16(16) to 16(30), Matthew begins to say *ea(t),* pointing to food, when he wants to eat. *Eat* is also the first word used to encode a process rather than a change of state. During this same period, at 16(21), Matthew encodes for the first time a (relatively) constant state of an Agent: He says *dirty,* pointing to a spot on his arm.

At 17(2), Matthew is reported to form his first sequence involving both Agent and Action or State. Watching the fish (whom he has just fed) eat,

Matthew says (*f*)*ishy*; *ea*(*t*). Matthew's next development is to produce a two-word Agent—Action-or-State utterance. At 17(12), Matthew is reported to have said *Daddy bye bye* after his father left for work. (This type of utterance has already been discussed under the Agent category.) Between 17(16) and 17(29), Matthew was recorded as saying *I see* when he wanted to see something. At this stage, there was no independent justification for segmenting this utterance. *See* is often reported in the literature and may serve as an Indicative marker. However, in this example, the Volitional context means that *I see* is a complex performative involving both Indicative and Volitional elements. This example is interesting in that *see* implies a Dative function for *I*.

Shortly thereafter, at Matthew VI—18(18), a two-word utterance occurs in which Action and resultant State each are encoded by a distinct word. In answer to the question *Where'd the ice go?*, Matthew answers *go bye bye*.

At the same time, Matthew uses *yeah* to affirm an Action or State of an Agent for the first time. In one of a number of examples, Matthew's mother asks *Is Bernice writing?* and Matthew answers *yeah*. In interpreting *yeah* as affirming *writing*, we are assuming that Bernice's identity is presupposed by Matthew, and, therefore, is not the element being affirmed. This seems like a valid assumption, as Bernice Laufer, the observer, was well known to Matthew by this time.

Matthew's first factitive occurred at Matthew VIII—20(26) as part of a conversational sequence. He is digging in the sand with a stick and says *house*, presumably referring to the result of his activity with the sand. (His mother then queries *house?* and Matthew replies *yeah*.) Thus, Factitives occur, but with rarity for Matthew as well as for Nicky.

Action or State of Agent reaches its highest productivity in isolated one-word form during Matthew VIII—20(26). Table 24 presents all occurrences from this session in order to convey the range of combinations involving Action or State of Agent.

The examples involving *no* and *yeah* deserve some explanation: *No* and *yeah* have here been used to deny or affirm an Action or State of an Agent, *no* for the very first time. Although Nicky had used *no* in denying an Object's identity, he never used *no* to deny an Agent's Action or State, nor did he ever affirm an Agent's Action or State with *yeah* or *yes*. An example of the expression of an Action and an Object occurs at Matthew IX—22(1) when Matthew, about to look out the window, says *see it*.

SUMMARY

Both Nicky and Matthew begin by describing their own Actions or States as they move, in an almost Performative manner. From here, their development proceeds in a number of directions. Both describe their own actions in a non-

Table 24
Instances of Action or State of Agent at Matthew VIII—20(26)

Preceding context	Modality	Event
M is about to run over to sand.		*look*
	M	about to get down *down*
	M	getting down *down*
	M	getting down *down*
	M	getting down *down*
	M	getting down *down, down*
	M	picks up crib *sleep*
	M	reaching towards mother *up*
	M	climbing up on block *up*
	M	climbing up *up*
	M	climbing up on slide *up*
	M	climbs up on slide *up*

Context	Action	Object	Utterance	Referent
Where did Ismenia go?			*bye bye*	
Where did baby go?			*bye bye*	
	M		finishes drinking / *finished**	his milk
	M		about to walk on / *walk*	block
	M gives	mother	*eat*	cookie
	M has given	pigeons	*eat*	bread
	M holding up whining, repeats	banana	to cut / *cut*	
	M holds up whining, repeats	banana for mother	to cut / *cut*	
	M touches		hot / *hot*	bench
	M touches		hot / *hot*	part of car
	M sitting in repeats		hot / *hot*	car
Are you wet?			*no*	
Did you play with baby?	M		*yeah*	
Did you have a good sleep?	M		*yeah*	
Can you do it?	M		trying to take out / *yeah*	key

Note: Asterisk (*) indicates two morphemes. Broken horizontal rules separate utterances that were not part of connected discourse.

verbal context before they do so in response to verbal context. Both boys also express a desired Action or State only after they have encoded their own current Action or State. From here, they go on to request Actions or changes of State from others, when they ask their mothers to pick them up or put them down; finally, they describe the Actions or States of other Agents. This sequence agrees with Guillaume's (1927) observation that children encode their own actions before those of others.

Almost none of the words first used to encode Action can be verbs in adult English, in which *up, down,* and *back* function as adverbs of direction and prepositions of location. When a child uses them in isolation, it is not clear whether they are referring to their direction of movement or the resultant location. *Down* said while jumping down could refer to the act of jumping or to its destination. It is thus difficult to decide on an objective basis whether *down* (or another word) refers to an Action or a resultant State; we have formed a single semantic category to cover both at this stage of development. It is probably most accurate to say that Action and resultant State are not differentiated, that the child is basically attending to change, as P. Harris has suggested (in a research seminar, Center for Cognitive Studies, Harvard, 1971). Action and resultant State are more differentiated aspects of the basic category of perceived change. The fact that the child, jumping down, encodes the event with *down* rather than *jump* suggests that the child is focusing on the *change* of State rather than the *Action* itself, thus reinforcing our hypothesis. In other words, at the initial stages, the child is encoding the contrast between starting point and end point and is unable to encode either the intervening process (Action) or end point (Location) in isolation. This could explain why *down* is used to signal change in either direction. Vertical movement always implies a contrast between 'up' and 'down'.

Both boys pass through a stage in which *down* is used when getting up or down. This agrees with the observations of Leopold (1949) and Lewis (1951) that there is a stage of confusion between *up* and *down*, where one word is used to signal the vertical dimension. This is similar to the case of *no*, in that one pole of a dimension is used to represent the entire dimension before it is restricted to a specific pole. This phenomenon has been demonstrated experimentally with older children acquiring other pairs of polar opposites (Donaldson and Balfour, 1968; Donaldson and Wales, 1970; H. Clark, 1971).

Whereas the earliest words referring to an Action of an Agent seem to encode a change of stage (e.g., *down*), later words encode intransitive processes (e.g., *dance*), transitive processes (e.g., *eat*),[8] and, last of all, constant states (e.g., *rest, dirty*). Factitives such as *cross* may represent object nominalizations, another line

---

[8]Although Ingram (1971) analyzes the development of transitivity, he does not discuss this particular phenomenon at all.

of development of expression of Action or State. The final development for both boys was the concurrent expression of an action and a direction or resultant state in sentences such as *get down* and *go byebye*.

Veneziano's (1973) data confirm this basic progression for children learning to speak Italian. She finds that pure action words like *tira* (pull and *sale* (go up) appear later in circumstances where words like *via* (away) had been used earlier. Still later, both types are combined in two-word sentences.

As with other functions, both Nicky and Matthew start out by expressing single words, later use words in sequences, and finally combine them in two-word sentences.

3.9 Object

Object involved in direct action or state change is a developmental outgrowth of the Performative Object, and presupposes the basic referential relationship between word and thing involved in Indicative Objects. Objects differ from Performative Objects in that Performative Objects are not themselves affected by performative gestures such as pointing and reaching, whereas Objects are directly involved in an action which involves change of state. It is thus the character of the action or state associated with a given utterance that determines whether it was classified as a Performative Object or a simple Object.

NICKY

For Nicky, the first clear instance of naming an inanimate Object of a direct action is reported in his diary, between 16(19) and 16(25) when he says *bar(fan)*, demanding a fan be turned on or off. This first example corresponds to what Guillaume (1927) identified as an "object of intended action." The first examples of his naming an inanimate Volitional Object occur during the same period, so it is perhaps best to think of the two types of Object as undifferentiated at this point, especially since both occur in a Volitional context. There are two examples of Object in the first observation session. In one, Nicky says *dat* (that), playing with some blocks. In another, Nicky picks up his ball and says *ball*. This example shows that Performative and Direct Action form a continuum, for picking up could also function as Indicative Action.

Between 18(8) and 18(16), Nicky produces his first sequence involving an Object and its Action when he says *ban* (pronounced as in French) (fan) followed by *ong*(on). His mother reports that he evidently expected the fan to be turned on after naming the Object. When nothing happened, he added the Action or State, and his mother complied. Both semantic functions making up the seq-

Table 25
Instances of Object at Nicky VI—22(21)

Preceding context	Modality	Event		
		N	pushing	truck
				truck
		mother	has made	truck
				truck
		N	playing with	teddy bear
				teddy
	whining	N	trying to put	teddy on bar
				teddy
		mother	has given N	spoon
				spoon
		N	picking up	
				spoon
		N	picks up	playdough
				playdough
		N	getting up on	chair
				chair
		N	has banged head on	chair
				chair
		N	sitting	on chair
				seat
		father	has just gone out and closed	the door
				door
		N	picks up	diaper
				diaper
		N	trying to put	diaper on bar
				diaper
	N repeats	Bernice	takes out	book
				book
		N	putting	wing piece in puzzle
				wing
		N	making	ball with playdough
				ball
		N	making	ball with playdough
				ball

Table 25 (continued)

Preceding context	Modality		Event		
		mother	cooking	meat	
				meat	
	N		chewing	meat	
				meat	
	N		drinking	milk	
				milk	
	N		has just flushed	poop	
				poop	
	N repeats	mother	making	bed	
				bed	
Do you hear the clock chime?	N hears	bell	ringing		
		bell			
		mother	cooking	stew	
				stew	
	N		picking up	piece of puzzle	
	repeats			*tummy*	
	N		putting in	tail piece of puzzle	
				tail	
	N		picks up	dog piece of puzzle	
				dog	
	N		picks up	goat piece of puzzle	
				goat	
N often uses round cover as a record.	N		picks up	round cover	
				record	

Note: Broken horizontal rules separate utterances that were not part of connected discourse.

uence had appeared earlier as isolated single-word utterances. In the next formal session, Nicky II—18(27), five sequences occur which include expression of an inanimate Object of action. One example is *cacoo* (record) followed by *on*, said while going toward, and pointing to, a record player that was turned off. During this same session, we find the first instance of expressing Object in response to verbal context. Nicky's mother asks *Do you want it on?* and Nicky responds *acacor* (record).

Nicky's first two-word utterance, combining an inanimate Object with its Action or State, is reported in Nicky's diary between 20(10) and 20(18) when he begins to say *boo(k) back* to accompany the putting of books, records, and toys back on their shelf. Evidently, the word *book* had an extended referential meaning at this stage. In this same period, a new type of sequence involving an Object is reported. Nicky says *mi(tten)* as his mittens are being put on, followed by *co(ld)*. It appears that *co(ld)* is being used to express the function or cause of the mittens.

Objects are most numerous at Nicky VI—22(21). Table 25 presents the examples from this session in isolated one-word form, enabling the reader to realize the large range of combinatorial possibilities of word and event.

There is one particular Object that deserves special mention, the Locative Object; that is, an Object that seems to function as the Location of an Agent. The only one-word examples occur fairly late in the period under study, at Nicky VI—22(21). Table 25 shows several examples occurring at this time. It is clear that the operational distinction between Locative and other Objects is difficult to make, as Locative Objects often seem to be just slightly larger Objects (e.g., *chair*) or to be both a Location and a manipulative Object (e.g., *door*). For this reason, and because the Locative Objects of this sort were rare for both boys, they have not been put in a separate category. A particular type of Locative, Location of Object, was defined in terms of a relation between two inanimate Objects. It was more frequent, as well as operationally distinct, and will be discussed as a separate category in a later section.

MATTHEW

In the case of Matthew, the first report of an inanimate Object directly involved in an action or state change occurs in his diary about a week after he first named an inanimate Object of Volition. At that time, 13(0), Matthew said *ba(ll)*, having just thrown it. Matthew first expresses Object during a formal session at Matthew II—14(10, 18). In one of the two examples, Matthew turns on a record player and says *ca(record)*. At 14(28), Matthew forms something like a sequence involving an Object and its Action. He says *car*, playing with toy cars and then *bye bye*, looking out the window. This sequence seems almost like a chain of association. Action or State of Object had already made its appearance in isolated form, so the sequence consisted of two preexisting semantic functions.

The next day, 14(29), Matthew forms two single-word utterances that seem to involve word combination *within* instead of *between* words. Matthew says *kye kye* playing with his toy cars and, at another time, *kye bye* while making the toy cars move. These utterances seem to represent some sort of amalgamation of *car* and *bye bye*.

The first example of a two-word utterance expressing Object plus its Action or State occurs at 15(27): *more meh* (milk) when he wants his bottle refilled.

Objects become most numerous at Matthew IV—16(2). Table 26 presents the examples from this session and illustrates the variety of combinations of named Objects with Actions or State Changes.

At Matthew VI—18(18), he first relates an Object to verbal context. Matthew's mother asks *What are you doing with that?* and Matthew answers *bu(tton)*, pushing a button.

There are few examples of Objects in isolated single-word form which could be considered Locative Objects: At Matthew IV—16(2), Matthew says *door* when he is about to go out a *door*. At Matthew VIII—20(26), Matthew says *stone* walking on a stone.

Numerous examples of two-word utterances expressing Object plus State change occur at Matthew VIII—20(26); they are presented in Table 27. Note that, in each of these, the process word identifies an Action or State of the Object rather than the Agent. Thus, these examples are continuous with examples from one-word speech, but distinct from examples discussed in Section 3.8, Action or State of Agent, such as *eat cookie*. Another interesting point about the examples depicted in the Table is that each one conforms to adult word order whether this requires Object first or last. Thus, Matthew seems to be acquiring syntax, as his underlying semantic—conceptual structures come to be expressed more fully in linguistic form.

INSTRUMENTAL OBJECTS

At 15(10), Matthew is reported to say *bu(tton)* after he pushes a turntable button and the record turntable has begun to revolve. Here, *bu(tton)* could be considered an Instrumental Object. In adult grammar, inanimate Objects may function as the Instrument of an Action, as well as its recipient. Fillmore identifies the Instrumental as "the case of the inanimate force or object causally involved in the action or state identified by the verb" (1968). In the case of one-word utterances, the action or state must be identified without the help of any verb, as we already have pointed out. Otherwise, however, the underlying concept guiding our search for the Instrumental case was the same as Fillmore's definition. In addition to the *bu(tton)* example, Matthew presented only one clear-cut case in isolated one-word form. At IV—16(2), Matthew said *(s)poon* while eating chips with a spoon. At 18(25), Matthew formed a two-word utterance involving a spoon as Instrument: Holding a spoon and pointing to the cabinet where his medicine was, he said *ea(t) (s)poon*. At Matthew VII—19(21), an Instrumental Object is produced as part of a complex sequence:

MOTHER	MATTHEW
	[Gives spoon to mother to cut an egg for him]

	cut
Cutting?	*a cut*
a cut	*cut*
[cuts the egg]	
Yeah, I'm cutting.	*yeah, spoon*

Although these individual examples are interesting, the Instrumental did not really achieve productivity. Nicky produced no clear examples of instrument at all. Thus, it seems best to consider it an, as yet, undifferentiated aspect of the Object relation.

Table 26
Instances of Object at Matthew IV—16(2)

Preceding context	Modality	Event		
		M	trying to push	button *bu (tton)*
		M	pushing	button on wall *bu (tton)*
		M	drinking	juice *ju (ice)*
		M	drinking	juice *ju (ice)*
		crayon *craw*	has fallen	on the floor
M looking at mother.		M	playing with	crayons *craw*
		M	turns	pages to crayon picture *craw* (crayon)
	M points to	crayons *craw*	have fallen	
		his book *boo(k)*	has fallen	
		mother	gives	book to M *book*
		mother	gives	spoon to M *poon*
		M	going to pick up	spoon *poon*

Table 26 (continued)

Preceding context	Modality	Event		
	M	eating with	spoon *poon*	
	M	pulling	car out of shelf *car*	
	M	about to go out	door *door*	
	M	about to close	door *door*	
	M	trying to open	refrigerator door *door*	
	mother	has closed	car door *door*	
	M	has closed	door on finger *door*	

Note: Broken horizontal rules separate utterances that were not part of connected discourse.

Table 27
Two-Word Utterances Expressing Object Plus State Change at Matthew VIII—20(26)

Preceding context	Modality	Event		
		M	puts	banana *(ba)nana*	down *down*
		M	has taken	tree piece *tree*	out *out*
		car *car*	has gone down *down*	slope	
M	watching	car *car*	coming *coming*		
M	reaching for	more *more*	ice *ice*		
M	reaching toward	empty *more*	cookie plate *cookie*		
M	whining, repeats	*more*	cookie		

Note: The syntax of two-word utterances has necessitated an extra column to describe the referential Event. Broken horizontal rules separate utterances that were not part of connected discourse.

SUMMARY

The expression of the Object develops out of the expression of Performative Objects, so it is hard to spot the earliest examples. The first examples we have for the two children illustrate the different forms an Object can take. The first example for Matthew is *ball*, an Object of his own action, which occurs relatively early. Nicky's first example is *fan*, which looks like a Volitional Object except that Nicky clearly wants a change of state of that Object. Thus, the action (change of state) is external to Nicky. This more externalized form of Object occurs relatively late in Nicky's development.

Once again, Objects are first expressed in relation to situational context, later in relation to verbal context. Use in sequences followed use in isolation and preceded use in two-word sentences. Instruments and Locations of Agents have been treated as types of Objects because of their rarity in one-word speech.

3.10 Action or State of an Object

As with the Action of an Agent, many of the early expressions of this category were ambiguous as to whether they referred to an Action or its resultant State. It is probably most accurate to say that, in the earliest examples, the boys basically are attending to Object *change* and are not differentiating among the aspects of *initial state*, *process*, and *resultant state*. Many past Actions undergone by Objects become present States, as in *broken*; without further syntactic cues, these often cannot be disambiguated. As with Actions of Agents, the first words used to encode Actions of Objects are often adult adverbs. Leopold (1949) offers many German examples that parallel our English ones. Constant States have been included in this category, although they will be carefully distinguished as we trace the microdevelopment of this semantic function.

States or attributes can be either intrinsic or extrinsic. For example, the sun is intrinsically hot, whereas a coffee cup is hot only temporarily and extrinsically. However, properties that are intrinsically true of an Object are also extrinsically true, so it is extremely difficult to identify intrinsic predicates in actual speech. From the point of view of the child's perceptual experience, the distinction between static and changing States seems to be more meaningful and operationally definable than the intrinsic—extrinsic distinction.

McNeill (1970a) has suggested that one-word speech begins with intrinsic predications. However, the preliminary observations of Matthew's sister Lauren, which he cites as evidence for this theory, actually support the counterhypothesis: *Hot* was used by Lauren to describe a current situation before being used to assert a general property (McNeill, 1970a, p. 24).

NICKY

Between 18(1) and 18(8), Nicky began to say *down* when shutting the cabinet door. At 18(13), Nicky said *ong* (on) as a statement of fact when his mother switched the fan off. Between 18(8) and 18(16), Nicky is reported to have said *ong* (on) in a whine when he wanted a light turned on or off. During this same period, Nicky was reported to begin forming a number of sequences of single words consisting of an Object and a desired Action or State. These already have been mentioned in Section 3.9.

Action or State of Objects becomes a productive semantic relation for Nicky at Period II—18(27). An example from this observation session will make clear the distinction between Action or State of Agent and Action or State of Object. At one point, Nicky pulls his train down and says *down*. Although Nicky is the Agent, it is the resultant Action or State of the Object that is encoded rather than his own: The train, not Nicky, goes down. Note, though, that this same lexical item was used earlier to encode Action or State of Agent.

There are new developments in expressing Action or State of Object in this session. For the first time, a *constant* or static State of an Object is expressed. Nicky says *bi(g)*, looking at a picture of big dogs. Also, for the first time, a process that does not involve change is expressed. Nicky says *hi* as his mother puts on his record that begins with the word "hi." Note that *hi*, originally a "pure" Performative, part of the act of waving, now is used to describe a record that starts with "hi."

During Session II, Nicky also expresses Action or State of Object in response to verbal context for the first time. In a sequence, Nicky says *(l)igh(t)*, pointing to a light; his mother answers *light, yeah,* and Nicky responds *ong* (on). In this example, the role of the context supplied by the mother may not have been important as it mainly repeated what Nicky had already said. Between 19(8) and 19(15), Nicky began saying *(h)ot* while blowing on cooked food. Here, the fact that Nicky is blowing on, rather than eating, the food constitutes behavioral evidence that he is referring to the Object's State rather than his own. About a month earlier, at Nicky I—18(4), there was a single example, discussed in Section 3.8, of *hot*, uttered as Nicky was starting to eat some hot soup. In that example, it appears that he is referring to his own State of feeling hot, rather than the State of the soup. We do not believe that the children use *hot* to name hot objects when this word first starts to be used because it would be the only instance of encoding of a constant State at that point in development. When the child's behavior indicates that he is saying *hot* in response to *feeling* hot, our operational definition of Action or State of Agent is fulfilled. This interpretation of hot as describing a *change* of State of Agent rather than a *constant* Object State would explain why it is used so early by some children

Table 28
Instances of Action or State of Object at Nicky VI–22(21)

Preceding context	Modality		Event		
N looking out the window			car	has gone by / *gone*	
Mother has picked up pin.			pin	is no longer there / *gone*	
	N	pointing to	needle of tape recorder	going to & fro / *seesaw*	
			needle of tape recorder	going to & fro / *seesaw*	
	N	pointing to	picture of bear	*seesaw*	on rocking chair
	N	points to	tape recorder	going round / *round-n-round*	
	N	looking for	tape recorder	going round / *round-n-round*	
	N	repeats	tape	going round / *round-n-round*	
			N	pushing around / *round-n-round*	spoon in dish
	N	points to	his	a round / *round-n-round*	rug
	N	points to	his	round / *round-n-round*	bowl of playdough
			N	about to take out / *out*	puzzle piece

Speaker	Nonverbal / context	number pieces	Child utterance	Mother
N	trying to take off	lid of can	*out*	
N	sliding down		*down*	
			crying*	
N	points to	meat		
N	giving to mother	stick	a long / *long*	
N	about to hold	block	black / *long*	Mother is giving piece to N. *What color is it?*
N	points to	block	red / *red*	*What color is that?*
N	points to	block	red / *red*	*What color is that?*
N	points to	block	orange / *orange*	*What color is that?*
N	points to	block	orange / *orange*	*What color is that?*
N	points to	block	orange / *orange*	*What color is that?*
N	about to hold	piece	black / *black*	Mother is giving piece to N. *What color is that?*
N	about to hold	piece	blue / *blue*	Mother is giving piece to N. *What color is that?*

Table 28 (continued)

Preceding context	Modality		Event		
Mother is giving piece to N. *What color is that?*	N	about to hold	orange *orange*		piece
What about that?	N	points to	green *green*		block
What about that?	N	points to	green *green*		block
What color is that?	N	points to	green *green*		block
	N	points	orange *green*		block
What color is that?	N	points to	yellow *yellow*		block
What is it?	N	points to	yellow *yellow*	picture of	sun
Mother is giving block to N. *What color is it?*	N	about to hold	yellow *orange*		block

Note: Asterisk (*) indicates two morphemes. Broken horizontal rules separate utterances that were not part of connected discourse.

(e.g., Matthew's sister Lauren) under such circumstances—before any other encoding of a static Object State.

Denial of an Object's Action or State in two-word form occurred at Nicky III—19(29): Nicky said *no record* to signify that the record was not turned on. In the period 20(10–18), the first two-word utterance combining Action or State with an Object word occurred; this was described in Section 3.9, Object.

At Nicky IV—20(23), Nicky expresses negative Action or State for the first time by responding *no* to a statement or question from his mother. In one example, Nicky's mother asks him *Does that one go in there?* (referring to an inlaid puzzle piece) and he replies *no*.

At this same time, a new type of Action or State begins to be expressed: Nicky refers to something in terms of its *purpose*. The example is Nicky's use of *dan(ce)* in reference to a dance record. Another example shows how Nicky can now employ old vocabulary, formerly used to signal change, to encode a permanent state. At Nicky V—21(17), Nicky points to a picture hanging on the wall and says *picture* followed by *on*. This use of *on* contrasts with the frequent earlier usage in connection with switching lights on and off. Thus, in encoding the Action or State of Objects, appreciation of change precedes appreciation of constancy.

Action or State of Object is expressed with greatest frequency in isolated one-word form at Nicky VI—22(21); Table 28 presents these examples to show the range of possibilities for this semantic function.

Particularly interesting are the examples involving *round-n-round*, which show how the same vocabulary item can be used either to encode a dynamic process (first four examples) or a constant State (last two examples).

MATTHEW

The first example in which Matthew expressed the Action or State of an Object was noted in his diary at 14(6), when he said *dow(n)*, having just thrown something down. His first sequence involving Action or State plus its Object, occurring at 14(28), was described in Section 3.9. At 14(29), Matthew is reported to relate Action or State of Object to verbal context for the first time. While playing with toy cars, Matthew's mother said *There's a car* and Matthew answered *bye bye*.

The first two-word utterance involving an Object and its Action or State is produced at 15(27) when he points and says *more meh* (milk). Thus, once again, both semantic elements of the two-word utterance, static State and Object, have been expressed in isolation before being syntactically combined.

The use of *light* to express the turning on or off of a light at Matthew IV—16(2) shows how, at first, the child encodes change of state without verbally dis-

Table 29
Instances of Action or State of Object at Matthew VI—18(18)

Preceding context	Modality		Event
		lamp	is of *light*
	M		has turned light on *light*
	M	looking into	container empty *gone* of juice
	M	points to	ring toy has no *gone* rings on it
Milk carton has been empty. (unaware now full)	M	pointing to	milk carton *gone*
	M		has taken off *gone* rings from toy
	M	looking at	record that was not turned on *on*
	M		about to push *byebye* car
	M		pushing *byebye* car
	M	points to	place where ceiling light going in circle *round-n-round*

What are you doing?	M			making go round *round-n-round*	rings
What's the record doing?	M	pointing to	record	making round and round motion *round-n-round*	with hand
		M		patting	his car *beepbeep*
		M		picks up	another ring *more*
	M	reaching for	juice	*pour*	
	M	looking at		hot *hot*	cereal
			mother	has closed *down*	aquarium cover
			mother	pulling up *down*	buggy
You're all wet	M			pulling down *down*	buggy
		M		throwing down *down*	his car

Note: Broken horizontal rules separate utterances that were not part of connected discourse.

137

tinguishing initial from final state. Later, Matthew uses *on* when he wants his music box turned either on or off. The first example of expression of the Action of an Object in a Volitional context occurred during this session, when Matthew went to a closed window and said *down*, asking for the window to be opened.

As these early examples show, Matthew, like Nicky, first encodes *change* of state rather than *constant* state. The first definite example of a constant state occurs at 16(17) when he says *dirty*, referring to milk in a dirty baby bottle. Clearly, constancy is relative in this example, for there is still an element of change or perceptual contrast: Matthew has, in the past, seen *clean* bottles and he may be noting the *change* from this reference point. But *dirty*, unlike earlier encoding of Object Action or State, does not signal any change in the current situation. Hence, it is being used to communicate a more constant state than has been the case in earlier messages.

At Matthew V—17(13), Matthew first expresses a negative Action or State: He tries to put a shape in a hole when it doesn't fit and says *no*, thus seeming to deny the state of fitting.

Matthew VI—18(18) represents the highest degree of productivity for Action or State of Object in isolated one-word form. Table 29 shows the great variety of combinations now possible. A particularly interesting sequence, the first example of nominalization, also occurs at Matthew VI. At one point during the session, Matthew points to a light on the ceiling moving in a circle and says *round-n-round*. Here Matthew is using *round-n-round* to describe for the first time a constant action process. Later he says *gone*; his mother asks *What's gone?*; and Matthew answers *round-n-round*. When queried about what he means, he points to the ceiling, where the moving light had been before. Thus, Matthew predicates *gone* of the 'round-n-round'. In this way, *round-n-round* becomes a moving entity rather than the movement itself; and a process parallel to nominalization has taken place. This shift in function of *round-n-round*, even within one single situation, makes it clear once again that the growth of semantic structure involves more than just the acquisition of new vocabulary.

Affirmation of an Action or State is first expressed at Matthew VII—19(21), when there are several examples. In one of them, Matthew's mother asks *Is it hot?* and Matthew answers *yeah*.

SUMMARY AND DISCUSSION

Both Matthew and Nicky develop the ability to express the *Action or State* of an Object after they have expressed the *Object* of an Action. The first examples for both boys are similar in that they both encode Actions or States where the child is the implicit Agent of the Action. In fact, both boys used the same word, *down*, although in quite different contexts. Encoding of Actions, which were completely separate from the child, followed as a later stage, another example of decentration.

The progression in types of Actions and States encoded is similar to that for animate Agents. The children first encode change without verbal awareness of a mediating process. Both Nicky and Matthew used a single word to describe a situation in which a light was turned either on or off. Leopold (1949) reports an identical usage in German for his daughter Hildegard. This is, of course, another example of the use of one pole to signal an entire dimension; in this case, the dimension of state change.

Following this, children encode both static states and processes occurring apart from a discernible change of state. The Action or State of an inanimate object was encoded first in an Indicative context, only later in a Volitional one.

As with other semantic functions, Action or State of an Object is first used in a nonverbal situation; subsequently, it is used in relation to a verbal context. Both boys expressed this relation first in isolated words, later in a sequence, finally in two-word form. Once again, the ability to relate single words to sentence structures provided by an adult precedes relating word to word in one's own sentences.

Guillaume (1927) had the interesting idea that a stage transitional between single-word utterances and sentences occurs in which a single *mot—phrase* (sentence—word) is related to different situations (e.g., different objects) whose common aspect is the act encoded by the single word. He felt that this combinatorial power of an Action word would cause it to be dissociated from any particular Object, for example. Guillaume is quite explicit in stating that object and action are not initially dissociated in one-word speech—the global quality so often attributed to single-word utterances—and he sees this as the prime barrier to multiword sentences. It is hard to test this idea with our data. For Matthew, for whom we have the earliest productivity data, Action or State of an Object does not become productive for almost two months after the first instance. That is to say, an Action is not initially combined with various Objects. Yet, other semantic function like Agent develop into two-word form without *ever* developing much productivity in isolated one-word form. Hence, Guillaume's hypothesis appears to lack general applicability. On the other hand, Action or State of Inanimate Object participates in the regular progression from situational to verbal context and from isolated single-word utterance to sequence and sentence that we have seen before. Hence, these progressions seem more promising avenues to explaining the transition to syntax.

3.11 Dative

Although the first examples of the Dative case occur relatively early, productivity is not arrived at until much later, and examples remain infrequent. This characteristic of the Dative case continues into two-word speech (Brown, 1973). The first examples for both boys correspond to the traditional notion of Dative, that is, the indirect object.

NICKY

For Nicky, the earliest instance of a Dative occurs during Nicky I—18(4) when, on two occasions, he gives a book to his mother and says *mama*. Between 19(15) and 20(3), some examples occur in which the Dative is a body part. For instance, Nicky says *han(d)* when he wants his wet hands dried. When body parts were passively involved in action, they were considered to have the function of Dative because of their animacy. Similar examples occur during the formal session in the interval, Nicky III—19(29).

The first sequence involving a Dative occurs at Nicky V—21(17). It is a conversational sequence, although the Dative is more closely tied to the non-verbal context.

MOTHER	NICKY
He's wearing glasses.	[Takes off mother's glasses]
	no gun (glasses)
You took my glasses off.	[Gives glasses to mother]
	mama

In this sequence *mama*, a Dative, encodes the animate recipient of an object from Nicky, the agent in the situation.

Nicky VI—22(21) represents the height of productivity of the Dative function in one-word form. The range of combinatorial possibilities of word and event is shown in Table 30. This Table includes the first instance of naming an animate Obect of someone else's Action: Nicky says (*f*)*ishy* when Matthew has gone to feed the fish. During this same session, the first nonconversational sequence involving a Dative occurs: Nicky says *ban(ana)* followed by *teddy* when he gives a banana to his teddy bear.

Nicky VII—23(21) finds the first example of Dative clearly tied to verbal context, this time in isolated single-word form: Nicky's mother asks *What are you doing?* and Nicky, moving his foot up and down, responds *toes*.

At Nicky VIII—24(23), the Dative is incorporated into a number of different two-word utterances. One example, part of a complex sequence, involves negative Volition plus Dative: Nicky says *no feet* as Matthew puts his feet up on a stool.

MATTHEW

For Matthew, the first Dative occurs relatively early. At 11(28), he offers a bottle to his father and says *dada*. The first Datives to appear during a formal

Table 30
Instances of Dative at Nicky VI—22(21)

Preceding context	Modality	Event		
		Matthew	has gone to feed	the fish *(f)ishy*
		N	pushes away	Matthew from chair *Matthew*
N	wants whines, repeats	knees *knee*	on	bar
		N	has rubbed	his eye *eye*
		mother	wiping	N's nose *nose*
		mother	wiping	N's face *face*

Note: Broken horizontal rules separate utterances that were not part of connected discourse.

session occur at Matthew IV—16(2), when Matthew goes to his mother, hugs her and says *mommy*. During this same session, Matthew uses a Dative in response to verbal context as part of a partly imitative conversational sequence. His mother says *We're going byebye and get Lauren,* to which Matthew imitatively replies *bye*. At that point, his mother affirms *Yeah, byebye;* Matthew responds with *lala* (Lauren), a Dative in relation to the verbal context.

Approximately 2 months later, there occur two examples of a benefactive type of Dative in which the beneficiary is removed from the situation in space and time: At 18(12), Matthew says *yaya* (Lauren) when he pours yoghurt in the kitchen and repeats it as he walks into the dining room to his sister Lauren. At 18(28), after Matthew's mother gives him a cracker, he reaches toward the cracker box saying *yaya* (Lauren); when he gets another cracker, he proceeds into the dining room and offers it to his sister.

At 20(3), an interesting example occurs. His mother asks *Do you want to go with Mommy?* and he answers *daddy*. This is an example of a comitative Dative, one which also involves paradigmatic substitution.

The next development is the incorporation of the Dative into a multiword utterance. At 20(19), Matthew says *a cookie* upon seeing a cookie his mother was holding out for him. After taking it, he held out his other hand and said *Yaya a cookie*. In this example, the word *cookie* encodes an element which would have been communicated by the presence of the cookie at an earlier point in development. The situation is practically identical to situations reported two months earlier; the only change is that Matthew is now able to encode more elements of that situation. This example is particularly interesting because it shows a sequence of functions, viz. Dative, Object, which is rarely reported in the literature (cf. Bloom, 1970; Brown, 1973).

SUMMARY

The first examples of Datives for both boys involve handing something to a parent. Later developments involve expressing a benefactive goal and expressing animate objects. In Matthew's development, the benefactive examples essentially represent a Dative who is removed from the present situation.

There are relatively few examples of Datives, so it is hard to discuss their development in any detail. Nevertheless, the sequence of development is in general the same as that for other functions, from use in isolation to use in a verbal context, and from use in sequences to use in two-word sentences.

3.12 Object Associated with Another Object or Location

Expression of the function Associated Object involves naming one object in relation to another one. The object named may or may not be present in the situation. In the earliest examples, the associated entity is fairly close to the present situation. With age, however, both boys become capable of denoting metaphoric relations. This category of utterances is the semantic basis for attribution in mature speech.

NICKY

Nicky is first reported to have expressed an Object associated with an Object or Location between 18(8) and 18(16): He says *poo*, putting his hand on his bottom when being changed, although he has not had a bowel movement. Thus, he seems to be expressing an association between feces (which he calls *poo*) and the anal area of his body. The next formal observation session brings several similar examples.

An interesting example is reported between 19(15) and 20(3), when Nicky puts his diaper (security blanket) on his head and says *hat*. This equation between the diaper and hat seems like an early form of metaphor. The possibility of *hat* being merely an overextension of the word to diapers is ruled out by the fact that Nicky already had a word for diaper (*bap*) in his vocabulary.

At Nicky III—19(29), Object Associated with Another Object or Location reaches the height of its productivity. Table 31 presents the examples from this session. One can see how Nicky is able to express entities somewhat removed from the present situation. For example, in the third entry in the table, there is no milk present in the situation to which Nicky's word could refer. (This usage is similar to *shoes* in Nicky IV, discussed in a later paragraph.)

Nicky IV—20(23) brings the first example of this semantic relation expressed in two-word form: Nicky says *ring tower* several times in a complex sequence, referring to a stacking ring toy. At one point, his mother asks him *What are you*

Table 31
Instances of Object Associated with Another Object or Location at Nicky III—19(29)

Preceding context	Modality		Event		
	N	points to repeats	his picture	drawn with	crayon *cray(on)*
	N	holding repeats	dish		without water *ba* (water)
	N	reaches for repeats	empty glass		*mil(k)*
	N	holding onto repeats	refrigerator door		*mil(k)*
	N	looking around	kitchen		*cheese*
	N	holding onto whining	refrigerator door		*apple*
	N	reaching toward whining	counter		*apple*
	N	has gone to whining	refrigerator		*apple*
	N	walks into	kitchen		*nana* (banana)
	N	has gone to	refrigerator		*(ba)nana*
	N	looking at	revolving tape recorder		*fan*

Note: Broken horizontal rules separate utterances that were not part of connected discourse.

going to make?, and he answers *ring tower.* This is the first semantic function in which a child has gone from single-word form to syntax without the intermediate stages of dialogue and sequence.

At Nicky V—21(17) we find the first example of an Associated Object used either in response to verbal context or incorporated in a sequence. The sequence is a complex conversational one and goes as follows:

MOTHER	NICKY
Should we read a book?	
Which book?	[Points to a picture of a bear]
	bear
Should we read about the bear?	*no bear*

Although the second part makes the first ambiguous, we consider that *bear* answers the question *Which?* and is therefore connected with *book.* This example illustrates how this category functions as the semantic basis of certain types of attribution. (In this usage, *bear* seems to function more as an inanimate than animate entity: Compare *the bear book* with *the bear's book.*) This is the only instance of this semantic function occurring nonimitatively in relation to verbal context.

An example that is more paradigmatic for association with a location is when Nicky (IV—20[23]) points to the observer's bare feet and says *shoes.* In some sense, Nicky is asserting that there is an association between shoe and foot. One could say that this assertion has a negative sense—be is remarking on the absence of the shoe. This may be correct, for he later said *shoe* on two occasions while searching for the observer's shoes. Yet, notice of absence must, logically, be based on a concept of habitual presence. The connection between 'shoe' and 'foot', furthermore, is enacted behaviorally by the painting gesture.

An interesting "metaphor" occurs at Nicky VI—22(21) when he holds up a container of playdough and calls it *meat* (even though he also has the word *playdough* in his lexicon). This metaphor clearly involves encoding an entity totally absent from the situation at hand. The first sequence that expresses both an Object and an Associated Object occurs during this same session: Nicky has made a garbage truck and he describes it by the sequence *truck; garbage.*

MATTHEW

At 14(29), Matthew says *caca* (cookie or cracker) while pointing to the door to the adjoining room where the cookies were kept. The first examples of Associated Object during a formal session occur during Matthew III—15(5,17). The examples from this session are shown in Table 32.

The earliest example of this function in two-word form occurs in Matthew's first two-word sentence at 15(23): Matthew says (*f*)*ishy ball* to refer to a ball

Table 32
Instances of Object Associated with Another Object or Location at Matthew III—15(5) & 15(17)

Preceding context	Modality		Event	
	M	reaching towards	counter	
				caca
	M	picks up	empty juice	glass
Cup had juice in it.		whining	*mil(k)*	
M has had some	M	holds up	empty juice	glass
orange juice.		whining	*mi(k)*	
	M	reaching toward	refrigerator	
				mil(k)

Note: Broken horizontal rules separate utterances that were not part of connected discourse.

with *fishes* in it. Because the fish in question are plastic rather than live and because the meaning is more attributive than possessive, it seems correct to classify this sentence as an Associated Object rather than Associated Being. This example of a two-word sentence is surprisingly early for such a late-appearing function and well deserves the name "fluke." However, Matthew used both *fishy* and *ball* independently at this period so there is no reason to suspect that *fishy ball* is an unanalyzed unit. The height of productivity for this semantic function in one-word form is reached in the following session. The relevant examples are given in Table 33.

At 18(11), an instance parallel to Nicky's *bear* book example occurs: Matthew says (*f*)*ishy*, then goes to get his fish book, which he brings back to his mother. One striking feature of this example is the use of a word to signal an intention requiring sustained action for its realization.

Matthew's first sequence involving an Associated Object goes as follows: while talking about some thread Matthew says *ki(te)* and, a bit later, *yaya* (Lauren). The connection was that, a while before, the thread had been used for kites and for repairing Lauren's sweater. Thus, each word referred to a different past use. Although *kite* represents an Object Associated with the thread, *yaya* (Lauren) is considered an Animate Being Associated with her sweater, a semantic function to be described in the next section.

Like Nicky, Matthew uses metaphorical associations: At Session VII—19(21) Matthew is playing on top of the portable dishwasher, which he calls an *airplane*. It is probably clear by now that the Association between two entities does not

Table 33
Instances of Object Associated with Another Object or Location at Matthew
IV—16(2)

Preceding context		Modality	Event	
	M	pointing to repeats	living room	where record player kept *krakor* (record)
	M	looking at	empty crayon *craw*	box
	M	reaching toward	kitchen	where spoons kept *(s)poon*
	M	pointing to whining, repeats	empty milk *ma* (milk)	cup
	M	runs to reaching toward whining, repeats	counter cupboard	where cookies kept *cookie*
	M	runs to reaching toward whining, repeats	kitchen cupboard	where cookies kept *cookie*

Note: Broken horizontal rules separate utterances that were not part of connected discourse.

just mean simple contiguity, but can be based on many different kinds of connection.

SUMMARY AND DISCUSSION

Both boys develop skill in expressing Objects Associated with Objects and Locations. In both boys, too, this semantic function shows a movement toward naming something increasingly remote from the object with which it is associated. Habitual Association seems also to underlie the expression of Nonexistence.

Because an Object Associated with another Object or Location is a relation necessarily involving two entities external to the child-speaker, it is, by definition, more decentered than any preceding semantic relation. Thus, the emergence of semantic functions manifests a progressive process of decentration. An Associated Object is distinguished from an overgeneralized name by the fact that the two entities do not resemble each other perceptually. Thus, if a child pointed to a spherical nut and called it *ball*, *ball* would *not* be categorized as an Associated Object. Obviously, this is a relative rather than absolute distinction.

Note that, for this function, the stages intermediate between single word and syntax, sequence and dialogue, are absent for both boys. This could be either because Associated Objects first emerge in single-word form at a point where two-word utterances are already a possibility, or it may represent nothing more than a sampling error. The pattern for later-developing semantic functions indicates that the former is more likely. The development from one- to two-word form confirms de Laguna's description of the development of the expression of properties. She claimed that the child first pointed to an object and named one of its properties, and later substituted the object's name for the pointing gesture in a two-word sentence; at this point the child had moved from implicit to explicit predication. Certainly we have traced a like development toward verbally explicit predication. However, many of our examples show that pointing is not the only gestural means for specifying the topic: Looking at as well as acting upon in a variety of ways are other possibilites frequently used. Whether or not the verbal specification of the topic in a two-word sentence *substitutes* for or *augments* pointing remains to be tested. Since our procedure stressed non-verbal cues necessary for semantic interpretation, and since pointing or other gestural specification of the topic would not be *necessary* to interpretation if the topic were already verbally encoded, our procedure had built-in bias against noticing and recording gestural cues occurring with two-word sentences. It would be most interesting, however, to do a study comparing the role of gesture in one- and two-word speech.

This category has no direct translation in most current grammatical theories, although it is clearly basic to the syntactic expression of attribution. The basic problem seems to be that no system of grammar allows two nouns to be in direct relation to each other. Thus, two entities cannot be in direct relation to each other. Bowerman (1973) recognized this problem in characterizing the structure of noun–noun combinations in two-word speech, and concluded that such relationships do, in fact, exist in the real world—as between, for example, an Object and its Location.

3.13 Animate Being Associated with Object or Location

When a child points to an object and names its absent owner, this word is generally interpreted as a possessive. Observers, at least since Bloch (1921), have been struck by this usage, probably because the word's referent is so distinct in form from the topic, specified by the child's pointing gesture. It is difficult, however, to say that the child has the precise concept of possession at this point, for it is not clearly distinguishable from the more general notion of Association. On the other hand, it is perhaps worth remembering that the possessive construction in adult speech can express many different notions. As in the case of Associated Objects, naming an absent owner could be taken as an assertion of nonexistence. However, once again such an assertion must be based on an underlying notion of habitual association. Lewis (1963) described one-word examples from much the same category under the rubric of "reference to the past." Like the preceding semantic function, this one, by definition, involves a relationship between two entities external to the speaker, and so is relatively decentered.

NICKY

Between 18(19) and 18(25), Nicky is reported to have said *lara* (Lauren) upon seeing her empty bed. This example illustrates how close this function is to Agent in an Agent–Object relation—'bed' being the Object in this instance. The next formal session, Nicky II—18(27), brings more examples of similar usages. For instance, he points to the door to Lauren and Matthew's house and says *Wawa* (Lauren), and a little later *Ma(tthew)*.

Nicky III—19(29) brings the first two-word utterance involving an Animate Being Associated with an Object or Location: Nicky says *ma* (my) *diaper* as he pulls down his diaper, thus realizing the Association between self and diaper with a first-person pronoun. Note how this two-word utterance is embedded as the Object of the Action of pulling, just as single-word utterances were embedded at an earlier time. This is the second instance where the intermediate stages of sequence and dialogue have been skipped and a child has gone straight from isolated one-word form to syntax. It appears that some generalization has taken place from other earlier developing semantic functions, so that these intermediate stages may be bypassed. Note, however, that the stage of expression in isolated single-word form still precedes incorporation in a two-word sentence.

Another feature of this example is that it is the first one in which Nicky is the Animate Being associated with something. As with the Agent function, self seems at first to be taken for granted as possessor, and so, expression of self in this role represents a new degree of decentration. This example also represents Nicky's first use of a pronoun. (Only first-person pronouns were used by Nicky during the period under study.) The first use of this function in a volitional context occurred at Nicky IV—20(23), when Nicky stood by the refrigerator and said *my b(al)oney*. His mother replied *Do you want some baloney? There isn't any.*

Sequences and the use of the single word in dialogue still occur nonetheless. The first sequence reported between 20(19) and 20(25) is an interesting one: Nicky says *daddy; mummy; daddy,* and so on, touching different clothes in the closet and naming their owners. An early use of this semantic function in dialogue occurs in the same period: Nicky has pointed to his mother's books and she has said *Those are mine.* At this point, Nicky points to his own books and says *Nini* (Nicky). These are both examples of paradigmatic substitution.

Other early examples of the expression of this semantic function in response to verbal context are shown in Table 34. This table presents all the isolated

Table 34
Instances of Animate Being Associated with Object or Location at Nicky IV–20(23)

Preceding context	Modality		Event		
Those are Vickie's.		N		picks up	Vickie's tapes *deedee* (Lady)
	N	hears	Lauren's *Wawa* (Lauren)		record upstairs
	N	points to	father's *daddy*		books
		N		picks up	daddy's bell *daddy*
What's up there?	N	points to	father's *daddy*		razor
	N	walking in	hallway to		Matthew's house *Matthew*
		N		picks up	toy Matthew has used *Mama* (Matthew)

Note: Broken horizontal rules separate utterances that were not part of connected discourse.

single-word examples from Nicky IV—20(23), the height of single-word productivity for this semantic function.'

An interesting example of paradigmatic substitution in a dialogue occurs at
Nicky VI—22(21): Nicky is asked, *Can Matthew have your teddy?* and he replies
Nicky. This example is particularly interesting because it looks as though there
may be some syntactic adjustment of the single word to the grammar of the
question. Immediately before, Matthew had taken his teddy and Nicky had
reacted with *my teddy*; yet his answer to *Can Matthew have your teddy?* is not *my*
but the more paradigmatic *Nicky.*

The possessive inflection *'s* appears at Nicky VII—23(21) on six reliable
occasions; three times in isolated single-word utterances, three times in single
words in sequences. Inspection of the examples given in Table 35 shows that,
even without the inflection, all the examples would have been categorized as
an Animate Object Associated with an Object or Location. Thus, the use of the
's inflection occurs in contexts parallel to those of one-word expressions of
Animate Being Associated with Object or Location. In some of the examples,
as when Nicky, getting something to put in his bag, says *Nicky's*, Nicky is the
Agent acting upon an Object in the situation. These examples confirm our
decision to treat the verbal expression of Agent acting upon a definite Object

Table 35
Use of the Possessive Inflection at Nicky VII—23(21)

Preceding context	Modality	Event		
		N	picks up	mother's cracker *mommy's*
		N	getting	something to put in his bag *Nicky's*
		Mother	takes	his egg *Nicky's*
		mashush mashush		
Yeah, that's Matthew's bear.		*te(dd)y bear*		
Teddy bear.		*mashush mashush*		
Ah.	N points to	Matthew's *mashush*		bear

Note: Broken horizontal rules separate utterances that were not part of connected discourse.

as part of the Animate Associated category whenever it occurs, for these examples show that such a situation can be realized by a possessive as well as by an Agent–Object sentence once the child is able to transcend the stage of single morpheme expression.

MATTHEW

Matthew's first instance of Animate Entity Associated with an Object or Location is reported at 15(29) when Matthew says (f)*ishy*, pointing to an empty fish tank. At Matthew IV—16(2), a similar usage occurs, but with the addition of verbal context: Matthew's mother asks *Are you going to tell us what we are going to have in here?*; he touches the empty fish tank and answers *fishy*.

The first sequence involving this semantic function is reported in Matthew's diary shortly thereafter at 16(21): Matthew says *daddy* followed by *door* when his father goes out the door. A sequence involving a more possessive type of association occurs at Matthew V—17(13): Matthew says *nany* (candy) followed by *Lara* (Lauren). His mother then asks *Does Lauren have candy?* and Matthew nods. This type of sequence demonstrates that Animate Being Associated with an Object is a semantic function in its own right, not merely the result of lack of vocabulary to name the Object in question. If, in this situation, Matthew intended only to name the Object in question (candy), he would have stopped after doing so, rather than adding his sister's name to form a sequence.

Matthew VI—18(18) brings the first possessive syntax as well as the first mention of self in this type of usage: Matthew picks up a book and says *my: my*. Mother queries *Your what?* and Matthew repeats *my*. *Mine* is used for the first time at Matthew VII—19(21), when he sees Lauren eating his medicine. Also at Matthew VII, the first two-word expression occurs: Matthew says *my hat*, holding his hat.

At Matthew VII—19(21), Matthew comes to his car and says *our car*, thus using a new possessive pronoun. The *'s* inflection never occurred during the period under study. The first recorded use of this function in a Volitional context was at IX—22(1), when Matthew said *mine* while reaching for a piece of paper.

SUMMARY

The function Animate Being Associated with an Object or Location appears relatively late in a child's development. Expression of this function implies a high degree of decentration, in that the child must associate two entities. Expression of an Animate Being Associated with an external Object develops after the expression of an inanimate Object in a similar relation. This decentration process is parallel to the expression of the Action or State of a nonego animate being after the expression of the Action or State of an external Object. Expression of the self in this function follows expression of others. This progression parallels the encoding of the self as Agent after the encoding of other Agents. The examples cited show that different types of association between an animate being and an object can be expressed.

Both children began by expressing the Associated Animate Being in one-word form. From there, Nicky passed directly to expressing it in two-word form, whereas Matthew passed through the customary stages of expression in dialogue and in sequences. The earliest examples of the possessive construction show the continuity of event structure between the expression of this function in one- and two-word form.

3.14 Location

Guillaume (1927) observed that children's one-word utterances sometimes refer to Locations. Our observations confirm his; however, to arrive at an operational definition of this category some further specifications are necessary. We have already noted that it is difficult to differentiate Objects from Locations in early utterances. Some objects with apparently locative functions have already been discussed in Section 3.9. In this section, we shall discuss only those examples in which a Location is clearly differentiated from an Object of Action in terms of situational structure. Similarly, it is sometimes difficult to differentiate an Action or State from a Location (cf. Section 3.10). Here, we discuss only Locations that are clearly entities rather than relational States.

NICKY

Nicky's diary reports the first example of Location of Object between 18(19) and 18(25): He says *bap* (diaper) to indicate the Location of some feces. This example is not entirely unambiguous, however, because indication of the feces occurs as an earlier utterance (not close enough to be part of a sequence) rather than in the ongoing situation. Location is expressed in a formal observation session for the first time at Nicky IV—20(23) when Nicky puts a pretzel in his mouth and says *mou(th)*. Location reaches the height of productivity as a semantic function at Nicky V—21(17). Table 36 presents all of the isolated single-word examples from this session. At the same time, the first sequence involving an Object and Location appears. It is a particularly interesting example, because it refers to a past event; Nicky says *bear* followed by *trolley* just after he has left his bear on the trolley.

Table 36
Instances of Location at Nicky V—21(17)

Preceding context	Modality		Event	
		N	is about to put	lamb on sofa *chair*
		N	is about to put	lamb on chair *chair*
		N	puts	toy on couch *chair*
		N	trying to balance	top on middle of ring *mid(dle)*
	whining, repeats	N	trying to balance	top on middle of ring *mi(dd)le*
		cover	is in	middle of toy *middle*
	N	gives whining, repeats		to put on	middle of ring *middle*

Note: Broken horizontal rules separate utterances that were not part of connected discourse.

During this same session, Nicky first uses a Location in response to verbal context. This occurs near the end of this conversational sequence: Nicky points to Bernice's glasses, saying *gla(sses)*. His mother answers *Yes, those are Bernice's glasses*, to which Nicky responds *mama*. His mother answers *Yes, mama has glasses*. At this point, Nicky points to his eye and says *eye*. "Eye" is considered in this example to be the Location of the 'glasses'.

An interesting instance of Location expressed in nomitative response to verbal context occurs in a sequence at Nicky VII—23(21). Nicky repeatedly exclaims *teddy*: His mother responds with a question: *Where's the other teddy?*, and Nicky repeats *room* in reply.

The first multiword of Location example occurs during the same session. In this example, Nicky, about to put a container in a truck, says *in the truck*. The use of a prepositional phrase makes this example strikingly adult. If, however, Nicky had said only *truck* in this situation, the utterance would still have been classified as a Location. Thus, syntactic expression of Location is growing out of the situational structures of the single-word stage. Note, too, that there is no lag between the use of Location in nonimitative response to verbal context and use of Location in multiword utterances.

MATTHEW

The first instance of Location expressed by Matthew is reported in his diary at 15(20), when he says *bo(x)* putting his crayon in his box.

No Locations are expressed in formal sessions until Matthew VII—19(21). The point of greatest productivity is reached at Matthew VIII—20(26). Table 37 presents the examples. The last example in this Table also shows the first use

Table 37
Instances of Location at Matthew VIII—20(26)

Preceding context	Modality		Event		
	M	points to	mother's mouth *mouth*	has	ice
	M	reaching for	cookie plate	to put on	table *table*
		M whining	M	climbing on	blocks *top*[a]
Where does it go?	M	points to	correct hole *here*		

[a] Because *top* expresses the Location of a block in the stack, it was considered to fulfill the criteria for locative.

Note: Broken horizontal rules separate utterances that were not part of connected discourse.

of Location in nonimitative response to verbal context. The first sequences involving Locatives also occur in this session. One nice example is the following conversational sequence:

MOTHER	MATTHEW
	kite
	[Something incomprehensible was said here]
	water
The kite went in the water?	
What happened to the kite?	
Did it go in the water?	*yeah*

There are no clear examples of the expression of Location of an Object in a two-word sentence by Matthew during the period under study.

SUMMARY

The differentiation of Location from Action or State on the one hand, and Object on the other, occurs relatively late for Matthew and Nicky. Both children expressed this function first in an Indicative context, later in a Volitional one. They both passed through a stage of expression of Location in sequences, but only Nicky offers an example of use in two-word form. Sequences typically involve an Object and a Location; however, Nicky's first multiword expression of Location is a prepositional phrase in which only State and Location are expressed.

3.15 Modification of an Event

This semantic function refers to words that modify an entire event rather than those having a specific relation to one element in the situation. The concepts underlying several types of adverbials are included—time, manner, and quantity.

NICKY

This final semantic function is unique in appearing first in two-word form: At Nicky III—19(29), Nicky points to a record that is playing and says *more record*. Here, *more* seems to refer to the duration of the playing rather than signifying another record. A similar example occurs at Nicky IV—20(23): Nicky says *more round* when his mother picks up a toy which he has been spinning.

Nicky's diary reports only one example of a word which modifies an entire event (other than expressions of Volition). This example occurs in a two-word sequence between 20(25) and 21(1): Nicky puts his hand on the toilet handle, saying *pull*; then he waits to pull it, saying *wai(t)*. Although *wait* is a verb in English, there is clearly an expression of time involved; *wait*, moreover, would function in relation to the entire event of Nicky pulling the handle even if considered a State element.

Not until Nicky VI—22(21), does Modification of an Event occur in one-word form during a formal observation session: Nicky says *good* when he swings himself over the gym bar. Modification of Events in two-word utterances is more frequent: for example, *no more* when his mother is wiping his face with a cloth; then *too hot*. The latter implies Modification in terms of quantity. Although one could say that *too* modifies a single adjective, it implicates a separate event in relation to which there is an excess: the wash cloth is *too hot* to wash Nicky's face.

During Nicky VII—23(21), his mother had finished reading a book when Nicky said *again*, clearly indicating repetition of the entire event—his mother reading the book. During this session, there are four examples of two-word utterances including *too*. For example, Nicky is trying unsuccessfully to balance a postcard on top of a toy when he says *too big*. Clearly, *big* modifies the postcard, but *too* relates it to the event of balancing on top of the toy.

MATTHEW

Around 18(1), Matthew begins to use the word *(a)gain* when he wants someone to do something for him another time. For example, At 18(22), he says *(a)gain* when he wants his mechanical train wound again. At Matthew VI—18(18), he affirms Modification of an Event with *yeah*. The situation is that his mother is giving him his medicine, and asks *Again?* Matthew answers *yeah*. This is the first example of Modification of Event in response to verbal context.

At Matthew VII—19(21), we find the first sequence involving Modification of Event. Matthew says *again*, referring to his mother lighting a match. His mother responds with a question, *You want to blow it again?*, to which Matthew replies *yeah*.

At 20(18), Matthew points to an overturned chair, which he had not seen topple, and says *happen*. Clearly, he means that a total event involving the chair has happened. This is quite a decentered message, for Matthew is in no way involved in the Event related to *happen*.

Matthew VIII—20(26) brings the height of productivity for Modification of Event in isolated one-word form. The examples are presented in Table 38. *Self* and *myself* function as manner adverbials, closely related to the Agent of the Action: In one instance, it is a question of Matthew getting out of the car by

Table 38
Instances of Modification of Event at Matthew VIII—20(26)

Preceding context	Modality		Event	
	M	by himself *self*	walking	on stones
	M	by himself *self*	about to get out	of car
	M	by himself *myself**	walking	on stones
Lauren has been given a piece of bread.	*too*		M reaching for	bread
M's hand is washed.	*again*		M holds out	hand

Note: Asterisk (*) indicates two morphemes Broken horizontal rules separate utterances that were not part of connected discourse.

himself; in another, of walking by himself on the stones. *Too* (Table 38) functions to indicate repetition of an event with a change of person. During this same session, the first instances of two-word utterances involving Modification of an Event occur: *back myself*, about to put duck piece back in puzzle; *down self* trying to get down by himself (on three different occasions).

SUMMARY

For both boys, Modification of Event is the last semantic function to appear. Nicky, but not Matthew, expresses it first in two-word form; this is the only time in our data that the one-word form has not preceded incorporation in a two-word sentence. It appears that, for Nicky at least, some syntactic generalization has taken place. Quantity-modification predominates (*again, too*) but both boys also express manner. Modification of Event has the most complex cognitive structure, for the event is embedded in a relation external to both event and speaker.

3.16 Questions

The existence of interrogative elements in the one-word period is somewhat problematical. It appears that distinctive intonation is the cue most often used in interpreting an utterance as a question. Question intonation is the last intonation pattern to develop, and is much rarer than imperative (Volitional) or Indicative intonation. Nevertheless, Menyuk and Bernholtz (1969) found clear-cut question intonation in their spectrographic analysis of the one-word utterances of a child between 18 and 20 months of age. Leopold (1953) and Tonkova-Yampol'skaya (1969) also report question intonation in the second year of life.

The early stages of language development are characterized by the fact that the child is more able to relate words to situational structure than to verbal structure. However, the Interrogative mode is distinguished from the Indicative and Volitional (imperative) in requiring a *verbal* response. Thus, it is not surprising that it should develop later and be used less frequently than the Indicative and Volitional, which require *attentional* and *action* responses, respectively. Interrogative can be considered a modality element in Fillmore's (1968) scheme.

The reader has probably noticed that questions were rare in our examples. We, therefore, thought it would be of interest to gather all the questions together in one place—the purpose of the present section.

In his thirteenth month, Nicky pointed to things, saying *ada* with the intonation of *what's that?*, seeming to expect to be told the name.

At 14(12), Nicky said *Dar?* (Dot, his mother's name) as he looked around the house and under pillows for his mother, who was in the hospital. Matthew once said *kaka* (record)—14(29)—when there was music coming from a hi-fi but no record playing, in a way that his mother interpreted as a question.

At 18(4), Nicky used *dat* apparently to ask for the names of objects, in a way which was intonationally distinct from pointing sentences. Rather than saying *dat* with a rising intonation contour, however, he said it with a certain excitement in his voice. The fact that he used a pronoun instead of a name might also have lead his mother to interpret these utterances as interrogative requests for a name. Between 20(10) and 20(18), Nicky is reported to say *daddy?* His mother replies *No, Daddy not here* and Nicky responds *wor(k)*. Between 21(1) and 21(8), Nicky said *gar* (glasses) in such a way as to be interpreted by his mother as *Where are your glasses?* At Nicky VII—23(21), Nicky said *garbage* in a questioning tone, looking toward the kitchen and holding a purse. In this same session, Nicky's mother says *Let's put your socks on*. Nicky repeats *put*. He goes on to say *shush?* (shoes). At Nicky VIII—24(23), there occur two instances of a two-word question *Who that?*, both times uttered upon hearing a noise (once the noise of a garbage truck). These are the only instances of questions, so their status in the total context of development is not clear.

3.17 Summary

Some notable features of semantic development during one-word speech have been commented on in the preceding sections. In this section, we shall bring together these observations and make some more general ones. Since these comments are based on the development of only two children, and are based on a sample of their total output, it is possible that some of them may not hold true for other children. However, it seems most worthwhile to look for all the parallels possible in order to emphasize points that are worthy of confirmation by other investigators. Tables 39 and 40 present many of the examples discussed in the text to enable the reader to relate this discussion to the examples discussed in previous sections.

At the beginning of language, there is a general passage from "pure" Performative utterances to more language-like ones. In other words, the first language sounds are part of the child's actions and are separated only gradually from those actions and from the immediate context. The first words that both boys used were Performatives. When they first started pointing out objects, the gesture of pointing was accompanied by a constant nonsense syllable. Only later were identifiable names connected with pointing. Likewise, the first expression of Volition was the Performative use of *no*. Only later was expression of Volition connected with reference to an external event through the encoding of the desired Object or State. Finally, expression of Action or State often had its roots in Performatives. The boys first described their own actions in ways that were essentially Performative. The word *down* first accompanied the action of getting down (or up), but later achieved more independence and could be used with nonpresent actions and object actions. Other words such as *hi* and *byebye* were used first as "pure" Performatives and later to fulfill other functions.

During these early stages of language use, there is a progressive change in children's use of gestures. At first, both Indicative and Volitional gestures are used with nonsense syllables, but not with adult words. When names are first used, they are associated with simple visual orientation. Later, children integrate the Performative gestures and the word into a conventional communicative act. At this stage, the relationship between words and gestures is reasonably stable; then children begin using a more diversified range of gestures, and speech becomes more independent of the gestural context.

A progression that was especially apparent at the beginning of language use was the tendency of Indicative use of a function to precede Volitional use of the same function. Both boys expressed Indication before they expressed Volition verbally. Of course, Indicative Objects preceded Volitional Objects. The first uses of other functions were similarly nonvolitional, as can be seen from Tables 8 and 9. The only exceptions are Nicky's use of Object and Matthew's use of Action or State of Agent and Modification of an Event. Of these, Modification of an Event occurs sufficiently late that the constraint may no longer be operative. The example of Action or State of an Agent occurs in imitative response to a question; the first nonimitative expression of this function is Indicative rather than Volitional.

Many writers have taken the view that language first serves to express desires.

However, this clearly is not the case. The reason Indicative uses precede Volitional ones is probably that, when a function is newly emerging, it disintegrates under conditions of too great drive or emotion. Hence, the use of a function in a highly emotional demand situation must wait for its prior establishment in nonemotional, Indicative usages. Many of the children's semantic functions developed first in contexts that had nothing to do with their primary needs, but that were independently interesting to them, such as the fish tank for Matthew and the fan and record player for Nicky.

Another developmental theme in our results is decentration. One progression is from the description of the child's own Actions and States to the description of other Agents' Actions and States. The simplest form of this progression is seen in the expression of rejection, where a child first rejects objects and actions that are directly related to himself, and, only later, demands that others not carry out actions that are indirectly related to him.

The expression of Action or State follows a more complex sequence. Children first express their own Actions in a Performative manner. The first nonego Actions or States they encode are those of Objects upon which they are acting. Later, they encode Actions or States that are independent of themselves. Children do not express Actions or States of nonego Agents until after they express the Actions or States of independent Objects. Later, children express the Actions of Agents that are completely external. Thus, the children move outward from themselves in the verbal expression of Actions and States. This movement outward constitutes a process of progressive decentration. As mentioned above, the expression of association seems to fit into this same sequence in that children express Associated Inanimate Objects before Associated Animate Beings. To express the Action of another requires a leap in the ability to perceive the world from the perspective of another person. Perception from the perspective of an Object could be considered an intermediate step. Thus, decentration is a pervasive principle ordering development within the one-word stage.

Another process of decentration relates to the child's objective awareness of himself. Children name other people before they name themselves. Other people are expressed as Agents long before the child expresses himself in a similar role. Similarly, children point out objects associated with other people before they verbally associate themselves with an object.

Another developmental progression involves the types of actions and states that children express. The earliest forms involve changes of state, whereas constant states and processes are last to be encoded. Two-word verb phrases may express both action and end state, as in *get down*. Hybrids like factitive verbs are also late to appear.

This progression from expressing variable states to constant ones confirms a hypothesis presented by MacNamara (1972). MacNamara's hypothesis, however, assumes a one-to-one relationship between vocabulary item and func-

Table 39
Temporal Sequence of Key Examples from Nicky

Age (Months)	Performative	Indicative Object	Volitional Object	Volition	Agent	Action or State of Agent
8	dada 8(19)					
9		dada 9(8)				
10						
11				nana 11(28)		
12	ada 12(7)	mama 12(7)				
13	hi 13(8)			mama 13(19)	dada 13(3)	
14			Dot? 14(12—18)			down 14(21)—15(18)
15			Kelly 15(19)—16(18)			
16			milk 16(19—25)	daddy; mommy; daddy 16(25)—17(1)		up 16(25)—17(1)
17						
18		. . . baby 18(4) mommy; dat 18(4) no 18(27)	. . . banana 18(4) mommy . . . shovel 18(4) awa pretzel 18(27)	mama . . . diaper 18(4) mommy; dat 18(4) . . . no 18(4)	Lauren 18(1—8) . . . Matthew 18(4) Matthew! 18(19—25) Lauren . . . Matthew 18(27)	up! 18(4) hot 18(4) . . . down 18(27)
19		no daddy 19(29) no eye 19(29)		no boot 19(15)—20(5) no diaper 19(29) no night-night 19(29)	owl . . . tootoo 19(29) hand 19(29)	. . . play 19(29)
20		Nicky 20(3—10) bee . . . boat 20(23)		don't 20(23) no want 20(23) no want it 20(23)		cross 20(3—10) jump 20(21)
21				no mouth 21(17)		touch 21(17)
22					Nicky 22(21) Nicky catch 22(21) mommy sleep 22(21)	rest 22(21) get down 22(21) mommy sleep 22(21)
23						
24						

Note: Spelling conventionalized. See individual sections for contexts and explanations of examples in Table. "12(12)" indicates diary; "*12(12)*" indicates session; ". . ." indicates verbal context; ";" indicates sequence; "!" indicates Volition (Omitted for Volition and Volitional Object).

Object	Action or State of Object	Dative	Associated Object	Associated Being	Location	Modification of Event
n! 16(19–25)						
an; on! 18(8–16) *. record 18(27)*	*down* 18(1–8) *fan; on!* 18(8–16) *big* 18(27) *light . . . on* 18(27)	*mama* 18(4)	*poo* 18(9–16)	*Lauren* 18(19–25) *Lauren* 18(27)	*diaper* 18(19–25)	
	hot 19(8–15) *no record* 19(29)	*hand!* 19(15)–20(3)	*hat* 19(15)–20(3) *milk!* 19(29)	*my diaper* 19(29)		*more record* 19(29)
ook back 20(10–18) *itten; cold* 20(10–18)	*book back* 20(10–18) *. . . no* 20(23) *dance* 20(23) *picture . . . on* 21(17)	*no glasses . . . mama* 21(17)	*ring tower* 20(23) *shoes* 20(23) *bear . . . no bear* 21(17)	*mommy; daddy; mommy* 20(19–25) *Nicky* 20(19–25) *my baloney!* 20(23)	*mouth* 20(23) *middle!* 21(17) *bear; trolley* 21(17) *mama . . . eye* 21(17)	*pull . . . wait* 20(25)–21(1)
hair 22(21)		*banana; teddy* 22(21) *fishy* (22(21) *. . . toes* 23(21)	*meat* 22(21) *truck; garbage* 22(21)		*teddy . . . room* 23(21) *in the truck* 23(21)	*no more!* 22(21) *too hot* 22(21) *again!* 23(21)
		no feet! 24(23)				

Table 40
Temporal Sequence of Key Examples from Matthew

Age (Months)	Performative	Indicative Object	Volitional Object	Volition	Agent	Action or State of Agent
7	*hi* 7(22)					
8	*pat* 8(6)	*dada* 8(12) ... *dog* 8(30)				
9			*mama* 9(16)			
10		*dog* 10(9)				
11				*nana* 11(24)		
12			*cracker* 12(23)	*mama* 12(8)		
13					*daddy* 13(3)	... *up!* 13(16)
14		*daddy ... mommy* 14(10, 18)				*night-night* 14(5) ... *down* 14(10, 18)
15				*mommy ... down* 15(11) *spoon* 15(5, 17)		*down!* 15(5, 17) *down* 15(5, 17)
16			*mommy X* 16(4—18) *mommy; daddy; mommy* 16(7—13)	*mommy X* 16(4—18) *mommy; daddy; mommy* 16(7—13)	*mommy; daddy* 16(17)	*byebye; door* 16(2) *mommy down!* 16(5 *dirty* 16(21)
17			... *fishy* 17(11)	... *yeah* 17(13)	*fishy; eat* 17(2) *daddy byebye* 17(12)	*fishy; eat* 17(2) *daddy byebye* (17(12 *I see* 17(16—29)
18		... *yeah* 18(18)			*gone ... birdie* 18(3)	*go byebye* 18(18) ... *yeah* 18(18)
19					*me light* 19(3) *mommy!* 19(14)	
20		*no ... bear* 20(26)	*I want some* 20(26)			*house* 20(26)
21						
22		*this one* 22(1)				*see it* 22(1)

Note: Spelling conventionalized. See individual sections for contexts and explanations of examples in Table. "12(12)" indicates diary; "*12(12)*" indicates session; "..." indicates verbal context; ";" indicates sequence; "!" indicates Volition (Omitted for Volition and Volitional Object).

162

Object	Action or State of Object	Dative	Associated Object	Associated Being	Location	Modification of Event
		dada 11(28)				
ball 13(0)						
car; byebye 14(28)	down 14(6)		cookie 14(29)			
kyekye 14(29)	car; byebye 14(28)					
	. . . byebye 14(29)					
more milk! 15(27)	more milk! 15(2b)		milk! 15(5, 17)	fishy 15(29)	box 15(20)	
			fishy ball 15(23)			
spoon 16(2)	down! 16(2)	mommy 16(2)		. . . fishy 16(2)		
	dirty 16(17)	bye . . . Lauren 16(2)		daddy; door 16(21)		
	no 17(13)	byebye Lauren 17(18)		candy; Lauren 17(13)		
. . . button 18(18)	round & round 18(18)	Lauren 18(12)	fishy 18(11)	my . . . my 18(18)		again! 18(1)
eat spoon 18(25)	. . . yeah 19(21)		kite 18(11)	mine 19(21)		again . . . yeah 19(21)
			airplane 19(21)	my hat 19(21)		
				our car 19(21)		
		. . . daddy 20(3)			top! 20(26)	happen 20(18)
		Lauren a cookie 20(19)			kite . . . water 20(26)	self 20(26)
						too 20(26)
				mine! 22(1)		

tion,[9] whereas we have shown that the basic progression is the development of semantic functions rather than lexical acquisition. In fact, many new semantic functions are first expressed by old vocabulary. For example, Nicky first expressed Action or State of an Object with the word *down*, a word he earlier had used to express Action or State of Agent. Matthew's first Agent was *dada*, a word that had functioned previously as an Indicative Object.

At the outset, we remarked that children express many relations that involve a single entity like Agent and Object and only later express relations that imply two entities such as Associated Object, Associated Animate Being, and Location of an Object. There is a similar progression from the expression of intransitive actions to that of transitive ones. It is possible that intransitive acts with an implicit Agent should be considered an intermediate stage of this progression. An example of this type would be the use of *down* to encode the action of an Object caused by an Agent. The development of the ability to encode both entities implies a developmental progression from one-place to two-place predicates.

The expression of the participants in an action before the expression of associations is also related to the fact that change is encoded before constancy. Children are late in developing the ability to make statements about relatively enduring states of affairs like possession or habitual location.

Another development is in the planning function of speech. The relatively late development of the benefactive function of the dative illustrates the use of a word to express the goal of fairly complex sequence of actions.

One feature of vocabulary development that has been noted several times is the use of one pole of a dimension to represent both poles. Thus, Nicky went through a stage where he said *no* to mean either *yes* or *no*. Both boys said *down* for *down* and *up* for a period, and similarly confused *off* and *on*. Another example comes from a sequence reported in Nicky's diary between 20(10) and 20(18). Nicky points to a hot object like a coffee mug and says (*h*)*ot* followed by *co*(*ld*), in sequence. Sometimes the words are stated in the opposite order. This type of sequence would seem to constitute evidence for the psychological reality of the dimension joining polar opposites. Leopold (1949) observed a similar use of *hot* for both hot and cold and reports Jesperson to have parallel examples. E. Clark (1973) has related such phenomena to a general theory of the development of referential meaning.

Bloom (1970) has distinguished three types of negation: rejection, nonexist-

---

[9]MacNamara also hypothesizes "that the child will not learn the name for states or activities until he has firmly grasped the name for at least some entities which exemplify such states and activities." This hypothesis is, of course, confirmed by the developmental precedence of Indicative Objects over Action or State. (Early Performatives are considered to be *part of* an action rather than *standing for* or *representing* one.)

ence, and denial. During the period under study, the children produced all three types, although not always in single-word form. The earliest use for both boys was in connection with forbidden objects: Nicky said *no no* at 11(28); Matthew *no no* at 11(24). This usage seems like a precursor of rejection. The next use was rejection, apparently first of objects and then of actions. Nicky rejected objects with *no* at I—18(4) and actions similarly at 18(8–16). Matthew rejected water at 11(28) with *na!na!*, and protested his mother's putting on his undershirt with *no!no!* at 13(22). At 18(15–21), Nicky said *no!* when he didn't want Lauren and Matthew to leave, thereby rejecting an action not directly related to him; we have no comparable example for Matthew.

The next type of negation that Nicky uses is nonexistence. Nicky used *no* at II—18(27) to express the fact that there was no milk in a glass. We have no similar examples for Matthew. Bloom makes the point that nonexistence is expressed where there is some expectation of existence. This is another example of Wason's (1971) general point that negation functions in a positive context. Bloom's (1970) treatment of nonexistence is, however, confused by the fact that she normally treats the use of *no* with an action word as an example of nonexistence. For example, she calls *no fit*, from Eric III—22(0), an example of nonexistence (p. 178). To us, it seems that such examples are better treated as denial of a state. This view is borne out by the fact that this type of utterance first appears at Eric III, when denial is also first expressed in multi-word form (p. 178). During this period, nonexistence of objects is syntactically differentiated in Eric's speech from utterances like *no fit* by the presence of *more*, as in *no more airplane*. Nicky's usage further confirms calling sentences like *no fit* instances of denial rather than nonexistence, in that the first examples of this type of negation and of what Bloom would recognize as denial both occurred at the same time: At III—19(29), Nicky said *no record*, to indicate that the record player was not on, and *no eye* to indicate that what he was drawing was not an eye. The first example of this type of denial from Matthew is in one-word form: At IV—17(13), he says *no* when a piece won't fit in a puzzle. Denial of objects comes later, at 20(26), in the following sequence:

MOTHER	MATTHEW
	[pointing to a bear]
	(*gi*)*raffe*
Is that a giraffe?	*no*
What is it?	*bear*

Denial of objects in single-word utterances can only occur in response to verbal context, as shown by this example and Bloom's tables (pp. 176, 183). However, Nicky's example, *no eye*, shows that verbal context is not necessary for its expression in multiword form. Matthew's first two-word example occurred at 20(26) and similarly lacked verbal context. In this example, he said *no tree* when a piece he was holding was not a tree and so would not fit in the tree position in a puzzle. Our data thus confirm Bloom's statement that an isolated *no* is most often used to express rejection, but do not appear to support her contention that negation is first used in two-word form to express nonexistence. Nicky's first two-word negatives functioned to reject objects or actions.

As was pointed out repeatedly, the use of almost every semantic function passes through a number of stages before it is first used in two-word utterances. Most functions appeared first in isolated, one-word form. From this point, there are two directions of development. One is the use of single words in relation to verbal, as opposed to nonverbal, context. The other is the use of single words in sequences, as opposed to in isolation. Conversational sequences might be considered a combination of these two developments. The exceptions to this order of development are relatively few.

With later-acquired functions, both boys occasionally skipped over intermediate stages of development on their way toward two-word sentences. In the case of Associated Object, Nicky and Matthew both jumped directly from isolated one-word examples to two-word utterances. In the case of Associated Animate Being, Nicky again jumped to two-word speech. Finally, in the case of Modification of an Event, Nicky skips the one-word stage altogether. There are two possible explanations for these exceptional cases of development. It is possible that our samples simply failed to include the missing types. However, it is equally possible that as children begin to form generalized syntactic rules, they need less time and practice to advance in their expression of a newly acquired function. Because all of the "missing steps" occurred late in the one-word period, the latter explanation seems more likely. By the time the boys were developing these last functions, they already were expressing many other functions in two-word form.

The frequency of sequences climbs for both boys until they make up about half of the total output at Nicky IV—20(23) and Matthew VII—19(21). Beyond this point, multiword sentences rose in frequency and gradually displaced sequences. Sequences involving repetition show no developmental pattern, and are present in varying numbers at all stages. This accords with E. O. Keenan's (1975) conclusion that repetition fulfills a number of different functions in young children's discourse in the course of development. Thus, repetitive sequences at different times may represent developmentally distinct functions.

A final observation in the development of early speech is the growth of the importance of paradigmatic responses and sequences. We noted earlier that, whereas most sequences describe different aspects of a single event, children later may name sequentially several objects or people that stand in similar relations to the context. One example involved Nicky's naming the owners of various pieces of clothing that were hanging in a closet. In another, he sequentially announced that Lauren and Matthew were coming. In sequences like these, a child seems to be exercising his understanding of the function, and deliberately expressing the parallelism.

Although such paradigmatic sequences are never common, they are formally similar to the paradigmatic way a child may contrast his own word with the verbal or nonverbal context. This type of usage was especially clear in the case of agent and associated animate being. In an example given in section 3.7, Nicky and his mother had been playing "Ring around the Rosy." At one point, Nicky broke away and said *Ma(tthew)*. This is evidently meant to parallel the situation where Nicky and his mother were agents in the game. In another example, discussed in section 3.13, Nicky responds to his mother's statement *Those are mine* by saying *Nini!* (Nicky's). The paradigmatic use of language develops relatively late, but it allows a child to communicate messages that might not otherwise be understood.

There is a similar progression in the answering of questions. Children first answer *wh* questions, such as *What do you want?*, in which the child's answer combines syntagmatically with part of the question. For example, the answer *banana* would imply the combination *I want a banana*. Later, the child answers questions in which his answer often implicitly substitutes for part of the question. If a mother asks *Do you want some milk?* and her child answers *banana*, *banana* here paradigmatically replaces *milk* in the Volitional frame. The fact that functions are almost always expressed first in isolation and only later in response to verbal context indicates that children do not answer questions they do not somehow understand. However, once a child has a function, he can make himself much clearer by using a word in relation to verbal context than by using it in isolation.

These different aspects of development during the one-word stage indicate that children are learning many things even before they have learned to put two words together. Even during the process of decentration, one-word speech is richly communicative. In fact, it is only through communication that children learn the forms of adult language. This theme will be pursued in the chapter that follows.

chapter 4

Cognition, Communication, and Information

4.1 Cognition and Language Development

T he developmental sequences noted in the preceding chapter are not autonomous linguistic developments; they are firmly grounded in the child's cognitive functioning. As Slobin has written:

> Language is used to express the child's cognitions of his environment—physical and social— and so a child cannot begin to use a given linguistic form meaningfully until he is able to understand what it means. It should be possible, then, to rank linguistic forms in terms of the psychological, or cognitive complexity of the notions they express [1973, p. 180].

Slobin goes on to state that, although conceptual understanding is clearly a limiting factor in linguistic expression, formal linguistic complexity must also play a role. In one-word speech, however, formal complexity is, of course, constant. We would expect, therefore, that semantic development of one-word utterances should occur in the same sequence as the requisite nonverbal cognitive development, but would lag behind it.

Several recent studies (Greenfield, Nelson, and Saltzman, 1972; Goodson and Greenfield, 1975) have shown that the development of verbal and non-verbal behavior have common structural sequences. For example, Greenfield,

Nelson, and Saltzman (1972) demonstrate that children from 1 to 3 years of age develop consistent strategies for combining seriated cups which are parallel in form and order of acquisition to sentence structures learned in the course of grammatical development. These studies have not, however, attempted to study the problem of what specific cognitive developments are necessary to the acquisition of a particular form of linguistic expression.

In Chapter 2, we presented evidence from numerous sources that the requisite nonverbal cognitive structures are present when children begin to talk. Ervin-Tripp (1971) suggested that understanding the order of development of conceptual relations can help account for the order of development within language. In this section, we shall show that the sequence we have observed in language development in fact does parallel earlier sequences in cognitive development.

In Chapter 3, we concluded that the child was able to encode change of state before process. This progression mirrors a much earlier progression in infant perception discovered by Mundy-Castle and Anglin (1969). They set up the moving visual display shown in Figure 2. Infants around 12 weeks of age anticipated the appearance of the object by horizontal eye movements from porthole to porthole. These infants had schematized the object's *change* of state. Older infants began to interpolate a trajectory between the two portholes; their eye movements did not go straight across, but in an arc, as if following

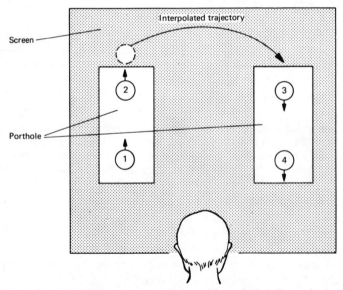

Figure 2 Mundy-Castle–Anglin apparatus. Arrows and numbers indicate object movement. [From *Development in Infancy* by T. G. R. Bower. W. H. Freeman and Company. Copyright © 1974.]

the path they imagined the object to be following. This behavior indicated an awareness not only of state *change* but also of a *process* intervening between initial and final states. Thus, semantic development repeats perceptual development in that children represent changes of state before they represent processes on a linguistic level.

One developmental sequence mentioned in Chapter 3 is from one-place to two-place predicates. Here, of course, we are defining predicate on an implicit cognitive rather than an explicit logical level. More specifically, early appearing semantic functions involve but a single entity—as in Object—whereas later ones involve two—as in Location of Object. If we look at the development of the corresponding action patterns during infancy, we see that they develop in the same order: the infant acts on an object before placing an object in a location. This sequence is reflected in the Cattell Infant Intelligence Scale (1940). For instance, lifting a cup (object) is a task that, according to the Scale, the average infant can do at 6 months of age, whereas placing a cube (object) in a cup (location) is not generally accomplished until 4 months later. Again, the earliest item in the Scale involving the manipulation of a single object occurs 4 months before the earliest item that could be considered placing an object in a location— banging a spoon on a surface. Thus, action development, as it relates to object manipulation, parallels development of the expression of semantic functions involving two objects, but precedes it in time.

Another developmental sequence is that the use of later words is often quite removed from the speaker's ongoing action, in structure as well as time. When Matthew reaches for a cookie and says *Lauren*, in an example of the Dative, he has, in a way, acquired some ability to do one thing and say another. More specifically, Matthew has acquired an ability to treat an immediate object (the cookie) as a means while expressing the goal (Lauren) of a fairly complex sequence of means—end relations. A similar sequence is reported by Piaget (1951) during the development of sensorimotor intelligence. At Stage III, a barrier between a child and a desired object is treated as a goal in itself. However, at Stage IV (8 months), the child is able to set aside a barrier in order to reach a more distant goal. The barrier has become a means to an end. Thus, the awareness of distant goals in relation to immediate objects is similar in cognitive and linguistic development.

The increasingly complex means—end relations that become possible as the sensorimotor period progresses involve what Sinclair calls "the embedding of action-schemes one into the other." Semantic development within the one-word stage also involves increasingly complex embedding. For example, the child can encode Indicative Objects early in the one-word period. In so doing, the child embeds an entity and its name is his indicative gesture, e.g., pointing. Later, the embedded element—what we have called the "referential event"— becomes more complex. For instance, the child becomes capable of pointing at something and naming a person associated with it, thus expanding the embedded event to consist of a relation between two elements. The most complex cognitive embedding in single-word utterances occurs in the last semantic function to develop, Modification of Event, in which one complete referential event embeds another. For instance, when Nicky says *wait* in connection with flushing the toilet, the act of flushing the toilet is cognitively embedded in the state of waiting.

More generally, the child progresses from encoding the present situation and immediate visual surroundings to encoding future intentions and past events. This broadening of the sphere of reference has been commented on by earlier writers (e.g., de Laguna 1927; Werner and Kaplan, 1963), but they often have missed its true extent.

Early performatives and indications refer to the situation at hand. However, when a child begins to express volitional objects, he necessarily makes reference to a potential situation that is different from the existing one. Early in their development, children learn to use names to ask for objects that are not visually present. They also use names to express their future intentions, as in the example given above involving Matthew and the cookie. In playing with his vocabulary, Nicky would occasionally remind himself of his security diaper or some other desirable object, and would set out to find it. This development of language use toward expression of increasingly remote future goals parallels the development of intentionality in infancy as described by Piaget (1951) and Bruner (1971).

There is a similar progression in the encoding of past events. Whereas Matthew first uses *down* only to refer to an immediate change of state, he later—15(10)—says *down* when his mother enters a room, to report that he has gotten down from something by himself. Still later—16(2)—he goes to find his mother to tell her the same thing. Such expression of past events parallels the development of representational skills toward the end of the sensorimotor period (Piaget, 1951). In fact, Matthew had first shown evidence of rudimentary representation, in the form of fantasy play, several months earlier, at around a year of age.

Parallels between sensorimotor and cognitive development and language development support the view that language is first inserted into a nonverbal cognitive framework. This view assumes an amodal or supramodal cognitive organization that can integrate information from different modes into a single cognitive structure. ("Modal" here refers to perceptual modes—auditory, visual, and enactive—not linguistic or emotional modes.[1]) Experiments with very

---

[1] These two senses are derived from different disciplines: sensory modes from psychology, attitudinal modes from linguistics.

young infants indicate that the earliest cognitive organization is, in fact, of this nature. For example, Bower, Broughton, and Moore (1970) have shown that newborn infants integrate visual and tactual information about objects. Aronson and Rosenbloom (1971) have also shown that 3-week-old infants integrate visual and auditory information. Other experiments by Bower (1974) and Aronson and Dunkel (unpublished, cited in Bower, 1974) indicate that babies are not able to respond differentially to information emanating from different modes until later in infancy. For instance, whereas 3-week-old babies cry when the sound of their mother's voice appears to emanate from a place to one side of her, older babies not only get upset but also orient back and forth between voice and face. The response pattern of the older infants shows that they can *differentiate* information from the two modalities. In contrast, the younger babies seem to have incorporated information from different modalities into an undifferentiated whole. Thus, the facts of infant perceptual development seem to support our assumption that the young child just beginning to learn language has the organizational capability to integrate a word with information from other modes. From our knowledge of perceptual development we would hypothesize that the ability to produce or comprehend a purely verbal structure differentiated from organization in other sensory modes would be a later development.

In relating language use to his cognitive organization of the world—in terms of Agent, Object, and so on—a child not only is able to communicate effectively with limited linguistic means; he also has the basis for further development of his linguistic skills. What the child knows—the world of his experience—is his basis for deciphering the unknown—adult language. Premack (1970) expressed a similar point of view when he wrote that "teaching an organism language amounts in part to mapping the built-in knowledge of its species." Of course, Premack was dealing with chimpanzees and we are dealing with human infants, but the basic problems involved appear to be the same.

4.2 The Transition from Words to Syntax

In the preceding chapter, we noted several characteristics of development during the one-word stage that appear to relate to the transition from one- to two-word speech. The first of these is the fact that most semantic functions originally were expressed in one-word form and then appeared in sequences before they were combined with other semantic functions to form two-word utterances. The second is the fact that the use of a function in nonimitative response to verbal context usually precedes its use in two-word utterances. Dialogue seemed to be the situation in which children could get the most accessible information about word combination in adult language, and sequences appeared to be the best opportunity to practice such combination. Thus, we decided to examine the children's earliest two-word utterances to see if their form could have been learned in these contexts.

By focusing on the earliest two-word utterances, we can study the transition to syntax while it is in process. Although the child needs to form many word combinations before it can be concluded that he has a generative rule, we envision the first examples as focal instances that form the ontogenetic and cognitive core of the general rule to follow. Here, we have taken Rosch's (1973) concept of the role of focal instances in concept formation and applied it to the domain of grammatical rules.

DIALOGUE

In examining the dialogue that precedes children's first two-word utterances, five patterns can be observed that could lead to early sentences. Three of these are adult-initiated and two are child-initiated. Of the former, one involves paradigmatic answers to questions. In these, the child's answer substitutes for a word in the mother's question. When the child produces longer utterances, they correspond to longer segments of the mother's question. A second type involves a syntagmatic connection between the child's answer and the final word of the mother's question. Finally, there is imitation, where the child repeats something the adult has said. In the category of child-initiated dialogue, there are replies in which the adult gives new information in response to something said by the child and expansions (to be described in more detail later) in which the adult repeats the same information in syntactically elaborated form.

Nicky

Nicky's first two-word utterances occurred at Nicky II—18(27). At that time, he used *awa* or *awada* to mean "want." (*Awa* and *awada* are treated as a single word rather than as "I want the" because none of the words *I, want,* or *the* had appeared up to that time either alone or in any other combination. The analysis of *awa* as a variant of *want* is supported by the frequency of preposed *a* in Nicky's vocabulary, e.g., *acacoo* for record.) A good nonimitative example of this type of utterance from Nicky II, is *awada cacoo* (want record) uttered while the record player was turned off. If we look back to dialogue occurring earlier, there are a number of examples of Nicky's mother asking questions including the word *want* and Nicky responding with an Object of Volition. The following examples occurred at Nicky I—18(4):

MOTHER	NICKY
Do you want some milk?	*(ba)nana*
What do you want?	*showel* (shovel)

In the first question—answer unit, Nicky makes a paradigmatic replacement of *milk* with *(ba)nana.* Thus, his answer *banana* replaces x in the pattern *want (some) x* in his mother's question, and his two-word sentences express the whole pattern. It should be remembered that *some* is relatively unstressed in this pattern. In the second example, his answer *showel* syntagmatically combines with *want* in his mother's question. Hence, Nicky could have discovered the formula *want* plus object by putting together question and answer. In fact, during Session II there are two instances of this sort of dialogue right before *awada cacoo* is first uttered. In both these examples, *want* occurs in the mother's question and an object is expressed in Nicky's answer; the examples are drawn from conversational sequences:

MOTHER	NICKY
Want some orange juice?	*chee(se)* [repeated; whining and pointing to refrigerator]
Do you want some orange juice?	*mee* (milk) [whining and pointing to cupboard]

Hence he has participated creatively in an appropriate model just minutes before uttering his own two-word sentence.

Two-word sentences are next reported in Nicky's diary between 19(15) and 20(3) and also occur in the formal session of this period, Nicky III—19(29). In this session, the *awa* pattern continues, *awa* alternating with *wa*, as in *awa recor, wa recor* (want record), thus confirming our interpretation of *awa* and *awada* as approximations of *want.* But more important is a new two-word pattern that emerges: a volitional *no* plus Object or Action—State. Table 18 presented the examples from this session in Chapter 3. Examples from the diary involving rejection of an Object are: *no accor* (record) *no mi(l)k, no shoe, no boo (t), no dock* (sock); an example involving rejection of an Action—State is *no nightnight.* Dialogue involving an Object or State in the the question and rejection with *no* in the answer can be traced back as far as Nicky I—18(4). Examples were presented in Table 17, Chapter 3. In fact, in Nicky III—19(29), the appropriate dialogue occurs immediately before the corresponding two-word utterance: During a conversational sequence, Nicky's mother asks *Do you want the dance record?* and he responds *no!* A few minutes later, his mother asks *Do you want to listen to it?*, referring to a record, and Nicky responds *no record.* Thus, in fact, he could have, put together the *record* from his mother's question with the *no* from his answer in the earlier exchange.

An example of the construction of a two-word utterance from dialogue occurs with a two-word utterance of the type *no* plus Action—State: Nicky's mother questions *byebye?* and Nicky replies *no byebye*. Here, Nicky merely has to add the word *no* to the question in order to produce his own sentence. This same type of dialogue takes place a second time in the same session when Nicky's mother asks *Do you want to dance?* and he replies *no dance*.

During the same session, Nicky produces a number of two-word utterances of the form *no x* which express nonexistence and denial rather than rejection— for example, he says *no daddy* when his father is absent (nonexistence) and *no eye*, drawing a picture that is not an eye (denial). These have no antecedents in dialogue. Perhaps what is occurring is a kind of generalization of the pattern *no x* to new situations on either semantic (negativity) or syntactic (the rule *no* plus x) grounds.

Still at Nicky III—19(29), Nicky uses a two-word utterance that cannot be traced back to dialogue: as he pulls down his diaper, he says *ma* (my) *diaper*. This utterance consists of what would be two contiguous words in adult speech. Hence, Nicky could have picked up this sentence by imitating a fragment from adult speech.

There is one remaining two-word utterance produced at this session for which no antecedents in dialogue could be found: Nicky says *more record*, while pointing to a record playing. Perhaps this utterance can be explained as a fragment of adult speech used in an incorrect context, for *more record* could occur in standard English under certain circumstances. Considering that we are dealing not with a complete record of Nicky's speech but with monthly samples, it is hardly surprising that there are occasional sentences for which no antecedents can be found in our record.

Matthew

The early development of Matthew's two-word utterances is somewhat different. Unlike Nicky's first productions, Matthew's first two-word utterances are all combinations that could occur as contiguous words in adult speech. The first example, noted in Matthew's diary at 15(23), was (*f*)*ishy ball*, referring to a large clear plastic ball with toy fish swimming inside. An adult could have referred to this object as a *fish ball*. The second example was reported in his diary a few days later at 15(27) when he said *mo(re) meh* (milk) when his 4-ounce bottle ran out of milk. (He was accustomed to having eight ounces at that time of day.) These could not be traced back to earlier two-person dialogue, but could, of course, have been learned as complete fragments from adult speech.

The next clearcut example of a two-word utterance occurs at 16(5) as *mommy dow(n)* which Matthew days when, coming out of anesthesia following a kidney operation, he wants to get down from his crib. This was Matthew's first *creative* two-word utterance, in that the two words he used would not occur *contiguously* in adult speech. Correlatively, we were able to trace the components of this utterance back to dialogue. At 15(11), Matthew is reported to say *mama*, starting down the stairs. His mother answers *what?* and Matthew replies *dow(n)*. This dialogue is somewhat different in that both components are produced by Matthew. Matthew's second word *down* is, however, stimulated by his mother's question. This example thus shows another way in which dialogue can contribute to the development of two-word utterances.

At 17(12), Matthew produces another creative two-word utterance: *daddy bye-bye*, uttered after his father has left for work. We were able to trace the components of this Agent plus Action—State utterance back to earlier dialogue, without any ambiguity. At Matthew IV—16(2), his mother asks *Are you going, Beulah?* as Beulah prepares to leave. Matthew responds with *byebye* (not addressed to Beulah as a farewell greeting, but describing her Action or State). Here it seems as though Matthew's answer adds the expression of Action or State to the Agent—*Beulah*—contained in the question. The two elements Agent and *byebye* are combined in the subsequent utterance *daddy byebye*.

Another two-word utterance is reported at 17(17) when Matthew says *jump down*. Antecedents to this utterance occur in dialogue at Matthew II—14(10, 18): Matthew's mother asks *Do you want to get up?* and he replies *down*. If we conceive of *jump down* as a combination of Action and State, then we can find a parallel combination in mother's question (*get*) plus Matthew's answer (*down*).

The next creative two-word utterance occurs at 17(18), when Matthew says *mo(re) ea(t)* when he wants to feed the fish thing in the morning. If we interpret *more* in this to mean "more food" (the most reasonable interpretation, since Matthew used *more* for substances and *again* for repetition of events), then we can find the components in earlier dialogue. In fact, just the day before, Matthew's father said *toe, toe*, to which Matthew responded *ea(t)*. This was part of a game routine in which his father would say *Eat your toes* and Matthew would do so. Hence Matthew has added *eat*, an Action or State of an Agent, to an Object expressed by his father. In all of these examples from Matthew, the word order of the two components in dialogue form is maintained in the subsequent two-word utterance. In the case of *more eat*, this leads to incorrect word order from the perspective of the adult language.

The same day, Matthew is reported to produce yet another two-word utterance. After he and his mother have returned home from taking Lauren to nursery school, he says *byebye yaya* (Lauren). We could interpret this as a reversal of the word order found in the earlier *daddy byebye*. It is more likely, however, that Lauren is an animate object (Dative) rather than Agent in this situation, and that Matthew is signaling this relation by putting *yaya* (Lauren) last rather than first in the sentence. It seemed worthwhile to look back to earlier dialogue to see if the components could be found in this same order in a situation having a parallel structure. We found them at the beginning of a conversational sequence occurring at Matthew IV—16(2):

MOTHER	MATTHEW
We're going bye bye and get Lauren	*bye*
Yeah, byebye	*lala* (Lauren)

(The rest of the sequence is not pertinent for present purposes.)

At 17(18), Matthew said *caca ong* while carrying a record to the record player. This sentence consists of combining an Object with an Action/State. Similar combinations occur in earlier dialogue, but with different vocabulary. Considering our limited sample, it would not be surprising to have missed dialogue involving the same vocabulary. The earliest instance involving different vocabulary is reported at 14(29) when Matthew and his mother are playing with toy cars: His mother says *There's a car*, to which Matthew responds *byebye*.

There was one more two-word utterance reported that same day: The (*f*)*ishy* (*l*)*igh*(*t*) was off. This seems merely to follow the pattern of (*f*)*ishy ball*, his first two-word utterance at 15(23), and therefore requires no further explanation of its developmental source.

Discussion

Matthew's transition to two-word speech appears to be based on imitation of fragments from adult speech and construction of new sentence types out of material contained in the two-person sentences of dialogue. Nicky resembles Matthew in these respects, but he seems to rely relatively more on dialogue. Where the roots of syntax seem to lie in dialogue, note how, in each case (except for Matthew's *caca ong* [record on]), the earlier dialogue contained at least one word which later appeared in a related two-word utterance—for example, *no* for Nicky, *byebye* for Matthew. In some instances, both words of a two-word utterance previously had been combined in the two-person semantic structure of dialogue—as with Nicky's *no acor* (record) and Matthew's *byebye yaya*. In Chapter 3, we found that dialogue was common as an intermediate form between the one- and two-word expression of semantic relations, here we have found that the earliest two-word utterances have close antecedents in dialogue and that dialogue supplies some of the specific forms of early child grammar.

Although our data are well suited to analyze the role of dialogue, a more complete and extensive record of adult input is necessary to delineate the precise role of imitation. A study by Bloom, Hood, and Lightbown (1974) on the role of imitation in the period between one- and two-word utterances complements our data in providing just such a record. They found that, when children imitated, they imitated linguistic material that would later enter spontaneous speech. For three of the four children they studied, the conclusion was that "imitation appeared to function for learning the semantic–syntactic relations in multiword utterances" (p. 413). The fourth child did not use imitation in this way, although he appeared to use imitation to learn new vocabulary.[2] Hence, the results of Bloom and co-workers confirm both our hypothesis about the role of imitation in learning syntax and our discovery about individual differences in the extent to which this mechanism is used.

Our hypothesis concerning the role of dialogue in the transition to two-word speech may help explain how children acquire the dominant word orders of their language (Bowerman, 1973). Most of the dialogue under discussion does maintain the word order of the child's subsequent two-word syntax. This is true for all of the examples from Matthew, as was mentioned previously. Nicky, however, presents some instances which do maintain word order, others which do not. An example of the first type occurs when his mother asks *Do you want some milk?* and Nicky replies *(ba)nana*; here, *want* precedes *nana* just as it does in his later utterance *awada* (want) *cacoo* (record). Dialogue involving *no* does not, on the other hand, maintain the word order of later two-word utterances, as the following exchange shows: Mother: *Do you want the dance record?* Nicky: *no!* His corresponding two-word utterance would, of course, be *no record*. It could be, however, that by the time Nicky starts forming two-word utterances consisting of *no* plus on Object, he already has established a model of word order for Volitional sentences from his earlier *awa x* pattern in which *awa*, like *no*, expresses Volition. He may therefore be less reliant on dialogue to provide information about word order.

Another possibility is that the child can learn from the dialogue he initiates. For instance, at Nicky I—18(4), Nicky whines *(ba)nana, (ba)nana*. His mother's answer is *No, you can't have a banana.* This response adds semantically to Nicky's *nana*; thus, this form of dialogue can also be considered a two-person semantic structure. In addition, the mother's response also provides a model of a negative

---

[2]Bloom and associates also explain how their results are actually in accord with Ervin's (1964) seemingly contradictory data on the role of imitation. Fraser, Bellugi, and Brown (1963), Slobin (1968), Slobin and Welsh (1968), Kemp and Dale (1973) have all found imitations to be gramatically progressive in comparison with spontaneous speech at later points in development. Dodd and Coots (1973) modeled pivot constructions involving *more* with 18–20 month-old children and reinforced the children for imitating them. Sometimes, *more* was in the initial position in the two-word utterance, sometimes in the final position. Children learned the order presented and were capable of learning a new order when the model changed. This study demonstrates that children can learn two-word constructions through imitation.

Lieven's unpublished data, cited by Ryan (1973), confirms this point. She "found that, despite the decline with age in single-word imitations, when multi-word utterances first appeared in the child's speech a very high proportion of these were either complete or partial imitations of the mother's previous utterances" (p. 439).

volitional utterance in which *no* precedes the Volitional Object.[3] In this way, it contrasts with the type of adult-initiated dialogue described previously:

MOTHER	CHILD
Do you want a banana?	*no*

In this type of dialogue, the word order *banana, no* does not match the child's emerging syntax. A perceptual advantage of both these types of sentences as a syntactic model is that the key words fall at the beginning and the end of the sentence, the two most perceptually salient positions.

As we mentioned in an earlier chapter, Brown and his colleagues (e.g., Brown and Bellugi, 1964; Cazden, 1965; Brown, 1973) have described certain adult responses to child utterances as "expansions." An expansion is an interpretation or "gloss" of a child utterance which adds words to the child's utterance, usually functors, while leaving word order intact. (This last condition is automatically fulfilled for one-word utterances, since there is no word order.) By this definition *No, you can't have a banana* is not an expansion since it explicitly contradicts the child's preceding verbal demand, *(ba)nana*. Could the child receive this same syntactic information from an expansion? It could happen only if the child's own negative, *no*, were to be expanded. Looking through the responses to Nicky's negatives in the formal observation sessions up to his first two-word negatives at Nicky III, we could find no instance of such an expansion. In the case of early negative two-word utterances, expansions of single-word utterances do not provide usable input for syntactic development, whereas other forms of dialogue do.

Cazden (1965) explored the possibility that adult expansions following the child's utterances would provide a source of syntactic information that the child could use in further linguistic development. This exploration failed, however, to yield positive evidence that expansion training at the two-word stage helps further the child's linguistic development. Yet the analysis of Brown, Cazden, and Bellugi (1968) and Brown (1973) suggests that expansions can be useful if they relate to the child's emerging competence in particular ways. Recent research (e.g., Newport, Gleitman, and Gleitman, 1975) has tended to show that the value of particular kinds of language input from the environment depends on exactly where the child is in the language learning process. Our idea is that various forms of dialogue may be differentially constructive at dif-

---

[3] Brown and Bellugi (1964) eliminate sentences of the type *No, you can't have a banana* as a possible model for the child's two-word negatives because *no* to some extent has a separate intonation contour from the rest of the sentence. It seems, however, that there is no evidence on this point one way or another. But if the child is capable of constructing syntax from dialogue, then intonational separation of the component parts would not seem to be an insuperable difficulty.

ferent points in development. Our analysis emphasizes adult-initiated dialogue at the one-word stage because, unlike child-initiated dialogue, it compels the child to relate his single-word utterance to other words, a necessary prerequisite to syntax. The child must actually construct the semantic relation. In contrast, when the child is exposed to an expansion or other response to his utterance, he may not respond at all. Thus, adult-initiated dialogue intrinsically involves active participation from the child. If, as Piaget claims, we know because we act, then the active participation in semantic structure required by adult-initiated dialogue should be an extremely effective way for children to gain information about their native language.

Another possible advantage of this particular environmental mechanism at this early stage is that adults talk to children long before they can respond, and continue to do so even though children may answer infrequently. An expansion or other verbal response to the child's utterance, in contrast, requires that the child first say something. This would seem a risky environmental device from a biological point of view: If the child says nothing, he misses just the linguistic input he needs to learn his language!

In terms of information processing, adult-initiated dialogue has another advantage for the child with limited memory capacity. To learn syntax from this source, the child need use only the last word from the adult utterance, and this word is, of course, the most salient one.

In adult-initiated dialogue, the adult provides a *part* of a semantic relation that the child can complete with his own verbal response. Questions are particularly well suited for this sort of completion. Our hypothesis is that one way of learning syntax is by completing a two-person semantic structure. In contrast to expansion, the emphasis in adult-initiated dialogue is on adult verbalization as *stimulus* rather than *response* to the child.

By discussing the various kinds of dialogue and their possible function in stimulating linguistic development, we hope to have shown that the child need not bring forth his original grammar from nowhere but may construct it from interaction with his linguistic environment.

THE ROLE OF SEQUENCES IN SYNTACTIC DEVELOPMENT

Before concluding that deferred imitation of adult speech and stimulation from adult—child conversation are the only mechanisms mediating the transition to syntax, we must investigate the role of our other transitional form, the sequence—a succession of single-word utterances encoding different aspects of the situation. Perhaps the child also joins the components of two-word utterances in these sequences, without linguistic input from the environment. We are excluding conversational sequences from this discussion since they were included in our analysis of the role of dialogue.

Some observations from Leopold (1949), described by Werner and Kaplan (1963), indicate that sequences may sometimes function as internalized dialogue where the child plays the role of interlocutor and respondent. Leopold reports that during the transition from one- to two-word utterances Hildegard said things like *dada? byebye!* That is, she first asked a question about a person and then answered it by verbalizing an Action or State in declarative intonation. This type of sequence provides behavioral evidence that the child can extract the role of the other as well as her own from a question—answer interchange: She can, in fact, process dialogue as a two-person sentence, just as we suggested in the preceding section. This type of sequence suggests that dialogue and sequence are related functionally as transitional forms. Thus, Leopold's examples are of theoretical interest, even though we did not find this type of sequence in our own data. This seems to indicate that sequences may have lesser importance as transitional mechanisms for Matthew and Nicky than they did for Leopold's daughter Hildegard.

Sequences do, in fact, seem relatively unimportant for Nicky's development, for we find no examples of sequences involving *no* or *awa* (want) before his first two-word utterances. While there are a number in which the Volitional *mama* is combined with an Object (for example, at Nicky I—18(4), *dan* (fan); *mommy* when he wants the fan turned on), Nicky never combines *mama* or *mommy* with a Volitional Object in his two-word utterances.

Matthew's data, in contrast, show some sequential antecedents for two-word utterances. *Daddy byebye* at 17(12) is preceded by *mommy, mommy, mommy; byebye* at 17(9) when his mother has gone downstairs. *Mo(re) ea(t)* at 17(18) is preceded by *nandy; eat* at 17(11); *caca ong* (on) at 17(18) is preceded by *babu* (bottle); *gong* (gone) at 16(30). All of the two-word utterances that had antecedents in sequences also had antecedents in earlier dialogue. This fact supports the notion that sequences may be closely connected to dialogue. In contrast, none of the two-word utterances we hypothesized as originating from imitation of fragments of adult speech could be traced back to sequences. Hence, our hypothesis about these residual cases may be correct, although we do not have the data to establish it with certainty.

In conclusion, it seems that sequences can also help in the transition to two-word utterances: The child first relates two successive words to two different aspects of the situation, for example, he may describe an Action and then name its Object; later, he relates the two words to each other directly, and syntax is born. Whereas Nicky seems to rely mainly on dialogue and secondarily on imitation in forming his earliest two-word utterances, Matthew draws his first two-word utterances from a mixture of three sources: fragments from adult speech, dialogue, and his own sequences. Sequences seem least important, however, as a source, because each two-word combination that could be traced back to a sequence could also be traced back to dialogue. The reverse was not, however, the case.[4]

SEQUENCES AND THE DEVELOPMENT OF THE EXPRESSION OF QUANTITY

A particular kind of sequence, the repetitive sequence, seemed to have a special role in the development of plural morphology. In their early indicative utterances, neither Matthew nor Nicky differentiated between single objects and groups of objects. Starting around 17(10), however, Matthew was observed to distinguish plural from singular situations by the use of sequences and gesture. For instance, looking at a picture book page depicting several balls, he would

---

[4] A thesis by Rodgon (1972) explored the transition from single-word utterances to combinatorial speech: The study generally confirms the analysis of the relational use of single words described in our preliminary reports (Smith, 1970; Greenfield, Smith, and Laufer, 1972). Rodgon attempted to influence the appearance of two-word sentences in the speech of children at the one-word level. In particular, she attempted to encourage the expression of subject–verb, object–locative, and possessive constructions. Her training procedure consisted of a combination of three techniques:

1. Expansion of the child's single-word utterances (in the form of both telegraphic two-word utterances and full sentences).
2. Questions in response to the child's single-word utterances, intended to stimulate the second word in a semantic relation (e.g., child: *mommy*; E: *mommy what?*).
3. Spontaneous adult modeling of combinatorial speech (both telegraphic and full sentences).

The training seemed to have some effect in stimulating combinatorial speech, as we would expect from our analysis; however, her results are difficult to use because of shortcomings of the experimental procedure. First, there is no control for natural maturation. Second, imitative combinations were not distinguished from spontaneous combinations in the data analysis. Third, Rodgon's training techniques combine all of the various kinds of input whose effects we have analyzed here. Because Rodgon mixed the different types of input together for all children, her study does not contribute to answering the question of what kind of input has what effect on which children in making the transition from single-word utterances to syntax.

Rodgon notes the absence of a correlation between earlier expression of a relation in single-word form and response to combinatorial training. However, her pretraining assessment of single-word utterances is based on a very small sample: about 48 minutes for 8 of the 10 children and about 36 minutes for the other 2. Samples of such short duration are inadequate to assess underlying competence. Even though our individual observation periods were roughly three or four times as long as Rodgon's sampling period, Nicky and Matthew often failed, in a given period, to express a semantic function that had been expressed many times earlier (see Tables 10 and 11). Sometimes, too, there was a delay between the first expression of a semantic function alone with mother to its first expression in the presence of an observer. Hence, Rodgon's very limited data are not adequate to test the hypothesis that the child is capable of expressing the components of a semantic relation in single-word form before being able to express the relation in a two-word sentence.

repeat *ball*; *ball*; *ball*; pointing to a different ball each time. Hence, his first analysis of the plural situation involves a kind of enactive representation, successive pointing, plus use of an old linguistic form, the sequence. Matthew did not use plural forms of nouns until more than 2 months later, at Matthew VII—19(21). During this session, he says *skates* while trying to put his skates on. He also used the plural form *peas* on two different occasions, both appropriate.

At 20(10), Matthew is reported to use another indication of quantity, *some*, when he indicated with his hand that he wanted some spaghetti on his plate and said *some*. It is interesting that expressions of quantity with the independent word *some* and with the bound morpheme -*s* appear so close together developmentally. This seems to indicate that, at this point in development, when other two-morpheme forms already exist, the addition of the second morpheme is not in itself problematical. At Matthew VIII—20(26), the plural -*s* and *some* continue to be used, while the word *many* appears for the first time, when Matthew says *many* to refer to the fact that he has several cookies on his plate. Thus, the development of plural expression for Matthew involves an enactive representation (successive pointing) and use of an old linguistic form (the sequence) as steps on the path to morphological combination (*s*) and a vocabulary of quantity (*some, many*).

4.3 Informativeness

Given that a situational structure always involves a relation between the child speaker and a minimum of one other component, how can we characterize which element is selected for verbal encoding? When development has reached a point where the full range of semantic functions are available, can we say anything about what element will be selected in what situation? We have already done this with respect to the Agent concept, pointing out that, at the one-word stage, it is only spoken under unusual conditions, such as conflict about Agency or an actual change of Agent. In such cases, the expression of Agent partitions alternatives that are perceived by the child. Under normal circumstances, the child takes the Agent for granted, while perceiving less certainty in the realm of Action or State change. Hence, this element is the one ordinarily encoded verbally. We suggest that this principle of informativeness can generally explain which element is selected.

Note that we are using informativeness in the information-theory sense of uncertainty. Uncertainty exists where there are possible alternatives. But we are defining uncertainty from the child-speaker's point of view, not from the point of view of the listener. Information in this sense, then, is relative to the child. An adult present in a given situation may, however, be able to understand the child because the child usually is referring to that situation, and the adult can see which alternatives are important for the child.

In this section, we shall examine two other situations to show that the principle of informativeness can explain which element of the situation a child encodes. We shall first treat Volition, then Action—State and Object situations.

VOLITION

Let us now apply the concept of informativeness to the Volitional situation and compare the expression of positive and negative Volition. The Volitional relation has two elements that are expressed in single-word utterances, Volition and its Object. A single-word utterance can, of course, express only one of these elements verbally; the other must be expressed nonverbally, through gesture or object. If we compare the contexts for expressing negative and positive Volition, rejection and demand, respectively, the probability of encoding the Object is much higher in the negative or rejection situation than in the positive or demand situation. A child does not reject something unless he believes it is coming his way. To put the comparison another way, the uncertainty of the Object is greater in the positive, or demand, situation. Thus, it follows from the principle of informativeness that the Object will be more frequently expressed in the positive, or demand, situation, Volition in the negative, or rejection, situation. And this is precisely the case. Once the ability to express both Volition and its Object in single-word utterances has developed, Objects predominate over Volition in the expression of demands, whereas Volition predominates over Object in the expression of rejection. We are here talking about single-word utterances in which only one element can be expressed. Taking the body of one-word utterances uttered in isolation for both boys from the time each has acquired the ability to express both positive and negative Volition and its Object,[5] the results, presented in Table 41 are quite dramatic. Positive Volition (demand) is usually expressed by means of the Object, negative volition (rejection) by means of Volition, more specifically by the word *no*. Hence, the prediction from informativeness is borne out; uncertainty leads to verbal expression. That is, we see that Object is expressed where it is relatively *uncertain*—in the positive case—but not where it is relatively certain—in the negative case.

In the latter case negative Volition—*no*—was the means for communicating the message. It was mentioned in Section 3.5 that negatives presuppose a positive context; the positive context would be the Object in the case of using *no* to reject something. If this is so, then our Object of rejection is both certain and presupposed. But is it possible to claim that relative certainty and presupposition are the same thing? In a limited but important sense, this appears to

---

[5]We have excluded all volitional utterances preceded by verbal context. The reason for this is that expressing the Object of Volition in response to question would involve repetition of the last word (e.g., *Do you want a banana? Banana*) and the effect of imitation might confound this analysis.

Table 41
Frequency of Expression of Volition versus Object in Positive and Negative Situations

	Positive Volition	Negative Volition
Nicky		
Volition expressed	28	10
Object expressed	44	0
Matthew		
Volition expressed	9	3
Object expressed	56	1

be the case. Specifically, we would like to argue for certainty–uncertainty as the perceptual–cognitive basis for the distinction between *presupposition* and *assertion* in language. But first it is necessary to define presupposition and assertion. The presuppositions of a sentence are "those conditions that the world must meet in order for the sentence to make literal sense" (Keenan, 1971, p. 45). Keenan distinguishes two kinds of presupposition, pragmatic and logical.

Pragmatic presupposition is the appropriate context for uttering a sentence. Presumably, then the *pragmatic assertion* would be the sentence itself. Although the presuppositions are not stated, a sentence makes no sense if they do not hold. For instance, using the familiar second person pronoun (*tu*) in a French sentence presupposes that you are addressing an intimate or an inferior (Keenan, 1971). Pragmatic presuppositions are assumed rather than stated. This parallels the situation in single-word utterances: What, from the child's point of view, can be assumed is not stated; what cannot be taken for granted is given verbal expression. And it is the relatively certain element that is assumed, the relatively uncertain one that is stated: The former is the psychological basis for presupposition, the latter for assertion.

Logical presupposition is closely related to pragmatic presupposition, but involves a relation between sentences rather than between a sentence and its nonverbal context. One sentence presupposes another just in case the truth of the second sentence is a necessary condition for the truth or falsity of the first. The major psychological relation between the two concepts of presupposition is that a pragmatic presupposition is represented nonverbally, whereas a logical presupposition is a linguistic form. The psychological basis for logical presupposition will be taken up later. At the moment, we shall be concerned only with the psychological origins of pragmatic presupposition.

As in the case of pragmatic presupposition in adult language, the child's utterance would make no sense, would be vacuous, were it not for the existence of this assumed or certain element. Rejection is meaningless unless there is something to reject. Hence, to reject something by *no* would be senseless were there no rejectable Object evident in a situation. Thus, the evident or "certain" element is the perceptual—cognitive basis of the pragmatic presupposition. Indeed, we see it as the psychological basis for the later operation of presupposition in mature language.[6]

Note the assymmetry in Table 41. Although either Volition or its Object may be expressed in a positive situation, the Object of Volition is almost never expressed in a negative situation. This assymmetry corresponds to Givón's (1975) linguistic finding that negative sentences are more presuppositionally marked than positive sentences. That is, negative sentences contain more *old*, less *new* information. One line of Givón's evidence concerns Objects: "while speakers may use affirmative sentences to introduce new objects into discourse for the first time, in negative sentences only objects which have already been *previously* mentioned in discourse may appear" (p. 3). Translating this notion into situational terms, we can say that the Object in a negative situation would have to be a given; in a positive situation, in contrast, it may or may not be. From this analysis, we would expect that the negative Object would never be expressed in one-word utterances, although the positive Object might or might not be. Applying this notion to Volitional expressions, we see, in Table 41, that the data conform to these expectations: Negative Objects are almost nonexistent, whereas positive Objects are often, but not always, used. Thus, discourse relations involving presupposition are prefigured by the relation of word to situational structure during the period of single-word utterances.

In the application of presupposition to single-word utterances, the difficult task is defining why, from a psychological point of view, certain elements, but not others, come to be presupposed. In defining presupposition in terms of relative certainty or uninformativeness, we make a step towards such definition. We must, of course, go further in specifying what will be perceived as relatively certain in a given situation, what will be perceived as relatively uncertain or informative. Thus far we have done so for two types of situation, one in which the child communicates a relation between an Agent and his Action or State, one in which the child communicates a relation between Volition and Object. For each type of situation we have been able to specify the circumstances in which one element would be seen as the more informative one (e.g., Action) and the circumstances in which the other (e.g., Agent) would be so perceived.

---

[6]According to Bates (1974) Antinucci and Volterra (1973) have done a presuppositional analysis of early negatives. Their paper has not been translated from Italian, but it appears, from Bates's description, that they would view the presuppositions of negative Volitional utterances much as we do. They apparently find that expressions of negative Volition in single-word form have much the same sorts of pragmatic presuppositions as we have found.

ACTION—STATE AND OBJECT

Now let us pursue this problem further by looking at the relation between Action or State and its Object at a point in development where both semantic functions are available to the child. In fact, a number of rules predict *which* element of a situation involving Object and Action—State will be expressed *when*:

1. When the Object is securely in the child's possession while it is undergoing its process or State change, it becomes relatively certain and the child will first encode Action—State.

2. In such a situation, the only exception occurs when an adult question changes focus to the Object by presupposing its Action or State. Then the child will express Object rather than its Action—State.

3. When the Object is *not* in the child's possession, it becomes more uncertain and his first utterance will express the Object.[7]

4. Once the most uncertain or informative element in the situation has been encoded, be it Object or Action—State, it becomes more certain and less informative. At this point then, if the child continues to encode the situation verbally, he will switch to expressing verbally the other aspect, heretofore unstated.

We used our data to test the validity of these rules for defining informativeness in the Action—Object situation. In order to have sufficient appropriate material to do so, we needed to have both Object and Action or State of Object reach a certain frequency. A total frequency of Action or State and Object categories 20 or above was the criterion for this characteristic. Because we wanted to examine the *order* in which the two functions would be expressed (Rule 4), we needed to have a certain frequency of sequences in the corpus. Our criterion for this characteristic was the occurrence of at least 15% of all utterances in nonrepetitive sequences. We then took the first two sessions for each boy in which these criteria were met. These turned out to be Nicky II—18(27) and III—19(29) and Matthew VI—18(18) and VII—19(21) (see Tables 5, 10, and 11). We needed to make sure that both Action—State and Object were available, in terms of vocabulary, to encode a particular situation, so that our results would not be biased by the lack of available vocabulary. We also wanted to ensure that both Action—State and Object were alternative semantic functions in a particular situation, and so we excluded static situations from our analysis; in other words, we focus on situations in which an Object is involved

---

[7]The notion that distance from the child would be a key factor in defining relative informativeness of the Object to its Action or State comes from Veneziano (1973).

Table 42
Object and Action–State Discourse at Nicky II—18(27)

Preceding context		Modality	Event	
	N	listening to	record *acacor* (from "Jimmy Crack Corn")	on
				ong (on)
Record off.	N	points to whining	record *acacoo, acacoo*	
				ong (on)
Record has just gone off. *You want another record or you want the same record?*	N	pointing to whining, repeats whining	record *recor(d)*	*ong* (on)
	N	points to	record *recor(d)*	is playing
Record player is off.	N	goes over to repeats	record player *cacord*	
N standing near record player, which is off.		whining	*cacoo* (record)	*on*
			cacoo	*on*
No record playing	N	goes over and points to repeats	record player *acacor*	*on*
Do you want it on?	N	repeats	*acacord*	
	N	hears	record *acacor*	go on

Note: Solid horizontal lines indicate intervening child speech.

in some sort of process or change of State. In each case, we analyzed that Action–Object combination that occurred most frequently in a given session. Thus, we in no way selected for examples that would be favorable to our hypothesis, nor did we in any way exclude examples that might disconfirm it.

Nicky

From Nicky II, the Action/State—Object combination that best met our criteria involved uses of *record* and *on*. The scenes involving these situations are presented in Table 42.

A pattern of semantic choice emerges from these scenes in which Nicky always first establishes the identity of the record. In some cases, the Action—State is a given, as when the record is playing (beginning and end of Table 42). Note that *ong*(on) either follows the establishment of the identity of the Object involved or is omitted altogether (middle and end of table). In other cases, the Action—State is not given; that is, no record is playing, but the record Object is always somewhat uncertain because it is never in Nicky's physical possession; in fact, Nicky is not permitted to handle records. Hence, Nicky always begins by establishing the identity of the Object. This analysis will become more convincing when we see that Matthew first encodes the Object unless he has the Object in his possession and is causing it to undergo some process or State change; at this point, he invariably switches to expressing its Action—State first.

The same principles apply to the scenes we have analyzed from Nicky III (Table 43). These involve *nut* expressing the Object and *gone* and *drop* expressing *Action—State*. Nicky first responds to the question *What's that?* with *nut*. His mother confirms that it is indeed a nut, and so the identity of the Object has been established when Nicky next announces *gone*. At the outset of the next

Table 43
Object and Action—State Discourse at Nicky III—19(29)

Preceding context	Modality		Event		
What's that, Nick?			N	playing with	nuts
					nut
Nut, that's right.			N	puts	nuts into cup
					gone
			N	picks up	nut
					nut
	hurray				
	N	looks at	nut	has dropped	
				drop	
			N	picks up	nut
					nut

Note: Solid horizontal lines indicate intervening child speech. Broken horizontal lines indicate intervening adult speech, but no intervening child speech.

scene, the Object is not certain because Nicky is in the process of picking the nuts up. Once he has established *nut* as the Object in question, he responds to the fallen nut by expressing its Action—State: *drop*. Note that there is a general tendency in both these scenes for Objects to be expressed before (and more often than) their Actions or States. This tendency merely reflects the fact that an Action or State presupposes an entity. If this entity is uncertain, it must be specified before its Action or State can be expressed meaningfully. Hence, under most circumstances, Objects are expressed more than their Actions or States.

Matthew

At Matthew VI, the semantic relation that best met the requirement of category availability was that expressed by the relations involving *car* and *byebye* or *down*. We looked at the use of these words in action situations to see whether his choice of Object (*car*) rather than one of the Action or State words (*byebye*, *down*) reflected informational properties of the situation. The relevant scenes involving Action or State of a car, are presented in Table 44. At the beginning of the first scene, Matthew names an absent Object. Its Action—State is known from the noise; uncertainty lies in the identity of the invisible Object. Hence, in choosing *car* rather than *byebye*, Matthew is encoding the most informative aspect of the situation. Once, however, the identity of the car is established by his utterance and his mother's questions (*What's the car doing? Where's it going?*), Action—State becomes less certain relative to Object, and Matthew responds *byebye*. In fact, dialogue turns pragmatic presupposition into a primitive form of logical presupposition, for the questions actually represent linguistically two possible presuppositions of Matthew's assertion *byebye*: *The car is doing; the car is going*. The relation of dialogue to the origins of logical presupposition will be discussed in more theoretical depth in the discussion section that follows. Next, Matthew wants his own car. He is at a distance from it, so his possession is relatively uncertain and he encodes the Object. Next, his car is not only in his possession, but its identity has been established by the preceding utterance. Uncertainty shifts to its Action—State, which he encodes with *byebye*. (The motor noise *hmm* and the word for honking *beepbeep* have been excluded because they seem to function more as "pure" Performatives than as Actions or States.) Following this, he hears an invisible car pass by outside, so he goes back to *car* rather than *byebye*.

In the next scene, his own car has fallen down and thereby become less certain for him, so he encodes the Object first rather than its Action—State. The concept that an assertion encodes new information while a presupposition contains old is the basis for some adult psycholinguistic experiments by Haviland and Clark (1974). Applying this notion to this example, we would be led to the prediction

Table 44
Object and Action–State Discourse at Matthew VI—18(18)

Preceding context	Speaker action		Object action	
	M	hears	car	going by outside
			car	
What's the car doing?				
Where's it going?	M			*byebye; byebye*
	M	pointing to	his car	
		whining	*car, car*	
You want your car?	M	about to push	his car	*byebye*
	M	pushing	his car	*byebye*
				hmm (car sound)
	M	patting	his car	*beepbeep*
	M	hears	car	going by outside
			car! car!	
	M	hears	car	going by outside
			car	
	M	looking for	car	has fallen down
		whining	*car*	
Whatcha doing?	M	throwing	his car	down
				down, down
	M	has thrown	car	down
			car	
	M	hears	car	going by outside
			car	
	M	looking for	his car	

Note: Solid horizontal lines indicate intervening child speech. Broken horizontal lines indicate no intervening child speech, but intervening adult speech. For clarity of presentation, speech event has been divided into Speaker action vs Object action instead of the usual Modality and Event.

that Matthew would have first encoded the "new" change of State, rather than the "old" Object (car). However, this prediction is incorrect; Matthew said *car* first, not *byebye*. This example shows that "informative" and "new" are not equivalent for Matthew. Although "car" is "old", it is uncertain because it is out of his grasp. Thus, for nonverbal context, no simple equation of informativeness with new information is possible—even though the perception of information functions as the psychological basis for the given-new contrast. Other attributes of the ongoing situation must also be taken into account.

Let us now continue our analysis with the next scene. Here Matthew has his car in hand and is throwing it down; Object has become relatively *more* certain, Action—State relatively *less*, and Matthew says *down*, as we would predict. (Although this utterance is preceded by a question, the particular question— *Whatcha doing?*—does not presuppositionally bias Matthew's response toward encoding either the Object or its Action or State.) Note that this scene is the only one that begins with the expression of Action— State rather than Object and, correlatively, is the only one so far that begins with the Object in hand. It thus confirms the importance of physical possession as a psychological criterion of certainty from the child's point of view. Once the car has been thrown down and its Action—State expressed, Object certainty decreases, and Matthew expresses the Object—*car*. In the next scene, Matthew again names an absent *car* which he hears going by outside. Finally, Matthew names the Object for which he is searching. Thus, Matthew's choice of Object or Action—State word accurately reflects the continually shifting balance between information and certainty.

At Matthew VII, the semantic relation that best met our criteria was the Object—Action/State relation expressed by *skates* plus *on*. The scenes we shall analyze are presented in Table 45. In these scenes, Matthew is having difficulty getting his skates on and off. Therefore, trying to look at the situation from Matthew's point of view, we conclude that Action—State is more in question, is less taken for granted, under present circumstances than is the Object. Hence, we would expect more frequent expression of Action—State than Object, which is exactly what we find. In fact, Action—State is expressed six times, Object only three. Let us compare these scenes from Matthew VII (Table 45) with those from Matthew VI (Table 44). In the latter, the Object was often out of hand, and, correlatively, was expressed relatively more often than in the former.

In the first scene presented in Table 45, Object is expressed when it is not yet in Matthew's possession, hence, relatively uncertain from his point of view. Next time the Object—(*s*)*ka*(*tes*)—is uttered, it is after *on*; in other words, Action—State has become a known because of Matthew's previous utterance. In the second scene, *skates* occurs at the one point that the skates are not in Matthew's hands. Here, the Object has become relatively less certain, and this uncertainty is resolved with *skates*. In the final scene, skates are all too much connected to Matthew, and he restricts himself to encoding Action—State— again in accord with the prediction from an informational analysis.

DISCUSSION

The preceding analysis of dynamic situations involving Objects and their Actions or States confirms the value of uncertainty or informativeness in

Table 45
Object and Action–State Discourse at Matthew VII—19(21)

Preceding context	Speaker action		Object action		
	M	goes over to and picks up	skates (s)ka(tes)		
	M	trying to put whining, repeats	skates (s)ka(tes)	on on	
	M	trying to put whining, repeats	skates	on on	
	M	has put down trying to put whining	skates skates (s)ka(tes)	on	
They go outside.					
Do you want to put your skates on?				yeah	
	M	holding onto skates whining		on, on	
a skate?	M	whining		on yeah	
	Mother	putting on skates			ashoe
	M	whining		on	
	M	whining			ashoe, ashoe
	M	tugging	skates	off on[a]	

Note: Solid horizontal lines indicate intervening child speech. Broken horizontal lines indicate no intervening child speech, but intervening adult speech. For clarity of presentation, speech event has been divided into Speaker action vs Object action instead of the usual Modality and Event.

[a] Another example of using one pole of a dimension to encode what, in adult speech, would be its polar opposite.

predicting the child's semantic choice. The fact that our operational definition of uncertainty in the Object–Action relation is so consistent with the data leads us to conclude that we may have described successfully the informational aspects of the situation, as they look from the child's point of view.

Thus far, we have talked about one-word messages in terms of the role of individual words in the structure of an event. Olson (1970), however, says that this is not enough. He defines a message as any utterance that specifies the event relative to the set of alternatives. He goes on to say that "a word or an utterance, since it not only specifies the perceived referent but also the set of excluded alternatives, contains more information than the simple perception of the event itself" (1970, p. 265). Although he was talking about much more mature linguistic competence, it seems very likely from our results that the child's word tells us something about the alternatives he is excluding. Olson (1970) goes on to say of one-word utterances in adult speech: "A single word is then an utterance in which all the other sentence constituents are assumed or agreed upon and hence have been replaced by pronouns or simply deleted" (p. 269). If we omit the proviso about replacement or deletion, and recognize that the child at this stage assumes constituents rather than agreeing upon them with others, this description fits the one-word speech of a presyntactic child perfectly! Perhaps, too, we should wonder if it is really necessary to posit a deletion process for adults. Thus, the 1-year-old child is as sensitive to the informative properties of the world as adults. He is, however, limited to expressing the single most informative element. He may also be egocentric in taking more elements of his own perspective for granted, but there is, in our data, no way of knowing this for sure.

A consideration of ellipsis in adult discourse demonstrates two important points of continuity: (*1*) between psycholinguistic functioning in infancy and adulthood and (*2*) between the role of verbal context and nonverbal situational structure. Consider the following example of adult dialogue from Holzman's (1971) article, "Ellipsis in Discourse" (p. 89):

QUESTION	ANSWER
When are you going?	*tonight*

Clearly, the single-word utterance is perfectly natural in adult conversation. In fact, it is appropriate in this example precisely because it supplies all the information the questioner was seeking and no more. This rule, put forth by R. Lakoff (1973), is based on Grice's (1968) notion of conversational implicature. The response presupposes the proposition "You are going sometime" contained in the question; this functions as "old" information. Only the "new" information is expressed in the answer.

In this analysis, we are now talking about logical presupposition, that which is entailed by both an assertion and its opposite. Here, the assertion is the answer *tonight*. The assertion and any conceivable "opposite" (e.g., *tomorrow*) would entail the proposition "I am going sometime," which is, therefore, presupposed. We have modified the notion of linguistic presupposition to have a discourse meaning. What was assumed or "given" in the situation in our earlier analysis is now encoded linguistically and "given" in the question.[8]

Adult–child dialogue at the stage of single-word utterances involves exactly the same process as that described for the adult–adult example just given. Compare this example from Nicky I—18(4):

QUESTION	ANSWER
What do you want?	*showel* (shovel)

Again, the answer supplies all the information the questioner was seeking ("new" information) and no more. What is presupposed from the question— "I want something"—is not expressed in the answer. Hence, single-word answers to questions follow the same principle as spontaneous single-word utterances: express the most informative element. The only difference is that, in dialogue, the presupposition is given in the verbal context whereas, in spontaneous utterances, it is given in the nonverbal context. When the child relates his single-word utterance to verbal context through dialogue, the distinction between "new" and "old" information does correspond to the distinction between more and less informative elements. In dialogue, the adult verbalization provides the "old" information which is presupposed by the child's reply. Adult comment or question thus takes the role of what the child had perceived as "given" or noninformative in the nonverbal situation. Gunter (1963) has proposed that such elliptical responses can be expanded into complete sentences by a series of syntactic transformations of the question. Because the transformations combine question and answer to derive the expanded answer (*I am going tonight* in the above example), Gunter's rules imply the linguistic reality in adult speech of the two-person sentence. Holzman (1971) points out that *nonverbal* context must be used to comprehend certain types of elliptical sentences in adult speech, what Gunter (1963) called "telegraphic ellipsis." As an example (p. 91):

Pretty dress	*Thank you*

Holzman states that understanding of (and therefore response to) the first remark depends only on following the speaker's gaze to a dress. The gaze identified who was wearing what dress; hence, any Indicative gesture—looking—forms an intrinsic part of the message, as in early single-word utterances. Here, perception of a person wearing a particular dress is pragmatically presupposed by the assertion *pretty dress*. Therefore, the same process of information analysis described for earliest child language operates in adult language. Osgood (1971) has suggested that in general (i.e., in mature language) the presup-

---

[8]In his paper "Toward a discourse definition of syntax," Givón (1974) discusses extensively the interactive nature of presupposition in dialogue.

positions required for a sentence are not, as linguists claim, other sentences, deleted from actual production, but rather perceived features of the referential situation. The difference between the child and the adult is that the child is capable of adding linguistic elements when they cannot be transmitted by context, whereas the child is not. Holzman concludes:

> Since telegraphic ellipsis is a feature of adult conversation, it cannot be looked upon as something which occurs at an early stage of the child's development of language and drops out later as his knowledge of syntax increases. He is acquiring the ability to produce sentences which conform to adult grammatical patterns and also the ability to combine linguistic and nonlinguistic information in his communication [p. 95].

Comparing sequences to two-word utterances proper, we see that the former lack the fixed word order of English syntax. In sequences of single words, focusing in turn on different semantic features of the situation, each word is related to its corresponding situational feature rather than to other words. This is essentially the suggestion made by Werner and Kaplan (1963). Our analysis of scenes involving the encoding of Objects and their Actions or States indicates that word order in sequences of single-word utterances in fact reflects the shifting pattern of uncertainty in the ongoing event, as seen from the child's point of view. If so, then the addition of English syntax means that the child has learned that a fixed word order rule must override the informational structure of the situation as a determinant of word order. It is interesting that this occurs at about the same time that Bower (1974) reports that cognitive rules override the structure of perceptual information in the development of the object concept.

According to a study by Hornby (1971), it is not until much later in development (around age 8) that children are able to use word order as a device to signal the distinction between presupposition (what he calls "topic") and assertion (what he calls "comment"). Since the youngest children in his study (age 4) showed an ability to make this distinction, albeit without word order, Hornby's results tend to reinforce our own (although it would be nice if he had also included younger children).

Later developments shows the same precedence of more informative elements and the tendency of uniformative elements not to be encoded. Both of the types of subjects which McNeill (1970a) and others (Bloom, 1970; Bowerman, 1973; Brown, 1973) frequently found missing in later speech, ego-subjects and subjects of intrinsic predicates, carry little information. Similarly, of the two English bound-morphemes *s*, the singular marker on the verb carries less information than plural markers on nouns and follows it in order of appearance (Jakobson, 1969). The failure to express uninformative or obvious elements also accounts for the otherwise unexplained condition on Bloom's (1970) reduction transformation, which deletes most frequently those elements that have appeared most recently. Thus, sensitivity to information content is a point of structural continuity between the one-word stage and later grammatical speech.

This view of one-word speech is borne out by the natural way in which it can explain one aspect of the subsequent development of two-word sentences as the appearance of elements previously taken for granted. If the young child expresses the more informative elements in his own speech, he also may show special sensitivity to such elements in speech comprehension. If so, then this notion may help explain why strict syntactic expansions may not be effective at the early stages: They tell the child nothing more than what he already assumes to be the case.

chapter 5

Different Views of Child Language

5.1 A Theoretical Postscript: Chafe[1]

A t the moment, no single linguistic theory seems adequate to describe all the psychological facts presented in Chapters 3 and 4. As the reader will have noticed, we departed from or modified Fillmore's (1968) framework in presenting certain aspects of our data and in formulating a psychological theory of early language development. In a number of such instances, Chafe's system, described in *Meaning and the Structure of Language* (1970), successfully analyzes phenomena that lie outside the scope of Fillmore's theory.

Before discussing differences between Fillmore and Chafe, we must point out the important similarities between their linguistic theories. Chafe's system resembles Fillmore's in that it views language as having not only a semantic base structure but also a concrete one. That is, Chafe, like Fillmore, differs from other generative semanticists in rejecting the notion of an abstract base structure, one which consists of contentless logical forms. In many respects, the two systems are similar, as in the notions of Agent, Instrument, and Location. In certain respects, Fillmore has advantages for psychological description of early

---

[1] We are grateful to Breyne Moskowitz for suggesting a specific comparison between Fillmore and Chafe and for outlining the areas in which Chafe's formulation would have advantages in terms of psychological description.

acquisition, for example, the division of the sentence into Modality and Proposition (although these needed to be translated from a linguistic to a cognitive level). The purpose of the present section is, however, to outline other respects in which Chafe's theory has advantages. Although it is a matter of debate among linguists as to whether a linguistic theory should have psychological validity, this section should, nevertheless, help complete the picture of relative strengths and weaknesses of different linguistic theories for psychological description, specifically of early language acquisition.

Chafe's treatment of verbs differs from that of Fillmore. Fillmore categorizes verbs according to the cases they may take, both obligatory and optional. Chafe says that this is not sufficient to specify types of verbs and classifies verbs according to the nature of the action or state to which they refer. This classification determines, in turn, the arguments (Fillmore's cases) a verb may take. We began with Fillmore's method, classifying Actions or States according to whether they were associated with Agents or Objects (as perceived in the situation rather than as linguistically expressed). We saw, however, that development was occurring *within* each of these categories. Hence, the relation of an action or state to an entity was insufficient to describe development of single-word expression of actions and states, just as Chafe claimed it was insufficient to describe verb structure of complete adult sentences. Although Chafe's typology of verbs does not quite fit the stages we observed, his concepts of state, process, and action are closely related. Most striking is his analysis of what we have called transitive action words (like *eat*). He terms such verbs action–processes, a compound of agent action and patient (object) process, with the emphasis on the agent.[2] Because of their intrinsically compound nature, they are more complex than other types of (underived) verbs and should, in consequence, be the last to develop; this expectation corresponds exactly to our results (Sections 3.8 and 3.10). Here, Chafe's theory leads to a valid empirical prediction which could not be derived from Fillmore.

A minor point is Chafe's definition of Location in comparison with Fillmore's definition of Locative. Edwards (1974) points out that, whereas Fillmore defines Locative as the location of the state or action, Chafe defines Location as the spatial position or orientation of the object. It will be remembered from Chapter

---

[2]Edwards (1974) points out that Chafe's classification of certain verbs in this category is problematical; for instance, the transitive use of *break*. We agree with Edwards that verbs like these "actually describe only the process undergone by the Object, with the Agent's activity not described at all" and we have not included such words in our own category of transitive action (cf. Sections 3.8 and 3.10). This problem in Chafe's treatment does not, however, invalidate the basic concept of the compound action–process, exemplified both in the use of certain verbs in single-word utterances and in Chafe's linguistic theory.

Fillmore later (1971) treated verbs in more detail, but his treatment is less systematic than Chafe's and the particular features he analyzed have little applicability to our data.

2 that we found it necessary to adopt a definition like Chafe's in order to distinguish Location clearly from Object and State on a behavioral level. In this sense, then, Chafe's concept of Location seems to have greater utility for the stage of single-word utterances.

Another advantage of Chafe over Fillmore for describing early language development is that his framework opens up the possibility of developing a theory that will integrate the child's knowledge of referential meaning (e.g., E. V. Clark, 1973; Greenfield, 1973) with his knowledge of structural or combinatorial meaning. This is because Chafe has related the semantic features of a word (referential meaning) to its semantic—grammatical role (combinatorial meaning). Although the two types of meaning ought not to be confused, they are obviously interrelated in the acquisition process. Chafe's theory gives definite indications for the systematic investigation of these interrelations present from the very beginnings of language development.

Most important, however, is Chafe's treatment of old and new information, which he ties to semantic structure. Whether a given semantic role in a sentence conveys old or new information affects its place in surface structure. For example, a patient (object) which conveys old information may be represented as a sentence subject rather than the usual object. This process is analogous to the role of uncertainty in determining which element in an event will be realized in the linguistic surface structure. Chafe includes selection from alternatives in his description of new information. Such alternatives are one form of uncertainty that we have described on a cognitive level at a remarkably early point in language development. Although Chafe's concept of new information has required expansion and specification in terms of the child's perception of a referent event, he makes an important connection between semantic structure and information structure. This connection gives linguistic justification to our view that the development from one- to two-word utterances can be seen as the addition of a second, less informative element to a single-word utterance.

At this point, it should be noted that Chafe's theory requires the same important modification for psychological description as did Fillmore's. Although Chafe explicitly states that base structures are conceptual in nature, he diagrams them as consisting of words rather than concepts. The base structure in our theoretical scheme is, in contrast, a purely cognitive or conceptual one, gradually filled in with words at the surface level of expression.

To complete our discussion of Fillmore and Chafe, there are subtle differences in their definition of specific cases where the psychological validation of one or the other conceptualization is a matter of future empirical test. Edwards' (1974) comparison brings forth such differences: Should Instrument be limited to things used by an Agent? If so, then inanimate things that appear to move on their own, automobiles, for example, can serve as Agents. This is allowed in Chafe's but not Fillmore's scheme. The fact that Chafe and Fillmore disagree in their classification of such inanimate forces mirrors the fact that they constitute a classification problem for our data analysis. It seems to us, though, that the problem needs to be solved psychologically, as well as linguistically: Do infants and adults perceive such things as cars and wind primarily as forces (Agent), primarily as inanimate (Instrument) or as both? Very likely there is developmental change in this perception.

5.2 Contemporary Work on Single-Word Utterances

Five studies of single-word utterances were undertaken simultaneously with ours. In this section, we shall attempt to point out their distinguishing qualities and characterize their findings. Ingram (1971), Antinucci and Parisi (1973), and Halliday (1973, 1974, in press) represent a swing in the opposite direction from the previous reluctance to interpret one-word speech. Nelson (1973) and Bloom (1973) represent more conservative approaches. We shall discuss other theoretical treatments of the subject, particularly as they relate to our own findings and theoretical view.

INGRAM

Ingram (1971) has applied a version of Fillmore's case grammar to some of the one-word utterances in Leopold's (1949) study and earlier sources. His treatment is necessarily limited by the quality of his data, but clearly demonstrates that semantic analysis of one-word speech is possible.

Like us, Ingram recognizes that single words can convey different meanings, and analyzes some of the development of those meanings in terms of his model. His analysis agrees with ours in regarding intonation and gestures like pointing and reaching as expressions of modality in single-word utterances. He also recognizes that, for instance, *ball* and *red* can encode different aspects of the same situation, and are thus not undifferentiated global messages. However, he differs from us in considering that the child's earliest utterances are global in character. For instance, he claims that, before the appearance of state words such as *red*, a child's use of names refers both to the object and the state.

Much of Ingram's treatment is a psychological account of semantic features, rather than cases. This is somewhat confusing, since features had no formal status within Fillmore's (1968) definition of case relationships. It is also unfortunate in that there is a very definite limit on the number of cases, but none whatsoever on the number of features, which proliferate in Ingram's treatment. Some conceptual dimensions such as animate—inanimate and ego—other, undoubtedly deserve to have systemic status. However, Ingram is led to deal with these concepts as features in the same way as he deals with the dimension large—

small. As a result of his orientation toward features, Ingram discusses the development of the Agent role in terms of the feature animate. However, his treatment is hurt by his failure to differentiate between the use of the name of an animate being in an Indication and in the Agent role. In essence, he assumes that animacy is a sufficient condition to demonstrate agency and so he does not demonstrate that his examples of Agents are distinguishable from other non-agentive uses of the same name.

One interesting aspect of Ingram's discussion of agency is his claim that agency is first perceived in beings that move themselves. He proposes that agency is only later recognized in beings that act upon external objects. This notion is confirmed by our data in which Nicky and Matthew's first Agents encode the instigators of self-made noise.

In general, Ingram fails to make any distinction between an underlying cognitive structure and its expression in linguistic form. Although there is undoubtedly a close relationship between the two, it is necessary to specify the relationship, rather than to assume an identity. Some examples of Ingram's failure to differentiate are his discussion of differentiated cries in the first 6 months in sentential terms, and his postulation of the categories noun and verb in semantic structures.

Ingram's treatment is ultimately limited by the paucity of his data. Because he is dealing with isolated utterances rather than complete corpora, he is able to show that a given interpretation is possible, but not that the distinction it reflects are structural within a child's speech at a given time. Although he is explicitly working within a Fillmore-type framework, the only cases he discusses are Agent and Object.

ANTINUCCI AND PARISI

Antinucci and Parisi (1973) discuss one-word utterances briefly in relation to later sentences within the framework of the generative—semantic version of transformational grammar. Their data is taken from observations of one child, Claudia, acquiring Italian between 15 and 19 months of age. Their treatment covers a later period of growth than does Ingram's, but shows many of the same weaknesses of excessive formalism and insufficient justification.

Antinucci and Parisi show how the meanings of one-word sentences can be represented and explicitly state that later sentences differ form earlier ones primarily in the amount of the underlying structure that is verbally encoded (lexicalized in their terms). Although they state that "the choice of which element(s) to lexicalize is considered arbitrary at this point" (p. 612), they leave open the possibility of discovery of criteria.

Antinucci and Parisi describe three methods for ascertaining the child's underlying semantic representation:

1. extralinguistic context;
2. verbal response to adult questions and requests;
3. combination of a given lexical item with other items.

But only the first type of evidence is present at the earliest period of single-word utterances, and only the first two types are present so long as the child is limited to uttering one word at a time. Hence, their combination of methods is not applicable to the period of single-word utterances. In fact, Antinucci and Parisi analyze single-word utterances from a time period in which longer (two- and three-word) utterances containing the same word are produced. They do not attempt to analyze single-word utterances before these words have entered into syntactic combinations.[3] Despite its value in showing the continuity between earlier and later speech, we have two interrelated objections to Antinucci and Parisi's approach. The first is the now familiar criticism that they do not attempt to demonstrate the psychological validity of the particular structures they propose. The second is that they do not attempt to show that their analysis reveals more about child language than alternate possible analyses. The devices they borrow from generative semantics are abstract and extremely powerful, and could be used to describe an enormous range of sentences that do not occur. For example, Claudia says *da* (give), giving something to her mother. According to Antinucci and Parisi, this utterance has the following underlying semantic configuration (p. 610):

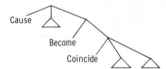

However, this structure tells us nothing about child language; it merely tells us what Antinucci and Parisi think the semantic structure of the verb *give* is. In particular, it does not explain why Claudia does not say, for example, *remind*

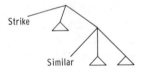

---

[3]Nevertheless, it is clear from Parisi's (1974) discussion of an earlier draft (1972) of this book that they have no principled objection to using the method of situational context either alone or in connection with the second method to deal with the earlier period of development.

which is, after all, formally simpler (cf. Postal, 1971). The fact that their semantic markers are formally content-free and highly embedded makes it extremely difficult for them to predict or explain which sentences a child will and will not use.[4] Antinucci and Parisi translate cognitive structure into logical structure without any evidence to suggest that the child possesses such a powerfully abstract tool.

The authors' justification for the above structure of Claudia's *da* (give) goes as follows: "When she says *da*, it is difficult to suppose that she does not know who must give, what must be given, and who must receive (p. 611). However, they say nothing about what justifies the translation from this kind of knowledge on Claudia's part to the formal structure that they posit. Indeed, it is precisely such knowledge of the referential situation that is represented in the more concrete type of semantic models, such as Fillmore's (1968). In these models, structure is directly related to the speaker's perception of the referential event. Hence, it remains closer to the nature of the psychological data.

NELSON

Nelson (1972, 1973) followed the language development of a rather large (18) sample of children between 1 and 2 years of age. The major source of data was mothers' records of vocabulary. Her study is not directly comparable to ours, but has yielded some interesting results on the one-word period. We shall discuss some of her results and then offer some criticisms of her use of her data to reveal the role of semantic functions in early speech.

One of the interesting results of Nelson's study was the identification of two different strategies for learning a language, referential and expressive. The strategy that she labels "referential" involves learning about things. Referential children use relatively more object words and build up a larger vocabulary before they start to combine words. Expressive children, on the other hand, learn more about themselves and other people than about objects. They acquire a more diverse vocabulary with more nonobject words, and start to make two-word sentences at an earlier point in their vocabulary development. According to her results, at the 50-word point, referentials had uttered from 0 to 5 two-

---

[4]A related criticism is that Antinucci and Parisi's semantic structures have unwarranted complexity. Schlesinger (1973) has put forth this criticism and Parisi (1974) has replied to it. To us the problem seems to be that whereas Parisi, in his reply to Schlesinger, defines semantic structure as "a cognitive structure which is constructed with the intention to communicate it . . . a subclass of cognitive structures," the child's semantic structure in their original article was full of specifically linguistic elements, like noun phrases (p. 612). Our way of representing structure avoids the pitfall of Antinucci and Parisi's original formulation by attributing minimal linguistic structure to the child necessary to account for the utterance while, at the same time, relating the linguistic function to a larger behavioral or cognitive structure derived from the total context of the utterance.

word utterances, expressives from 6 to 18. First-born children tend to be referentials, while later-born children tend to be expressives.

On the basis of these definitions it is possible to show that Nicky represents the referential type and Matthew the expressive. Table 46 shows the results of dividing up the nonrepetitive uses of semantic functions in our data according to whether they represent entities (objects) or relations (nonobjects). It can be seen that for Nicky the encoding of objects predominates (63.25% on the average) whereas for Matthew object encoding does not occupy the dominant place (47.33% on the average). In addition, we found that, at the 50-word point, Nicky had made 1 two-word utterance, Matthew 6. Thus, the data for the two boys bears out the classification we would expect on the basis of the fact that Nicky is a first-born and Matthew is not. The significance of this result is that it demonstrates that the developmental sequences we found to be common to the two boys do not result from similar language-learning strategies. The fact that they used demonstrably different strategies indicates that our results should have general validity across different classes of children. By putting together Nelson's findings with ours, we have new information in the early stages about how individual differences operate within the confines of more general processes of language acquisition.

Nelson obtained some crude figures that support our contention that mother–child dialogue is important for syntactic development. She found that the proportion of questions in the mother's speech to the child at 13 months was highly correlated to comprehension at 20 (although not 15) months of age. The proportion of questions at 24 months is significantly correlated to the mean length of utterance at 30 months. In contrast, proportion of maternal expansions showed no relation to any measure of syntactic complexity. Although these correlations leave much unexplained and do not relate to exactly the same time period as that covered by our study, they do corroborate our suggestion that verbal stimulation of child speech may be more important than verbal response to it at the early stages of language learning.

Nelson's other results are severely limited by her use of mother's vocabulary records as a source of data. These records do show that changeable states (e.g., *all gone, dirty, hot*) are more frequent in early usage than invariant attributes (e.g., *red, round, pretty*), and, correlatively, that the most common object words encode entities that change or can be changed by the child (e.g., *dog, cat, clock, ball*). However, the vocabulary records lead her to the tentative conclusion that a given word usually served only a single semantic function. Several factors probably influenced this conclusion. One is that mothers were asked to focus on the first use of a given word, not on changes in its usage. Another is that her classification system lumped together categories that ours distinguished. For example, our Indicative Objects and Objects of Action would both be included in her category Nominals. Thus, a word that was used in these

Table 46
Proportion of Nonrepetitive Uses of Object Words

Nicky

	Observation period and age							
	I	II	III	IV	V	VI	VII	VIII
	18(4)	18(27)	19(29)	20(23)	21(7)	22(21)	23(21)	24(23)
Total object words	19	53	59	55	54	81	70	29
Total	45	72	81	77	99	135	110	44
Percentage	42	74	73	72	55	60	64	66

Matthew

	Observation period and age								
	I	II	III	IV	V	VI	VII	VIII	IX
	12(15)	14(10)	15(5)	16(2)	17(13)	18(19)	19(21)	20(26)	22(1)
	12(22)	14(18)	15(12)						
Total object words	2	12	30	39	31	29	44	33	15
Total all words	10	18	53	65	63	79	84	73	38
Percentage	20	67	57	60	49	37	52	45	39

distinct functions would be considered to have a constant function in Nelson's scheme. For these reasons, her data do not seem sufficient to test the hypothesis of constant word function. She herself recognizes this point and calls for direct study of the question. We have carried out just such direct study, and our results clearly demonstrate that, contrary to the notion of constant word function, a given word often serves multiple semantic functions in the period of one-word speech.

Nelson's system has a number of weak points. One is that her categories are not illustrated with functional descriptions, but with vocabulary lists, so it is often hard to tell how appropriate her categorization is. For example, *outside* is classified as a locative modifier, whereas *out* is classified as a demand for action. However, it is quite possible to imagine both words being used in the same way. Another is that it is inconsistent. She states that if "a child said *door* when he wanted to go outside, this was classified as an action word" (p. 15). Yet on the next page under the definition of a nominal, it is stated that a nominal may be used in a relation involving an object. It seems that *door* used in this way could, according to Nelson's own definitions, equally well be considered an action word or a nominal (door as object of action) or even a locative modifier (door as a location of action). Because of these differences and problems, Nelson's study cannot be used to draw conclusions about the development of semantic functions.

HALLIDAY

Halliday's approach to early language development is made from within a framework quite different from our own. For this reason, we will not attempt to deal with all the possible issues that his treatment raises but will emphasize the point of agreement and disagreement between his approach and ours that seem most interesting. Our comments are based on his papers "Early Language Learning: A Sociolinguistic Approach" (1973), "Learning How to Mean" (in press), and "A Sociosemiotic Perspective on Language Development" (1974).

Halliday's analysis is based on a diary of the development of his son, Nigel. His approach is more functional and less structural than our own, although the difference is one of degree. Because of this orientation, Halliday accepts as language any consistent use of vocalizations, an attitude which leads him to begin his study at a much earlier stage than we have covered. Halliday's definition of language may also have influenced his data: The fact that Nigel's parents accepted (i.e., interpreted) his non-English vocalizations as language more than did Matthew's and Nicky's may account in part for why "made-up" words seem to have been so much more persistent and prevalent in Nigel's speech. Halliday's functional approach leads him to stress the continuity of the child's earliest speech with mature adult language. He also emphasizes the interdependence of vocalization and context in actual language use.

Halliday hypothesizes that, at first, each distinct form serves a single function. At around 15—16½ months, Nigel first combines two different intonation patterns with a single word to construct different messages. The final stage of development is achieved when a given utterance simultaneously fulfills an interpersonal and an ideational function. Halliday considers that grammar is required for this state. However, we would point out that the distinction between interpersonal and ideational functions is analogous to the distinction between modality and proposition in Fillmore's terms. We have already argued that single words incorporate analogues to these two aspects.

Halliday views both dialogue and sequences of single-word utterances as intermediate in the development of grammar. Like us, he notes that, at first, children can only respond to questions in which the answer serves a function already in his linguistic system. Halliday views the primary significance of dialogue as functional: It allows the child to master the purely communicative functions of language. In contrast, we consider that the communicative function of language has been mastered long before the onset of dialogue: The child has been using language from the beginning to direct the attention and action of others—in other words, to communicate. He has also responded in these ways to the linguistic communication of others from the emergence of the earliest words (Greenfield, 1973) and even before (Huttenlocher, 1974). In our view, the developmental achievement of dialogue is structural rather than functional: For the first time word is combined with word. In early question—answer dialogue, the child contributes but a single word, but his word is related semantically to the adult's question. Later he, in a sense, internalizes the role of the adult questioner, forming word combinations by himself. Dialogue is thus the two-person model for the child's earliest grammar. We also disagree with Halliday's statement that, in early dialogue, the child cannot reply to a question whose answer is unknown to the questioner. His examples are all equally compatible with the view that the answer must be present in the situation, and, therefore, obvious to the child, although not necessarily to the questioner. There is no evidence that the child just beginning to engage in dialogue knows what his listener does and does not already know.

It is unfortunate that Halliday does not describe any objective bases for distinguishing different types of utterances. As a linguist, he provides extremely detailed transcriptions of the sounds Nigel makes, but does not describe the overall contexts in which he uses them. His six functions (instrumental, regulatory, interactional, personal, heuristic, and imaginative) are never operationally defined. We do not know what situational features led to the classification of an utterance in one functional category rather than another. In general, his empirical method is inadequately described. Halliday does not see the necessity of explicitly relating the child's vocalizations to his nonlinguistic behavior or explaining their relationship to cognitive functions. In fact, he takes the untenable position that the child uses language to construct his conceptual framework. We, of course, see early language as based upon a pre-existing conceptual framework.

BLOOM

Of the studies discussed in this chapter, Bloom's (1973) study of one-word speech is probably the closest to our own in terms of range and type of data. She draws her data from a diary kept on the speech of her daughter Allison, supplemented by four 40-minute videotape recordings of Allison and audio recordings of three other children. Children's speech is regularly related to the context in which it is used. As was probably apparent from our discussion of interpretation in Chapter 2, Bloom's views on one-word speech are quite different from our own, and her conclusions differ accordingly. Although Bloom conceives of her study as focusing on the period of single word utterances, her emphasis was on the transitional period between one- and two-word speech. Thus, her videotaped corpora begin 2 months after Allison's first two-word sentences. Bloom has earlier diary data, but the diary is not described in very much detail, and relatively little data is presented from it. The supplementary audiotapes from three other children apparently represent only the tail end of single-word utterances. Hence, it is not surprising that Bloom's conclusions about developmental change within one-word speech are, in the main, limited to the later part of the one-word period.

Several of Bloom's findings about order of development support our own: The use of a person's name to indicate that person preceded use of that name to indicate possession, and the use of *no* to reject objects preceded its use to assert nonexistence. On the other hand, Allison used *again* relatively early (12 months) to announce or request the repetition of an event. This usage occurred before the function we have called Animate Being associated with an Object, and thus constitutes a discrepancy from the order we observed. However, this word was used only three times during this early stage, and then disappeared; it did not reappear until the end of the second year. Other comparisons of sequence cannot be made because too little early data is presented and because Bloom's data are classified differently from ours.

At one point, Bloom reaches a different conclusion from us about developmental sequence, one which appears to be falsified by her own data. She states that "Relational *function* forms occurred earlier, persisted, and were used more often [in the first half of the second year] than the *substantive* forms, which came to predominate in the last half of the second year" (p. 139). But Allison's first words were not function forms, but substantives—*Mama, Dada, Mimi,* and *Baby*—at 9 or 10 months (p. 97); these particular substantives were, moreover, persistent throughout the period under study. There are a greater number of different substantives than function words at the first video session (16 months), although function words are used more often. Thus, Bloom's data show that substantives carrying a labeling function constituted the first word usage to appear. This finding is, of course, in accord with our own results. Bloom's seeming self-contradiction on this point stems from the fact that the word "substantives," in the context of this quote, was intended to refer to class words alone, not to person names (Bloom, personal communication, 1975).

Bloom has an interesting analysis of developmental sequence in the use of successive single-word utterances which complements the information presented in Chapter 3. It should be pointed out, though, that her definition of successive single-word utterances was somewhat broader than our definition of sequence. Bloom's definition of successive single-word utterances included utterances on a single topic, even if the action context shifted (*chained* successive single-word utterances). Under our definition, such a shift would automatically end a sequence. Hence, our definition more closely resembles Bloom's *holistic* sequence, in which several aspects of a *single* situation are expressed in successive single-word utterances. Thus, our observation that sequences increased with development corresponds to Bloom's observation that holistic successive single-word utterances came to predominate over chained utterances in Allison's speech.

In her earlier book, *Language Development* (1970), Bloom had posited a topic—comment order for successive single-word utterances in which topic represented "given" and comment represented the "new" aspects of an event. In *One Word at a Time*, however, she concludes that the topic—comment account is inadequate because word order is variable: Sometimes the topic precedes the comment as in *juice; more*, but other times, comment precedes topic as in *more; juice*. Bloom claims that the order of successive single-word utterances was unpredictable. This conclusion is at odds with our analysis of Object—Action/State scenes in Chapter 4. There we pointed out that, whereas relative uncertainty is a concept that is psychologically basic to the concept of newness in discourse analysis, what appears new in the nonverbal situation may not correspond to the most uncertain element from the child's point of view. In Bloom's analysis, the object is always the topic; in ours, the object is often, but not always, the most uncertain element. Hence, although we agree that word order is variable, it is not unpredictable. Following the lead of Veneziano (1973), we have shown that in Action/State—Object scenes, the child will often encode the object first unless the object is already in hand. Another prediction from the uncertainty concept is that where the child is causing several objects to undergo the same action or change of state, the encoding of Object name rather than Action—State would remain likely after the first object. A related prediction would be that, where the child is selecting one object among several to undergo a state change,

Object would be encoded.[5] To further confirm our analysis, we looked at examples of Object—Action/State scenes from Allison II and III, the two sessions in which Allison made many holistic successive single-word utterances. In general, our criteria lead to successful postdiction of utterance order. In ten out of sixteen instances, the results are clearly as expected.[6] An interesting pair of examples from II and III respectively are (P. 199):

MOTHER	ALLISON
	[A taking doll and pul-
	ling at its blanket]
	off/
Off?	*blanket/*
Blanket	

Here, Allison is acting on the object (blanket); hence, object is taken for granted and its Action—State encoded first. Compare this scene at Allison III (p. 227) (Allison has been talking about her mother taking a shower):

MOTHER	ALLISON
	[A touching A's head]
	hat; on
With a hat on, yes. [shower cap]	

Here the hat (shower cap) is not even present; it is, therefore, very much in question, and so is expressed before its Action—State.

Of the six remaining cases, only one is a clear disconfirmation of our expectation about order. Three of these cases involve events in which Allison wants her mother to change the state of some object that Allison has in hand, and the Object is encoded first. For example, Allison twice said *diaper/on* in a situation in which the diaper was in Allison's hand, but Allison wanted her mother to change her. Because Allison is using language to affect the behavior of her mother, it seems that she may be looking at the situation from her mother's point of view: Since her mother does not have the object in hand when the sequence begins, it first must be identified before the desired Action can be described. Hence, these three examples all conform to the same pattern, one that constitutes

[5]We did not give these rules in Chapter 4 because none of the situations we had available for analysis involved either a single action on multiple objects or object selection for state change.

[6]The specific utterances involving Object plus Action—State are contained in the following events:

Allison II: 27, 28, 30, 59, 77, 80, 85. All were considered positive examples of our informativeness analysis, except 30 and 80; 30 required the extension of the principle as described in the text, while 80 was ambiguous.

Allison III: 14, 16, 24, 27, 53, 55, 71, 74, 85. Of these, 27, 53, 55, 71 and 75 were positive instances; 16 and 24 required an extension; 14 was ambiguous and 16 was a negative example.

a simple extension of the principle that the Object will be encoded first unless it is in hand.[7] Two other examples are ambiguous in terms of our criteria and no judgment can be made. Hence, Bloom's data generally confirm our notion that word order is predictable from an informational analysis of the situation from the child's point of view. Allison, like Matthew and Nicky, first will establish what an adult would consider to be the topic if it is not already established cognitively by virtue of its close relation to the Agent who is to act upon it, usually herself. Although word order in Allison's sequences is variable, it is much more predictable than Bloom's analysis indicated.

The two types of sequences are seen as early as stages in the developmental process culminating in grammar. Here is the sequence of stages as Bloom views it:

> (1) Perceiving and participating in certain action schemata, with single-word utterances occuring as successive chainings, as each word comments on or referst to the object or movement that holds the child's attention [*chained* successive single-word utterances]. (2) The ability to hold a whole event in mind, with successive single-word utterances beginning to occur in holistic networks that include different aspects of relations in such events [*holistic* successive single-word utterances]. (3) Awareness of meaning relations between words as the child begins to understand and use words in relation to such holistic representation of events, and begins to develop semantic categories of words. (4) Awareness of the relative *order* between such semantic categories for coding the meaning relations that linguistically represent the cognitive categories of events in thought [1973, 122–123].

During the first two stages cited, children are expressing conceptual relationships, not semantic ones. The development in their speech is due to an improved conceptual representation of the situation. Children begin to understand semantic relations during the third stage above; for two-word speech, children must know both semantic relations and grammatical ordering relationships.

This account of development is based upon a sharp division between "the meanings of particular words or the meaning relations among words (*semantics*) and the underlying cognitive structures (*concepts* or thoughts) that represent the relations among persons, objects and events in the world" (1973, p. 21). We, in contrast, have used "semantic" to express the meaning relation between a single word and a cognitive representation of real-world events. On one level, this is merely a terminological difference from Bloom, but on a deeper level, it

---

[7]In a recent article, Nelson (1974) has suggested that functional relations (i.e., the actions that an object can undergo, etc.) are basic to the acquisition of vocabulary. Her treatment of the problem is interesting and merits more discussion than is possible in this context, but leads to some conclusions that are falsified by our data. In particular, it suggests that objects will be named first in the context of actions and other functions. However, we have shown that the earliest use of names is to label objects in a nonaction context. Thus, Nelson's theory will need to be modified if it is to deal accurately with the origins of language.

reflects a theoretical difference. Bloom seems to envisage two *separate* but parallel structures, a cognitive one and a linguistic one. But how can the organization and representation of perceived reality constitute the cognitive underpinnings of language (p. 21) if the two structures are entirely separate? Our view is that the single-word utterance is a functional part of the cognitive organization of a particular referential situation. Accordingly, we have used the term semantic function to indicate the structural point at which the child's word fits into the cognitive structure of a given event. In claiming that the word is part of the cognitive structure of an event, we are saying something about *how* non-verbal cognitive organization is used in the language learning process.

At times, Bloom seems unsure about whether the child is aware of conceptual relations at all unless she produces a *sequence* of single-word utterances. However, this uncertainty is at odds with her description of the inherently relational nature of individual words like *gone, more,* and *up,* which she calls *function* forms. Bloom implies that these words are used in relation to objects, persons, and events even when used in isolation.

Bloom does not think, however, that substantive words encoding entities can be used relationally if they occur in isolation. This view can be seen in a number of ways. For example, she criticized McNeill's (1970a) interpretation of an example of Greenfield's from Matthew's older sister Lauren. In this example, Lauren said (*ba*)*nana* while looking at the top of her grandparents' refrigerator. (Although there were no bananas on the refrigerator, Lauren's mother kept bananas in that place at home.) McNeill states that, in this example, the child is using language to indicate location. Even though we agree that the child is relating the banana to its habitual location, the word *nana* represents not the location but the object. Thus, we would classify this utterance as an Object Associated with Another Object or Location. Our whole classification scheme implies the importance of a distinction between an underlying conceptual or semantic relationship and the form of its linguistic expression (e.g., Agent and Action—State are two separate semantic categories although both participate in the same semantic relation between an Agent and its Action—State). But this criticism is different from Bloom's. We shall now present Bloom's objections and see how they relate to our present treatment of this and other kinds of speech events. First, Bloom asks whether *nana* is merely a substitute for the word *refrigerator,* which Lauren may have lacked in her vocabulary (p. 94). Lauren, in this example, however, was not just looking in the direction of the refrigerator, but specifically at its top. Her visual attention constitutes behavioral evidence that she was not simply making general reference to the refrigerator but was tying the word *nana* to a particular location.

At a later point (p. 137), Bloom asks whether *nana* might not have functioned as a request. The answer, in our scheme, would be decided on the basis of behavioral cues, such as intonation pattern. In any case, the classification of *nana* in this example as a request would not affect placement in our category system, which cuts across the Indicative and Volitional Modes. Finally, Bloom brings up the possibility of *nana* as a statement of nonexistence (one of the functions she recognizes). Our view is that recognition of nonexistence in this case must be based on recognition of an habitual association between bananas and refrigerators; hence, our semantic categorization in terms of location is the more basic or "necessary" of the two possibilities.

A second example of Bloom's reluctance to impute relations to the child can be seen in her treatment of the relation we have called Associated Animate Being (p. 98–100). Bloom notes the relationship between the person and the object, but notes that often the child could not name the object and suggests that "it is possible that the *meaning* of the word Daddy was extended or enlarged to include phenomena such as objects associated with Daddy, or events in which Daddy acted" (p. 100). However, this is a confusion of referential and combinatorial meaning.

A similar example of her confusion of types of meaning occurs in her discussion of function words, when she says "the use of function words to apply across classes of objects may be similar to the early instances of over-inclusion of word reference..." (p. 111). In other words, she does not recognize that words like *more* and *all gone* can legitimately combine with a variety of objects to form different messages, just as they would in later sentences.

Another aspect of Bloom's critique of concepts of one-word speech is her treatment of intonation. She notes that various observers have found the analogues of adult intonation patterns in one-word speech. However, she suggests that there is no behavioral evidence to indicate that children intend a difference between questions and statements, and claims that early sentences, although distinguishable from sequences, do not show sentence prosody. That is, she claims that sentence prosody is learned after syntax, and that "the occurrence of question, statement and exclamation contours in the use of single-word utterances cannot be taken as unequivocal evidence of an inherent notion of 'sentence'" (p. 61). We would agree that it is inappropriate to argue from prosody to syntactic intuitions; it is also possible that prosody temporarily drops out when syntax first appears. Bloom's attack on the continuity of prosody functions is overstrong, however. Our data does not provide much evidence on questions, but they show clear prosodic continuity between one-word and later speech in the distinct expression of statements and demands. There is often moreover, clear behavioral evidence of a Volitional intent when the child uses a whining intonation. For instance, the whining child also will repeat the word until the indicated demand has been satisfied. Similarly, statement intonation has distinctive behavioral correlates, e.g., looking at something that has been named with no attempt to gain possession of it.

The final aspect of Bloom's treatment of one-word speech that we shall discuss is her view of the nature of restrictions on early speech. If memory or motor-performance factors played a part in the limitation of early speech to single words, this would provide some explanation for why early speech differs so radically in appearance from later speech. At the same time, it would lend credibility to the view that there is substantial underlying continuity between these stages. In contrast to this view, Bloom contends that children at the one-word stage do not produce longer utterances because they do not know how to express conceptual notions by means of syntactic–semantic relations (p. 55). Because Bloom does not see structural continuity between single-word utterances and later speech, she attacks the notion that nonlinguistic performance factors play any role in determining the form of early speech. Now, there is obviously some truth to Bloom's position. Children at later stages of development must know more about syntax than those at early stages. However, we do not accept the implied negative evaluation of children's capabilities at the one-word stage, and shall argue that Bloom's evidence does not fully support her position.

Bloom claims that children know about ordering relations between words and can produce strings of words before they know how these ordering relations can express conceptual relations. To show this, she cites Allison's use of *wídə*, a "meaningless" final-position pivot, which occurred during the video-taped session at 16 months. However, at this age, Allison was already producing two-word utterances and had been doing so regularly for 2 months. For example, during the video-taping session, she uses *more* as an initial word in combination with four different substantives. Thus, *wídə* provides no evidence on memory for word order *before* the child is capable of producing two-word sentences.

Bloom also argues that the existence of a stage during which children produce sequences of single-word utterances that encode different aspects of a single situation but do not combine these utterances into multiword sentences shows that children at the one-word stage do not know how semantic notions are encoded linguistically. In Section 5.4, we shall take up some evidence regarding the relative abilities of children in comprehension and production that bears on this question. Here, we shall deal with other aspects of Bloom's position.

Bloom's argument that restrictions at the one-word stage are purely linguistic takes strength from her demonstration that many later single-word utterances arise in those very situations that children do not know how to encode linguistically (pp. 127–129). However, the confirmation is less than complete in that the restriction at 22 months of a sizable number of utterances to single-word length could not be explained in this way (p. 127). Similarly, we find that, at 16 months, Allison could use the word *more* and the sentence *more cookie*. If one-word sentences arose only in situations involving linguistic inadequacy, we should expect *more* to be used in situations that involved different conceptual relations from those in which *more cookie* was used. However, this is not the case; there are numerous examples in the transcriptions in which no difference can be detected. Thus, we conclude that lack of linguistic knowledge need not be the sole explanation for the limitations on early speech.

The plausibility of there being performance restrictions on early speech is increased by the presence of performance restrictions on two- and three-word speech. Bloom explicitly refers to the existence of constraints on the surface form of utterances in later speech. For example, she refers to a two-word limit as a limiting factor at one period of speech development (p. 124), and again to a three-constituent limit during the last taping session (p. 126). It is inconsistent of her not to allow that similar constraints on length of output might have some effect at the one-word stage. In fact, it seems likely that children pass through a stage during which they find it difficult to integrate two independent words under a single sentence intonation contour. There is ample evidence that children's motor skills and construction activity pass through similarly limited stages before they achieve the hierarchical organization characteristic of mature forms of activity (cf., Werner, 1948; Bruner, 1971; Greenfield and Schneider, 1975); it is unlikely that language use is independent of such restrictions. Bloom is correct that some sequences result from situations that the child does not know how to encode sententially, but other sequences are used even while the child has the corresponding syntactic ability. In these cases, the child is evidently restricted by some grammar-independent difficulty, and attends more to informational structure than to syntactic rules in formulating his or her message.

5.3 Referential and Combinatorial Meaning

In Chapter 1, we distinguished referential and combinatorial meaning. Referential meaning is what the word alone denotes or encodes, and combinatorial meaning is the result of using a word in a specific combination with other elements. Our study focused on establishing a pattern of development of combinatorial meaning during the stage of single-word utterances. E. Clark (1973) and Nelson (1972, 1973) have, in contrast, described the development of referential meaning during this period.

Of course, the two types of meaning are just different aspects of the same phenomenon of speech. A word's referential meaning comes into play only when that word is used in a speech act. Similarly, a combinatorial meaning cannot be expressed independently of some vocabulary with specific referential meaning. In studying combinatorial meaning, we have tried to specify the different ways in which words can be used. Thus, a person's name used as an Agent *refers* to an animate being but has a structural relation to an Action.

Likewise, a word in the Action or State function refers to a change of state or a process, and so on, while having a structural relation to a particular entity. In Chapter 4, we showed that the concept of informativeness could explain which functions or combinatorial meanings were expressed in a given situation. Here, we shall show that informativeness is also significant for referential meaning.

E. Clark (1973) has advanced the idea that referential meaning is a function of semantic features, meaning components which define the word's field of reference. The development of referential meaning is the acquisition of semantic features. Thus, a young child whose definition of clock was restricted to the feature "round" might overextend the meaning of clock to coins. As more features were acquired, the child's field of reference (extension) for the word *clock* would narrow down to resemble that of the adult. An example from our data would be the use of a term for one pole of a dimension to denote the whole dimension. Clark assumes that one pole of the dimension can be considered positive (unmarked), the other negative (marked). Positive refers to the extended end of the pole away from Ego. She then cites early diary data to indicate that the "positive" (unmarked) term is acquired first: *on* before *off, in* before *out, up* before *down*. H. Clark (1973) elaborates on this notion, specifying that "the positive member specifies the assumed normal direction or relation, and the negative member specifies its direction or relation by negating the assumed one" (p. 55) and suggests that, although unmarked should precede marked in comprehension, marked terms may precede in production. For Matthew, *on* precedes *off* in accordance with the diary data, but *out* precedes *in* in contradiction to the diary data; the developmental sequence of *down* and *up* is ambiguous. Such inconsistency fails to support any simple theory of vocabulary development. However, H. Clark's suggestion seems to us to be on the right track, since it is based on the idea the child would not need to express the unmarked concept, that is, the assumed relation.

Let us develop this idea further. Our notion is that the child first expresses what is relatively uncertain or informative, and that informativeness can explain facts about lexical development as well as about choice of semantic function.[8] Applied to polar opposite states, uncertainty would be change. Hence, the first pole to develop in each pair would be the one representing change from the normal state. Matthew generally used *on* when he wanted something turned on, such as his music box, which usually was off. Matthew first uses *out* in

---

[8]Press (1974) has further demonstrated that the featural representation of a word meaning varies for young children as a function of the alternatives it is partitioning in a particular situation, even when the word's referent remains constant throughout. This study is, in fact, a nice experimental demonstration of Olson's (1970) notion that words are basically used to contrast one possibility with others present in the situation.

reference to getting pennies out of a bank, again a deviation from normalcy. For Nicky, *on* precedes *off*, just as for Matthew. *Up* and *down, in* and *out* appear at about the same time. Thus, it appears that features are not generally normal (unmarked, certain) or abnormal (marked, uncertain), but one or the other depending on the structure of the situation in which they are used. Recently Banks, H. Clark and Lucy (1975) have made a parallel discovery for adults: Up is the unmarked pole for balloons, down the unmarked pole for yoyos. Thus, informativeness turns out again to operate similarly in both adults and children.

5.4 The Relation between Understanding and Speaking

Huttenlocher (1974) has done the first naturalistic longitudinal study of comprehension. Her study shows generally that children are far more advanced in comprehension than production. These results are all the more striking in that the data she has reported come from the early one-word period, before the children were producing single words in sequences. Two children have thus far shown an ability to respond relationally to information presented in adult speech. For example, Craig was able to carry out a command of the form *Give (show) Jane (Mommy, etc.) the bottle (apple, cookie, etc.).* (The words in parentheses show the other alternatives tested in the same situation. To be credited with carrying out a command, the child must discriminate the correct alternative from other posibilities present in the situation.) In order to succeed in this task, Craig must not only identify the referents of key words (e.g., *give, Jane, bottle* in the above example) but also the relations among them, as Huttenlocher points out. Thus, the child shows, at very least, evidence of relating three individual lexical items to a representation of the situation in terms of the functional role of each item. This is evidence that a child who is restricted to producing single words in isolation has a richer underlying conceptual structure to which the word can be related. It also shows that parts of this structure that are not expressed in the child's own utterance are specifically semantic in the sence of being potentially related to linguistic elements. Another interesting aspect of this situation is that the Agent—Craig—is not expressed in the command. The syntax of adult imperatives "assume" the Agent just as children usually do in their early speech.

Huttenlocher also found that being able to locate the referent of an object name preceded the ability to respond to relational information about action roles—the same progression we found in production. Huttenlocher's data essentially confirm Greenfield's (1973) finding that identification of referents is the earliest form of comprehension response to a purely linguistic sign.

Even more interesting is the comprehension stage following Craig's ability to respond appropriately to a command like *Give Jane the bottle.* At this point, he was able to respond differentially to sentences like *Show the baby's bottle to mommy* and *Show Craig's bottle to the baby*. In short, Craig could assign *baby* the roles of possessor and recipient. To do so required syntactic processing, at very least processing of information about word order. Thus, a stage of syntactic comprehension occurs in the one-word stage, but follows a stage in which the child relates individual words to the situational structure as he perceives it.

There is a body of informal observation to the effect that not all children pass through a stage of single-word utterances. These observations seem most frequent for working class children and children in non-Western cultures. J. H. Smith (1970) carried out an analysis of some of M. Bullowa's longitudinal sound film data in order to gain information about one-word speech from other children. These children were all from working class backgrounds, and it was striking how rarely they spoke before being able to produce word combinations. Although it was difficult to adapt data that had not been collected specifically for this purpose and although the corpus from even the most verbal child was small (collected at weekly half-hour sessions), the sequence of semantic functions followed our findings, in so far as there was comparable data. What Huttenlocher's findings show is that, even if all children do not overtly pass through the stages we have been describing, they are most likely doing so covertly, on the level of comprehension. Single-word utterances, where they are produced in abundance, are just one more clue to the nature of the underlying process of language acquisition.

5.5 Conclusion

In this study, we have attempted to demonstrate the communicative nature of early speech. Parents, in fact, understand their children to express a wide variety of messages. At the same time, we have attempted to show that there is an objective basis for this feeling on the part of parents. Children do seem to be expressing a relatively limited number of semantic functions, a number that increases with time as their cognitive and linguistic capacities develop. These facts do not imply, as McNeill (1971) has concluded, that the concept of a sentence is present from the beginning, but rather that children at this stage can construct messages by combining linguistic and nonlinguistic elements. Such messages are the basis for the syntactic concept of a sentence which follows. In the case of Volitional messages, it is generally clear that the child intends to communicate. We believe the child also intends Indicative utterances to have an effect on the listener—sometimes only to capture the listener's attention— but this question needs to be resolved by careful study of how children attend to others and respond to listeners' response or lack of it.

The one-word period may be static in syntactic form, but it is a period of remarkable growth in content and function. Indeed, it is an example of the principle Slobin (1973) revived from Werner and Kaplan (1963): "New forms first express old functions, and new functions are first expressed by old forms". Thus, old vocabulary often is used to express a new semantic function. Even more generally, an old form, the single-word utterance, is used first to express many new semantic functions. Conversely, two-word sentences, a new form, at first express old functions previously expressed by single-word utterances.

Children are able to communicate because they are not dependent solely on words but use their words with gestures, action, and intonation, within a context they share with their listener. As Ryan (1974) has pointed out, "these clues are similar to what we use in trying to understand adult speech, in cases of ambiguity, lack of proficiency in the language, distortion, etc." (p. 202). However, we would go further and suggest that these contextual and nonlinguistic clues are used by adults in ordinary processes of comprehension, even when special problems of ambiguity do not arise. Much recent work in psycholinguistics (e.g., Bransford and Johnson, 1973) and linguistics (e.g., G. Lakoff, 1971) indicates that adult linguistic structure is not independent of contextual structure but is often integrated with it and dependent on it. In this sense, there is a clear continuity between adult language and the earliest stages of child language. Of course, adults, unlike young children, have developed the ability to deal with structures independent of context and content, as in symbolic logic, but this appears to be an almost conscious departure from the ordinary processes of verbal comprehension. (See Henle, 1962, for a demonstration of how difficult this is even for untrained adults.) In other words, our conclusion is that the communication process during the period of single-word utterances is continuous with that occurring at later points in development—although new sources of information, in the shape of vocabulary and grammar, are added and integrated with the basic processes.

By paying close attention to children's intonation, gesture, action, and visual attention, we have tried to establish an objective basis for interpreting their speech. Of course, this is difficult, since the process of interpretation is understood poorly even for adult speech. What emerges clearly is that children use their words in systematic combination with nonverbal elements; it remains less clear exactly how many varied kinds of messages they do intend at different stages. One way to approach this problem will be to approach child language with more precision and more equipment, watching for attentional patterns, gestures and intonations that escaped our broad transcriptions of sight and sound. A second approach, to which we have referred repeatedly in our discussions, will involve research into what nonlinguistic distinctions children are capable of making.

In order to study the emergence of the Agent function in one-word speech, we were forced to make a number of assumptions about the relationship between

Agency and animacy in children's cognition. While these seem on the whole reasonable to us, how much more satisfying it would be to know on the basis of independent evidence when children attribute agency to a person or thing, how they regard self-moving inanimate objects like cars, and when they regard an Action as the doing of some Agent. These questions are amenable to empirical investigation, but the work has just started to be done.

Another area of investigation that will certainly bring results for child language is relationship between verbal and nonverbal interaction in infants. For instance, Bruner's (1975) study of the connection between early verbal indication and the preverbal deployment of attention on adult—infant inter- action points one direction for investigation of the beginnings of naming.

Another direction is toward further investigation of language as an inter- active communication process. This, of course, involves a focus on the uses to which language is put, effects of utterances as well as their causes. Pragmatics in philosophy and linguistics can give this direction of investigation a theoretical framework. Articles by Ryan (1974) and Bruner (1975) and Bates's (1974) thesis (to be published as a book) are all good examples of the usefulness of pragmatics for the study of the development of communicative competence.

In showing that children do express definite semantic functions in their speech, we believe we have provided a better basis for discussing how it is that a child learns language. Semantic functions in single-word utterances give substance to the idea that grammar learning must be based on meaning. In our study, we have tried to look at how a child uses adult speech to make the leap from single words to syntax; we have not even considered the problem of how the communicativeness of the child's utterance interacts with the acquisition of semantic functions in single-word speech. Ryan (1974) presents a valuable theoretical discussion of this problem.

By examining the role of verbal interaction in early speech, we have tried to show that such interaction provides a means for the child to learn the basic syntax of early sentences. Verbal interaction provides a context in which children can combine words before perfecting the skills necessary for syntactic production. Syntagmatic combinations between his own speech and that of an adult is one source of knowledge about syntax; observation of word order where his speech is paradigmatically coupled to his mother's is another.

Many authors (e.g., Ervin-Tripp, 1971) have speculated on the structural continuity of single-word utterances with later speech. We believe that by studying the semantic functions that children express at both stages we have given the idea of continuity an empirical basis. At the same time, by explicitly dealing on a semantic level instead of a syntactic one, we avoid the concep- tual problem that has plagued much recent work on child language.

Our examination of children's use of isolated single-word utterances and sequences shows that child language is sensitive to the informational structure of an event. That is, children encode those aspects of the event that are most uncertain, from the child's own point of view, and fill in other aspects with temporally and developmentally later utterances. Obviously, this principle carries over into later child language, where the problem of "deletion" has been so much discussed. This, of course, explains the frequent deletion of the subject in speech around the three-word level. The subject, often taken for granted, is, therefore, less informative than other constituents of the sentence that resist "deletion." Items which are not expressed need not be present in a grammatical sense, but only semantically, as part of a child's internal structuring of the event. Dialogue follows this pattern of information analysis on a new level. What was assumed or presupposed from the situation in a spontaneous utterance is now presupposed because of its linguistic expression in the previous sentence. Again, this process follows principles which hold for adult conversation.

The presence of so many points of continuity between early language and mature speech leads one to conclude that the basic organization may be the same: Perhaps the structure of adult language has an underlying basis in cognitive organization. This suggestion has been made by Osgood (1971) and is substantiated by much recent work on semantic memory (e.g., Bransford and Franks, 1971) and comprehension (e.g., Greenfield and Westerman, 1974).

Slobin (1971) notes that "we are just beginning to sense the intimate relations between linguistic universals and cognitive universals, and are far from an adequate developmental theory of either" (p. 299). In this study, we have shown that the intimate relationship of cognition and language is present from the very beginning of language development. Further, by showing that presumed universal characteristics of later speech are present in one-word speech as well, we have added support for their universality. In particular, we have provided support for what Slobin (1971) calls the "language definitional universals" of communicative functions (e.g., asserting, denying, and requesting) and semantic relations (e.g., Agent, Object), and also have shown that these are based on what seems likely to be a universal cognitive organization.

Campbell (1966) suggests that language follows the human perceptual system in naming units that have the unity described by gestalt principles. This point is substantiated by children's early language. Not only do the children name more entities than relations; early names always refer to whole objects rather than object parts or attributes.

Our study has confirmed many of the phenomena of the early diary accounts. For instance, examples of all of our semantic functions appear in Leopold's (1949) study, as do examples of our Indicative and Volitional modes. We have also presented a whole corpus of data illustrating de Laguna's (1927) point that words function as sentences because the missing elements are supplied by the situation. Our developmental sequence of semantic functions is, in part, an elaboration of Werner and Kaplan's progression from identifying predications to predications of action to predications of attributes. Finally, we have provided empirical support for the notion of structural continuity between one- and two-word speech, noted by de Laguna (1927), Guillaume (1927), Leopold (1949), and Werner and Kaplan (1963). While a few researchers like Grégoire (1937) and Werner and Kaplan (1963) distinguished semantics from syntax, others like the Sterns (1907; W. Stern, 1930) confounded the two levels and mistakenly tried to identify parts of speech in the one-word period. By adapting a semantic theory of grammar (Fillmore, 1968) for application to the presyntactic period of development, we were able to describe structural continuity between one- and two-word speech without attributing syntactic characteristics to utterances that are, in fact, presyntactic. In this way, our study bridges the theoretical and empirical gap between the early diary studies of single-word utterances and recent grammatical studies of language development after syntax (e.g., Bloom, 1970; Bowerman, 1973; Brown, 1973).

To those who have eyes as well as ears, the language that children speak is neither strange nor incomprehensible. It shares many features with adult speech but can use those features only in a limited way. To overcome these restrictions, it relies on a system of nonlinguistic communication that already existed but that becomes more powerful with the addition of language. As the restrictions on its use decrease, language can begin to express more that previously depended on nonlinguistic factors for its communication, and becomes the vehicle of communication with which those who have only ears are familiar.

References

Antinucci, F., and Parisi, D. 1973. Early language acquisition: A model and some data. In C.A. Ferguson and D. I. Slobin (Eds.), *Studies of child language development*. New York: Holt. Pp. 607–618.

Antinucci, F., and Volterra, V. 1973. Lo sviluppo della negazione nel linguaggio infantile: Uno studio Pragmatico. In *Studi per un modello del linguaggio. Quaderni della Ricerca Scientifica.* Rome: Consiglio.

Aronson, E., and Rosenbloom, S. 1971. Space perception in early infancy: Perception within a common auditory–visual space. *Science, 172,* 1161–1163.

Austin, J. L. 1962. *How to do things with words.* Oxford: Oxford University Press.

Banks, W. P., Clark, H., and Lucy, P. 1975. The locus of the semantic congruity effect in comparative judgments. *Journal of Experimental Psychology: Human Perception and Performance 104,* 35–47.

Bates, E. 1974. Language and context: Studies in the acquisition of pragmatics. Doctoral dissertation, University of Chicago. To be published by Academic Press.

Bloch, O. 1921. Les premiers stades du langage de l'enfant. *Journal de Psychologie, 18,* 693–712.

Bloom, L. M. 1970. *Language development: Form and function in emerging grammars.* Cambridge, Mass.: M.I.T. Press.

Bloom, L. M. 1973. *One word at a time: The use of single word utterances before syntax.* The Hague: Mouton.

Bloom, L. M., Hood, L., and Lightbown, P. 1974. Imitation in language development. *Cognitive Psychology, 6,* 380–420.

Bloomfield, L. 1933. *Language.* New York: Holt.

Blount, B. G. 1969. Acquisition of language by Luo children. Unpublished doctoral dissertation, University of California, Berkeley.

Bower, T. G. R. 1965. The determinants of perceptual unity in infancy. *Psychonomic Science, 3,* 323–324.

Bower, T. G. R. 1966. The visual world of infants. *Scientific American, 215,* 80–92. Offprint no. 502.

Bower, T. G. R. 1967. Phenomenal identity and form perception in infants. *Perception and Psychophysics, 2,* 74–76.

Bower, T. G. R. 1971. Perceptual and intellectual world. In *Developmental psychology today.* Del Mar, Cal.: C. R. M. Pp. 107–129.

Bower, T. G. R. 1974. *Development in infancy.* San Francisco: W. H. Freeman.

Bower, T. G. R., Broughton, J. M., and Moore, M. K. 1970. The coordination of vision and touch in infancy. *Perception and Psychophysics, 8,* 51–53.

Bowerman, M. 1973. *Early syntactic development: A cross-linguistic study with special reference to Finnish.* Cambridge: Cambridge University Press.

Braine, M. D. S. 1963. The ontogeny of English phrase structure: The first phase. *Language, 39*, 1—13. [Reprinted in C. A. Ferguson and D. I. Slobin (Eds.), *Studies of child language development.* New York: Holt, 1970. Pp. 407—429.]

Bransford, J. D., and Franks, J. J. 1971. The abstraction of linguistic ideas. *Cognitive Psychology, 2*, 331—350.

Bransford, J. D., and Johnson, M. K. 1973. Considerations of some problems of comprehension. In W. G. Chase (Ed.), *Visual information processing.* New York: Academic Press. Pp. 383—438.

Brown, R. 1973. *A first language: The early stages.* Cambridge, Mass.: Harvard University Press.

Brown, R., and Bellugi, U. 1964. Three processes in the child's acquisition of syntax. *Harvard Educational Review, 34* (Spring), 133—151. [Reprinted in E. H. Lenneberg (Ed.), *New directions in the study of language.* Cambridge, Mass.: M.I.T. Press, 1964 Pp. 131—161. Also in B. Sutton-Smith (Ed.), *Readings in child psychology.* New York: Appleton, 1973. Pp 153—165.]

Brown, R., and Berko, J. 1960. Word association and the acquisition of grammar. *Child Development, 31*, 1—14.

Brown, R., Cazden, C. B., and Bellugi, U. 1968. The child's grammar from I to III. In J. F. Hill (Ed.), *Minnesota Symposium on Child Psychology.* Minneapolis: University of Minnesota Press, 1967. Pp. 28—73.

Brown, R. W., and Fraser, C. 1964. The acquisition of syntax. In U. Bellugi and R. W. Brown (Eds.), *The acquisition of language. Monographs of the Society for Research in Child Development, 29*(1), 43—79.

Bruner, J. S. 1971. The growth and structure of skill. In K. J. Connolly (Ed.), *Motor skills in infancy.* London: Academic Press. Pp. 63—94. [Reprinted in J. M. Anglin (Ed.), *Beyond the information given.* New York: W. W. Norton, 1973. Pp. 245—269.

Bruner, J. S. 1975. The ontogenesis of speech acts. *Journal of Child Language. 2*, 1—19.

Buhler, C., 1931. *Kindheit und Jungend: Genese des Bewusstseirs*, Leipzig: Hirzel.

Buhler, K. 1926. Les lois générales d'evolution dans le langage de l'enfant. *Journal de Psychologie, 23*, 597—607.

Cattell, P. 1940. *Infant intelligence scale.* New York: Psychological Corporation.

Campbell, D. T., and Walker, D. E. 1966. Ostensive instances and entativity in language learning. Unpublished paper.

Cazden, C. B. 1965. Environmental assistance to the child's acquisition of grammar. Unpublished doctoral dissertation, Harvard University.

Chafe, W. L. 1970. *Meaning and the structure of language.* Chicago: University of Chicago Press.

Chomsky, N. 1957. *Syntactic structures.* The Hague: Mouton.

Chomsky, N. 1965. *Aspects of the theory of syntax.* Cambridge, Mass.: M.I.T. Press.

Clark, E. V. 1970. Locationals: A study of the relations between "existential," "locative," and "possessive" constructions. *Working Papers in Language Universals* (Stanford University), *3*.

Clark, E. V. 1971. On the acquisition of the meaning of *before* and *after. Journal of Verbal Learning and Verbal Behavior, 10*, 266—275.

Clark, E. V. 1972. On the child's acquisition of antonyms in two semantic fields. *Journal of Verbal Learning and Verbal Behavior, 11*, 750—758.

Clark, E. V. 1973. *What's in a word? On the child's acquisition of semantics in his first language.* In T. E. Moore (Ed.), *Cognitive development and the acquisition of language.* New York: Academic Press. Pp. 65—110.

Clark, H. H. 1973. Space, time, semantics, and the child. In T. E. Moore (Ed.), *Cognitive development and the acquisition of language.* New York: Academic Press. Pp. 27—64.

Cohen, M. 1952. Sur l'étude du langage enfantin. *Enfance, 5*, 181—249.

de Laguna, G. A. 1927. *Speech: Its function and development.* New Haven, Conn.: Yale University Press. [Reprint ed. 1963, Bloomington: Indiana University Press.]

Dewey, J. 1894. The psychology of infant language. *Psychological Review, 1,* 63–66. [Reprinted in A. Bar-Adon and W. F. Leopold, *Child Language: A book of readings.* Englewood Cliffs, N.J.: Prentice-Hall, 1971. Pp. 34–35.]

Dodd, D. H., and Coots, J. H. 1973. Environmental control of a pivot construction. Paper presented at the meeting of the Western Psychological Association, San Diego, April.

Donaldson, M., and Balfour, G. 1968. Less is more: A study of language comprehension in children. *British Journal of Psychology, 59,* 461–472.

Donaldson, M., and Wales, R. 1970. On the acquisition of some relational terms. In J. R. Hayes (Ed.), *Cognition and the development of language.* New York: Wiley. Pp. 235–268.

Edwards, D. 1974. Sensory-motor intelligence and semantic relations in early child grammar. *Cognition, 2*(4), 395–434.

Ervin, S. 1961. Changes with age in the verbal determinants of word-association. *American Journal of Psychology, 74,* 361–372.

Ervin, S. 1964. Imitation and structural change in children's language. In E. H. Lenneberg (Ed.), *New directions in the study of language.* Cambridge, Mass.: M.I.T. Press.

Ervin-Tripp, S. 1971. An overview of theories of grammatical development. In D. I. Slobin (Ed.), *The ontogenesis of grammar.* New York: Academic Press. Pp. 189–212.

Fillmore, C. J. 1968. The case for case. In E. Bach and R. T. Harms (Eds.), *Universals in linguistic theory.* New York: Holt. Pp. 1–90.

Fillmore, C. J. 1971. Types of lexical information. In D. D. Steinberg and L. R. Jakobovitz (Eds.), *Semantics: An interdisciplinary reader in philosophy, linguistics, and psychology.* Cambridge: Cambridge University Press. Pp. 370–392.

Fraser, C., Bellugi, U., and Brown, R. 1963. Control of grammar in imitation, comprehension, and production. *Journal of Verbal Learning and Verbal Behavior, 2,* 121–135.

Givón, T. 1974. Toward a discourse definition of syntax. Unpublished manuscript, University of California, Los Angeles.

Givón, T. 1975. The presupposition of negation in language: Pragmatics, function, and ontology. Unpublished manuscript, University of California, Los Angeles.

Gleason, H. H. 1961. *An introduction to descriptive linguistics.* Rev. ed. New York: Holt.

Goodson, B. D., and Greenfield, P. M. 1975. The search for structural principles in children's manipulative play: A parallel with linguistic development. *Child Development,* 734–736.

Greenfield, P. M. 1968. Development of the holophrase: Observations on Lauren Greenfield. Unpublished paper.

Greenfield, P. M. 1973. Who is "Dada"? Some aspects of the semantic and phonological development of a child's first words. *Language and Speech, 16,* 14–43. [Reprinted in H. C. Lindgren (Ed.), *Children's behavior,* Palo Alto, Cal.: Mayfield Publishing, 1975. Pp. 4–16.]

Greenfield, P. M., May, A. A., and Bruner, J. S., 1972. *Early Words: Language and action in the life of a child.* New York: Wiley.

Greenfield, P. M., Nelson, K., and Salzman, E. 1972. The development of rule bound strategies for manipulating seriated cups: A parallel between action and grammar. *Cognitive Psychology, 3,* 291–310.

Greenfield, P. M., and Schneider, L. 1975. Building a tree structure: The development of hierarchical complexity and interrupted strategies in children's construction activity. Unpublished paper.

Greenfield, P. M., Smith, J. H., and Laufer, B. 1972. Communication and the beginnings of language. Unpublished draft.

Greenfield, P. M., and Westerman, M. 1974. Some psychological relations between language and action structures. Unpublished paper.

Grégoire, A. 1937. *L'Apprentissage du langage.* Paris: Droz.

Grice, H. P. 1968. The logic of conversation. Unpublished manuscript, Berkeley, Cal.

Gruber, J. S. 1973. Correlations between the syntactic constructions of the child and the adult. In C. A. Ferguson and D. I. Slobin (Eds.), *Studies of child language development*. New York: Holt. Pp. 440–444.

Guillaume, P. 1927. Les débuts de la phrase dans le langage de l'enfant. *Journal de Psychologie*, *24*, 1–25. [Reprinted in C. A. Ferguson and D. I. Slobin (Eds.), *Studies of child language development*. New York: Holt, 1973, Pp. 522–541.]

Gunter, R. 1963. Elliptical sentences in American English. *Lingua*, *12*, 137–150.

Haith, M. M. 1966. The response of the human newborn to visual movement. *Journal of Experimental Child Psychology*, *3*, 235–243.

Halliday, M. A. K. 1973. Early language learning: A sociolinguistic approach. Paper presented to IXth International Congress of Anthropological and Ethnological Sciences, Chicago.

Halliday, M. A. K. 1974. A sociosemistic perspective on language development. *Bulletin of the School of Oriental and African Studies*, *37*(1), 98–118.

Halliday, M. A. K. In press. Learning how to mean. In E. Lenneberg and E. Lenneberg, (Eds.), *Foundations of language development: A multidisciplinary approach*. New York: Academic Press.

Harris, P. 1971. Understanding one another before we speak. Unpublished paper, Harvard University.

Harris, Z. S. 1951. *Structural linguistics*. Chicago: University of Chicago Press.

Haviland, S. E., and Clark, H. H. 1974. What's new? Acquiring new information as a process in comprehension. *Journal of Verbal Learning and Verbal Behavior*, *13*, 512–521.

Henle, M. 1962. On the relation between logic and thinking. *Psychological Review*, *69*, 366–378. [Partially reprinted in P. C. Wason and P. N. Johnson-Laird (Eds.), *Thinking and reasoning*. Harmondsworth: Penguin Books, 1968. Pp. 93–107.]

Holzman, M. S. 1971. Ellipsis in discourse: Implications for linguistic analysis by computer, the child's acquisition of language, and semantic theory. *Language and Speech*, *14*, 86–98.

Hornby, P. A. 1971. Surface structure and the topic–comment distinction: A developmental study. *Child Development*, *42*, 1975–1988.

Huttenlocher, J. 1974. *The origins of language comprehension*. In R. L. Solso (Eds.), *Theories in cognitive psychology*. Hillsdale, N. J.: Lawrence Earlbaum Associates.

Ingram, D. 1971. Transitivity in child language. *Language*, *47*(4), 888–910.

Jakobson, R. 1969. The paths from infancy to language. Heinz Werner Lectures, Clark University, Worcester, Mass.

Katz, J., and Fodor, J. A. 1963. The structure of a semantic theory. *Language*, *39*(2), 170–210.

Keenan, Edward L. 1971. Two kinds of presupposition in natural language. In C. J. Fillmore and D. Langendoen (Eds.), *Studies in linguistic semantics*. New York: Holt. Pp. 45–52.

Keenan, Elinor O. 1975. Making it last: Repetition in children's discourse. In *Proceedings of the First Annual Meeting of the Berkeley Linguistics Society*. Berkeley. Pp. 279–294.

Kemp, J. C., and Dale, P. S. 1973. Spontaneous imitations and free speech: A developmental comparison. Unpublished paper, University of Washington, Seattle.

Kernan, K. 1969. The acquisition of language by Samoan children. Unpublished doctoral dissertation, University of California, Berkeley.

Lakoff, G. 1971. On generative semantics. In D. D. Steinberg and L. A. Jakobovitz (Eds.), *Semantics: An interdisciplinary reader in philosophy, linguistics, and psychology*. Cambridge: Cambridge University Press. Pp. 232–296.

Lakoff, G., and Ross, J. R. 1967. Is deep structure necessary? Unpublished paper, Cambridge, Mass.

Lakoff, R. 1973. Questionable answers and answerable questions. In B. Kachru, R. B. Lees, Y. Malkiel, and S. Saporta (Eds.), *Papers in linguistics in honor of Henry and Renee Kahane*. Champaign–Urbana, Ill.: University of Illinois Press.

Leopold, W. F. 1939—1949. *Speech development of a bilingual child: A linguist's record.* Vol. I (1939). *Vocabulary growth in the first two years.* Vol. 2 (1947). *Second learning in the first two years.* Vol. 3 (1949). *Grammar and general problems in the first two years.* Evanston, Ill.: Northwestern University Press.

Leopold, W. F. 1953. Patterning in children's language learning. *Language Learning, 5,* 1—14. [Reprinted in A. Bar-Adon and W. F. Leopold (Eds.), *Child language: A book of readings.* Englewood Cliffs, N.J.: Prentice-Hall, 1971. Pp. 135—141.]

Lewis, M. M. 1951. *Infant speech: A study of the beginnings of language.* New York: Humanities Press.

Lewis, M. M. 1963. *Language, thought and personality.* New York: Basic Books.

Lukens, M. 1896. Preliminary report on the learning of language. *Pedagogical Seminary, 3,* 424—60.

Lyons, J. 1967. A note on possessive, existential, and locative sentences. *Foundations of Language, 3,* 390—396.

Lyons, J. 1970. *Noam Chomsky.* New York: Viking Press.

MacNamara, J. 1972. Cognitive basis of language learning. *Psychological Review, 79,* 1—13.

McCawley, J. D. 1968. The role of semantics in a grammar. In E. Bach and R. T. Harms (Eds.), *Universals in linguistic theory.* New York: Holt.

McNeill, D. 1966. Developmental psycholinguistics. In F. Smith and G. A. Miller (Eds.), *The genesis of language.* Cambridge, Mass: M.I.T. Press.

McNeill, D. 1970a. *The acquisition of language: The study of developmental psycholinguistics.* New York: Harper.

McNeill, D. 1970b. The development of language. In P. H. Mussen (Ed.), *Carmichael's manual of child psychology.* Vol. I. New York: Wiley. Pp. 1061—1162.

McNeill, D. 1971. Explaining linguistic universals. In J. Morton (Ed.), *Biological and social factors in psycholinguistics.* London: Logos Press.

McNeill, D., and McNeill, N. 1968. What does a child mean when he says "no"? In E. M. Zale (Ed.), *Proceedings of the Conference on Language and Language Behavior.* New York: Appleton. Pp. 51—62. [Reprinted in C. A. Ferguson and D. I. Slobin (Eds.), *Studies of child language development.* New York: Holt, 1973. Pp. 619—627.]

Menyuk, P., and Bernholtz, N. 1969. Prosodic features and children's language development. *Quarterly Progress Report of the Research Laboratory of Electronics* (M.I.T.), *93,* 216—219.

Miller, W., and Ervin S. 1964. The development of grammar in child language. In U. Bellugi and R. W. Brown (Eds.), *The acquisition of language. Monographs of the Society for Research in Child Development, 29*(1), 9—33.

Mundy-Castle, A. C., and Anglin, J. 1969. The development of looking in infancy. Paper read at Society for Research in Child Development, Santa Monica, Cal., April.

Nelson, K. 1972. Semantic structures of the earliest lexicons. Paper delivered to Eastern Psychological Association, Boston, April.

Nelson, K. 1973. *Structure and strategy in learning to talk. Monographs of the Society for Research in Child Development, 38*(1—2) (Serial No. 149).

Nelson, K. 1974. Concept, word, and sentence: Interrelations in acquisition and development. *Psychological Review, 81*(4), 267—285.

Newport, E., Gleitman, L., and Gleitman, H. 1975. Mother's language and child syntactic acquisition. Paper presented at Stanford Child Language Research Forum, Stanford, Cal., April.

Olson, D. 1968. Language acquisition and cognitive development. Paper presented at the International Conference on Social—Cultural Aspects of Mental Retardation, Nashville, Tenn.

Olson, D. 1970. Language and thought: Aspects of a cognitive theory of semantics. *Psychological Review, 77,* 257—273.

Osgood, C. E. 1971. Where do sentences come from? In D. D. Steinberg and L. A. Jakobovitz (Eds.), *Semantics: An interdisciplinary reader in philosophy, linguistics, and psychology.* Cambridge: Cambridge University Press. Pp. 497—529.

Paloma, J. 1910. A child's vocabulary and its development. *Pedagogical Seminary, 17,* 328–69.

Parisi, D. 1974. What is behind child utterances? *Journal of Child Language, 1*(1), 97–107.

Piaget, J. 1923. *Le langage et la pensée chez l'enfant.* Neuchatel and Paris: Delachaux and Niestlé. [M. Gabain (Trans.), *The language and thought of the child.* London: Routledge and Kegan Paul, New York: Harcourt, 1926.]

Piaget, J. 1951. *Play, dreams, and imitation in childhood.* New York: W. W. Norton. [Original French publication, 1945.]

Piaget, J. 1966. Need and significance of cross-cultural studies in genetic psychology. *International Journal of Psychology, 1*(1), 3–13. [Reprinted in J. W. Berry and P. R. Dixon (Eds.), *Culture and cognition: Readings in cross-cultural psychology.* London: Methuen, 1974. Pp. 299–306.].

Postal, P. 1971. On the surface verb "remind." In C. J. Fillmore and D. T. Langendoen (Eds.), *Studies in linguistic semantics.* New York: Holt. Pp. 181–270.

Premack, D. 1970. A functional analysis of language. *Journal for the Experimental Analysis of Behavior, 14*(1), 107–125.

Press, M. L. 1974. Semantic features in lexical acquisition. Paper presented at the Stanford Child Language Research Forum, Stanford, Cal., April.

Preyer, W. 1890. *The mind of the child.* Part 2. *The development of the intellect.* H. W. Brown (Trans.), New York: Appleton. [Originally published as *Die Seele des Kinder,* Leipzig, 1882.]

Rodgon, M. M. 1972. An investigation into the nature of holophrases and the beginnings of combinatorial speech. Unpublished doctoral dissertation, University of Chicago. (in press. Cambridge, England: Cambridge University Press).

Rosch, E. H. 1973. On the internal structure of perceptual and semantic categories. In T. E. Moore (Ed.), *Cognitive development and the acquisition of language.* New York: Academic Press. Pp. 111–144.

Ross, J. R. 1970. On declarative sentences. In R. A. Jacobs and P. S. Rosenbaum (Eds.), *Readings in English transformational grammar.* Waltham, Mass.: Ginn. Pp. 222–272.

Ryan, J. 1973. Interpretation and limitation in early language development. In R. A. Hinde and J. Stevenson-Hinde (Eds.), *Constraints on learning: Limitations and predispositions.* London: Academic Press. Pp. 427–443.

Ryan, J. 1974. Early language development: Towards a communicational analysis. In P. M. Richards (Ed.), *The integration of a child into a social world.* London: Cambridge University Press. Pp. 185–214.

Salapatek, P. H., and Kessen, W. 1966. Visual scanning of triangles by the human newborn. *Journal of Experimental Child Psychology, 3,* 155–167.

Schlesinger, I. M. 1971a. Learning grammar: From pivot to realization rule. In R. Huxley and E. Ingram (Eds.), *Language acquisition: Models and methods.* New York: Academic Press. Pp. 79–89.

Schlesinger, I. M. 1971b. Production of utterances and language acquisition. In D. I. Slobin (Ed.), *The ontogenesis of grammar.* New York: Academic Press. Pp. 63–101.

Schlesinger, I. M. 1973. *Relational concepts underlying language.* Paper prepared for NICHD conference on language intervention with the mentally retarded. Wisconsin Dells, Wisconsin.

Sinclair, H. 1970. The transition from sensory–motor behavior to symbolic activity. *Interchange, 1,* 119–126.

Sinclair, H. 1971. Sensori–motor action patterns as a condition for the acquisition of syntax. In R. Huxley and E. Ingram (Eds.), *Language acquisition: Models and methods.* New York: Academic Press. Pp. 121–130.

Sinclair-de Zwart, H. 1969. Developmental psycholinguistics. In D. Elkind and J. H. Flavell (Eds.), *Studies in cognitive development: Essays in honor of Jean Piaget.* New York: Oxford University Press. Pp. 315–336.

Slobin, D. I. 1968. Imitation and grammatical development in children. In N. S. Endler, L. R.

Boulter, and H. Osser (Eds.), *Contemporary issues in developmental psychology*. New York: Holt. Pp. 437–443.

Slobin, D. I. 1970. Universals of grammatical development in children. In W. Levelt and G. B. Flores d'Arcais (Eds.), *Advances in psycholinguistic research*. Amsterdam: North Holland Publishing. Pp. 174–186.

Slobin, D. I. 1971. Developmental psycholinguistics. In W. O. Dingwall (Ed.), *A survey of linguistic science*. College Park: University of Maryland. Pp. 298–410.

Slobin, D. I. 1973. Cognitive prerequisites for the development of grammar. In C. A. Ferguson and D. I. Slobin (Eds.), *Studies of child language development*. New York: Holt. Pp. 175–225.

Slobin, D. I., and Welsh, C. A. 1968. Elicited imitations as a research tool in developmental psycholinguistics. *Working Paper No. 10*, Language Behavior Research Laboratory, University of California, Berkeley.

Smith, C. S. 1970. An Experimental approach to children's linguistic competence. In J. R. Hayes (Ed.), *Cognition and the development of language*. New York: Wiley. Pp. 109–135. [Reprinted in C. A. Ferguson and D. I. Slobin (Eds.), *Studies of child language development*. New York: Holt, 1973. Pp. 497–521.]

Smith, J. H. 1970. Development and structure of holophrases. Unpublished honors thesis, Harvard University.

Stern, C., and Stern, W. 1907 (4th rev. ed., 1928). *Die Kindersprache*. Leipzig: Barth.

Stern, W. 1930. The chief periods of further speech development. In *Psychology of early childhood*. (A. Berwell, Trans.) London: Allen and Unwin. [Reprinted in A. Bar-adon and W. Leopold (Eds.), *Child language: A book of readings*. Englewood Cliffs, N. J.: Prentice-Hall, 1971. Pp. 45–51.]

Stevenson, A. 1893. The speech of children, *Science, 21*, 118–120.

Strawson, P. F. 1952. *Introduction to logical theory*. London: Methuen.

Sylva, K. 1971. In the beginning, there was the Word ... and what on earth did it mean? Unpublished manuscript, University of California, Santa Cruz.

Tonkova-Yampol'skaya, R. V. 1969. Development of speech intonation in infants during the first two years of life. (M. Vale, Trans.) *Soviet Psychology, 7* (3), 48–54. [Reprinted in C. A. Ferguson and D. I. Slobin (Eds.), *Studies of child language development*. New York: Holt, 1973.]

Veneziano, E. 1973. Analysis of wish sentences in the one-word stage of language acquisition: A cognitive approach. Unpublished master's thesis, Tufts University, Medford, Mass.

Wason, P. C. 1971. In real life negatives are false. Unpublished paper.

Werner, H. 1948. *Comparative psychology of mental development*. Chicago: Follett.

Werner, H., and Kaplan, B. 1963. *Symbol formation*. New York: Wiley.

Author Index

233

Subject Index